ETHICS IN SPORT MANAGEMENT

Joy T. DeSensi, Ed.D.
University of Tennessee

Danny Rosenberg, Ph.D.
Brock University

Fitness Information Technology, Inc.
P.O. Box 4425, University Avenue
Morgantown, WV 26504-4425

Library of Congress Card Catalog Number: 95-83627

ISBN: 1-885693-04-4

Cover Design: James M. Williams/Micheal Smyth
Copyeditor: Sandra R. Woods
Printed by: BookCrafters
Production: Pepper Press

Printed in the United States of America
10 9 8 7 6 5 4 3 2 1

Fitness Information Technology, Inc.
P.O. Box 4425, University Avenue
Morgantown, WV 26504 USA
(800) 477-4348
(304) 599-3482 (phone/fax)
E-Mail: FIT@access.mountain.net

Sport Management Library

The Sport Management Library is an integrative textbook series targeted toward undergraduate students. The titles included in the Library are reflective of the content areas prescribed by the NASPE/NASSM curriculum standards for undergraduate sport management programs.

Forthcoming Titles in the Sport Management Library

Case Studies in Sport Marketing
Communication in Sport Organizations
Financing Sport **(Now Available)**
Fundamentals of Sport Marketing **(Now Available)**
Legal Aspects of Sport Entrepreneurship
Management Essentials in Sport Organizations
Sport Facility Planning and Management
Sport Governance in the Global Community **(Now Available)**
Sport Management Field Experiences **(Now Available)**

ABOUT THE AUTHORS

Joy T. DeSensi is with the Cultural Studies in Education Unit in the College of Education at The University of Tennessee, Knoxville. Her primary research interests are theoretical foundations of multiculturalism, gender, race, and ethnicity in sport, and ethics, and leadership in sport management. She has made numerous national and international presentations and is the author and coauthor of book chapters and articles that appear in *Quest*, *Journal of Sport and Social Issues*, *Journal of Sport Management* and the *Journal of Physical Education, Recreation and Dance*. She is currently Editor of the *Journal of Sport Management*, serves on the Editorial Board for *Quest*, and is a Past President of the Philosophic Society for the Study of Sport.

Danny Rosenberg, Ph.D. is an assistant professor in the Department of Physical Education at Brock University, St. Catharines, Ontario, Canada. His primary research interests are in the areas of sport and physical education philosophy, sport ethics, sport history, and sport management. He has authored or co-authored articles in journals such as the *International Journal of Physical Education, Canadian Journal of History of Sport*, and *Strategies*. His works have also appeared in book chapters and in several conference proceedings. He taught at Roanoke College in Virginia and in the sport management program at Bowling Green State University in Ohio. Dr. Rosenberg also serves on several professional committees in both Canada and the U.S., and is a reviewer for the *Journal of Physical Education, Recreation, and Dance*. He earned his degrees from the University of Western Ontario and the University of Tennessee, Knoxville.

TABLE OF CONTENTS

Part II - Personal and Professional Ethics

PART III - Sport Management Ethics Applied

FOREWORD

In the contemporary world, it is often difficult to remember that sport management ultimately is a service provided by one human being for another. It is even harder to act on this knowledge. Why? Because sport managers often do not come face to face with the people they are affecting. Because "bottom-line" mentality encourages impersonal decision making. Because other managers are playing fast and loose with the rules and one feels compelled to do the same, no matter how this affects consumers.

Some say these factors and others make it easier for managers to be amoral, to scan the administrative horizons for what works—whether or not these policies are also morally sound. Policies tend to replace relationships, legal contracts substitute for personal trust, effectiveness and efficiency stand in for caring about what kind and quality of progress are made. In such an environment, sport managers may be successful in producing certain results, but they may also be impoverished in their ability to produce the best outcomes in a human world.

Joy DeSensi and Danny Rosenberg have written a text that reminds professionals in sport management positions and students heading there that ethics not only can inform business and management decisions but also must do so. In addition, these authors provide the tools needed for making ethically proper decisions. They do both in a distinctive way.

DeSensi and Rosenberg respect readers' rights to pick and choose among different philosophic systems and positions. Thus, the book has an eclectic flavor. No one size fits all, and readers are encouraged to find the kinds of thinking and types of standards that suit their own backgrounds, personalities, and intellects.

In addition, these authors respect the complexity of ethics. Each kind of ethical reasoning, they point out, has its strengths and weaknesses. Although much progress has been made in ethics, in all probability no one philosopher, system or position is sufficient. DeSensi and Rosenberg want readers to reach ethical conclusions thoughtfully and critically.

In this book the authors help readers build a background in ethics. They devote nearly a third of the text to developing the vocabulary, perspectives, and reasoning methods of ethics per se. Although they acknowledge that everyone already possesses some of these skills, they insist that ethical problem solving challenges the best of us. This is not a text for those who want to dive into the deep pool of ethics problems before, in fact, they are ready to swim.

DeSensi and Rosenberg also show a respect for the literature (the relevant research in philosophy, management, and sport ethics) that precedes their work. It is not that they believe these earlier contributions provide all or even most of the desired answers. It is rather that progress is made, they think, in relationship to previous scholarship--to both its strengths and weaknesses. Readers of this text will learn of many previous writers who tried to formulate principles and strategies for acting well in business and sport contexts.

The book is practical. Should organizations write ethics codes and expect all employees to abide by them? How can sport marketing be done in a morally sound way? How might sport managers develop their ethical reasoning skills? Do women at the highest levels of moral thinking operate differently than men do? DeSensi and Rosenberg offer thoughtful answers to these and a host of other day-to-day issues in sport management.

Most important the authors, by writing this book, remind us all of what it can mean to be called a **good** sport manager. On the one hand, it may signify that the individual is effective, shrewd, gutty, prudent or, more broadly, competent. On the other, it could mean that the administrator is fair, caring, sensitive to the rights of others, and concerned about improving human existence.

DeSensi and Rosenberg want the term *good* to mean both. They believe that a world that calls for ever higher levels of technical administrative competence also cries out for more sophisticated ethical thinking and higher levels of moral courage. In the following pages they invite their readers to fortify their managerial, fiscal, and leadership skills with nothing less than good ethics.

R- Scott Kretchmar
Pennsylvania State University
July, 1995

PREFACE

Sport management may be broadly understood as a field interested in the organization and administration of specific sport-related areas. These areas may refer to the functions and leadership qualities of, and decision-making processes employed by, a sport manager; the staging of athletic events; the marketing of sport; dealing with sport personnel; sports equipment and clothing; school and community sports; legal and governance aspects of sport; and other similar concerns. The management of sport may take place in the private as well as the public domain. That is, it may be carried out for profit, as in professional franchise sport, or it may be viewed in terms of providing a social benefit, as in municipal recreation departments.

In each of these spheres, the delivery system of sport, which includes consumers, participants, and employees, must be guided by sound ethical principles. Because ethics deals essentially with standards of right and wrong, decisions and conduct within sport management often reflect moral judgments. Is it right to offer this sport service or some alternative? Is it fair to organize a league that is exclusionary? Are spending and pricing policies equitable, or do they favor one group over another? Are certain rules established in the best interest of all who participate in a given sport? Are specific sport practices discriminatory in terms of gender, race, religion, and the like? Are evaluations, negotiations, and the terms and conditions of working within sport reasonable and fair? Sport managers face these and a multitude of other important questions in the course of their everyday responsibilities.

The preceding questions, however, are decidedly distinct. They challenge sport managers to consider value issues with regard to sport, especially in the treatment of sport participants, consumers, and employees. Values, such as goodness, fairness, justice, equity, and rights, form the foundation of many managerial decisions and actions. Unfortunately such value considerations are sometimes overlooked and even undermined. Yet, ethical questions inevitably arise at every organizational level, and those in charge of managing sport must recognize and deal effectively with such problems just as they do when confronted with technical queries.

This book then offers a detailed and comprehensive account of sport management ethics. As far as the authors are aware, no extended treatment of this topic exists in the established literature, and so one purpose here is to fill this void. More important, as university professors who work in sport management, we are concerned about the moral development and reasoning skills of our students. Too often we hear them parrot conventional wisdom and media cliches with little thought given to the ethical weight and implications of their assertions. We firmly believe, therefore, that ethics can be taught and studied toward the goal of improving one's moral judgments and behavior. The main point here is not to serve up conclusive answers, but to provide sport management students with some basic tools so that they enter into ethical discourse intelligently.

This text would be helpful and useful to both undergraduate and graduate students studying sport management as a specialized area of interest. It is our sincere conviction that students who choose this emerging subdiscipline should acquire a basic understanding of ethics in order to realize the expansive nature of this topic in sport management and also to assess their own moral beliefs and character. Even those who teach general and specific sport management courses, where ethics may comprise a course unit or theme, will find this text a good resource. Teachers may select particular theoretical, professional, and applied subjects to suit the needs of their courses and students.

Before we discuss these specific topic areas, a brief word about the title is in order. We employ *sport* in a broad sense to cover many physical activities, from traditional games like football, baseball, basketball, and soccer to fitness, aerobic, and running pursuits. Our guiding principle for the use of the word sport is that it refer to a socially recognized form of physical endeavor. In conjunction with this use of sport, such pursuits need to be acceptable to the degree that they require some type of formal organization. Here, *management* will refer to organizational and administrative tasks assumed by a network of individuals who operate within an established institution to implement physical activities on a wider social scale. Such persons may work in professional franchise sport, in private enterprises, in sport-related media, in school and community sports, in sport-governing bodies, and in governmental agencies. Finally, as mentioned above, ethics involves principles of right and wrong that are implicated in our judgments and actions.

The title, therefore, makes explicit that the organization and administration of established physical activities must be guided by serious moral considerations and reflection. We also maintain that sport management ethics is not an oxymoron, even though numerous ethical problems in contemporary sport originate within its bureaucratic structure. If the institutional nature of sport is morally flawed in some areas, then addressing ethical issues directly may provide the means for sport managers to rectify and improve the moral character of sport. Once the meaning of the title has been clarified, the organization and main themes of this work follow accordingly.

The book is divided into four main parts. The first is entitled "Sport Management and Ethical Theory." After a short introductory chapter, chapters 2 and 3 supply a detailed exposition of the basic concepts and problems in ethics, as well as major ethical theories. This division provides the main theoretical foundation for the remainder of the book.

The second part is called "Personal and Professional Ethics." Chapters 4 and 5 examine these two areas respectively, whereas chapter 6 considers models and codes of ethics. Ultimately, ethics is instantiated by what people say and do. The topics in this part focus on ethical responsibilities of sport managers as social agents who work in highly interactive environments.

The third part is entitled "Sport Management Ethics Applied." Here, the nature of ethics is examined in specific areas of sport management. Chapter 7 deals with the functions of sport managers; chapter 8 is concerned with moral issues and decision making; chapter 9 considers sport marketing; chapter 10 elaborates on personnel management; and chapter 11 investigates legal and governance aspects of sport.

The fourth part of the book contains a single closing chapter that considers the future of sport management ethics. Although tentative and speculative, this chapter offers a glimpse into what may lie ahead and how sport managers ought to conduct themselves ethically in the coming years.

A number of other helpful features are part of the structure of this text. Every chapter, except chapters 1 and 12, begins with an objectives statement, and there are also occasional key-concepts boxes to highlight main ideas. At the end of the chapters, questions for consideration are provided so the reader can review the content of each chapter. There are also numerous examples introduced throughout the book to clarify specific points and make the discussion more meaningful.

As in all literary ventures, we could not have produced this work without the assistance, guidance, and support of many individuals. Initial ideas and suggestions were provided to us from a roundtable discussion held by several members of the North American Society for Sport Management during its annual meeting in the spring of 1992 in Knoxville, Tennessee. We wish to thank the participants of that group: Eric Kjeldsen, Dot Lovett, Mary Hums, and Linda Schoonmaker. Our appreciation is extended to the production staff of Fitness Information Technology for their excellent handling of our manuscript, and to its president, Dr. Andrew C. Ostrow, for his diligence in seeing this work to its completion. The comments and advice of our reviewers, Jan Rintala and Steve Mosher, were extremely helpful, yet as customary, we bear full responsibility for the contents herein. Our deep and sincere thanks is extended to Janet B. Parks, the Sport Management Library Series Editor, who unfailingly kept us on track, not without considerable prodding, and who supplied us with constant encouragement.

Deep appreciation is expressed to Dr. Michael Lusk and Camille Hazeur, University of Tennessee, Knoxville, whose persistent efforts with the preparation of this manuscript were always accompanied by genuine warmth and patience. Special gratitude is extended to Camille Hazeur, Director of Diversity Resources and Educational Services, who also offered invaluable insights for chapter 10 of this text.

We are delighted that R. Scott Kretchmar was willing to write the foreword.

He is a highly respected professor and scholar in physical education and sport studies, especially in sport philosophy, and these qualities make him an ideal candidate to comment on this work. We have known Professor Kretchmar for many years, and we value his luminary knowledge and insight in ethics.

This book is dedicated to Professor Earle F. Zeigler, who has profoundly touched both our personal and professional lives. He has been a teacher, mentor, colleague, and dear friend to both of us, and there are few words that can express the honor and privilege we feel in knowing him.

There are, of course, other people in our lives about whom we care deeply and who have made enormous sacrifices while we wrote this book. We would individually like to express our thoughts about others dear to us.

I wish to thank Columbia and Vincent DeSensi, whose spirit is always with me and serves as a guiding force; family who care; and my friends and colleagues, who always offer encouragement, motivation, friendship, and affirmation.

Joy T. DeSensi
The University of Tennessee
Knoxville, TN

I should like to thank my wife, Etty, for her patience, love, and support, and our children, Leah, Rafi, and Orah, for simply being there.

Danny Rosenberg
Brock University
St. Catharines, ON

PART I

SPORT MANAGEMENT
AND ETHICAL THEORY

Wade Austin, (1985). Reprinted with permission.

CHAPTER 1

INTRODUCTION

Chapter Objectives

- to become aware of ethical concepts in sport
- to consider the place of sport in society
- to reflect on one's personal beliefs
- to become familiar with the ethical concerns associated with sport management
- to establish the value of studying ethics
- to explore personal and professional ethics
- to characterize social responsibility

Ethical Concepts in Sport

Hatred of the opponent should be used to inspire athletes to become more intense and increase performance.

Winning is everything, and we must do whatever that takes. Everyone else cheats. Why shouldn't we?

We obeyed all the rules and finished last in the conference. Now there isn't a rule we haven't broken, and where are we? We're playing in the biggest bowl game ever.

Players are commodities—buy, own, sell, trade. It's all in the game. Sport should originate and be carried out with a concern for the rights of others.

To take a bribe is a violation of the cathedral—the sports cathedral.

Fair play and sportsmanship—that's what sport is about.

Concepts involved with the theme of ethics pose numerous problems for individuals not formally versed in the theoretical areas of philosophy and specifically ethical theory. The application of ethical rules in everyday life and in sport contexts presents even more difficulty for individuals. We propose that the area of ethics, particularly within sport, has suffered because there is a general lack of understanding or appreciation for ethical theories and their relevance to sport and that the ethical theories proposed are normative and thus difficult to operationalize. Although these are not justifiable reasons for not employing ethics in our own behavior, they may be reasons why individuals have not pursued study in this area. Because ethics deals with the study of morality and the standards of morality that individuals should follow, questions of value and concepts of rightness and wrongness are considered within this topic. As a normative area of study concerned with how individuals ought to act, ethics is prescriptive. That is, ethics tells people how to act. Questions in ethics applied to sport are not limited to the contestants and concepts, such as sportsmanship, the taking of performance-enhancing drugs, the treatment of opponents, and the paying of collegiate athletes (Morgan & Meier, 1988). Sport managers are also responsible for addressing ethical questions, such as those pertaining to professionalism, equity, legal management, personnel issues, team ownership, responsibilities of professional team franchises, and the social justice associated with all levels of sport. These issues must be taken into consideration and approached logically. Rational decisions on the part of the sport manager are imperative to ensure the integrity of sport.

The purpose of this text is to present the concepts and theories associated with ethics. As a result, individuals in the sport setting, specifically the administrator, but also the players, spectators, and other clientele will be aware of the individual's obligations, responsibilities, and rights, and be able to base decisions on sound ethical moral judgment, or both. This text will also apply ethics and ethical theory to the sport management setting through the presentation and analysis of various scenarios.

The overall topic of ethics is a critical issue in today's society. This is especially evident as the abuses in sport settings are revealed. It is imperative that future sport managers be exposed to the study of ethics and that this area not be perceived as trivial, irrelevant, or too difficult to work through. Sport managers must accept responsibility for knowledge in this area in order to ensure that they will serve and preserve sport in an ethically sound manner.

Although much literature exists regarding the philosophical examination of ethics, little is available regarding a truly applied nature of this area in sport management, a scarcity that makes the understanding of such knowledge difficult. When examining the factors affecting ethical and unethical behavior and how these factors enter into the process of decision making, there are few sources to which people can turn. The research that is available does not easily lend itself to model building in this area. What does exist are descriptive accounts of particular cases of decisions to act either ethically or unethically and surveys regarding manager's attitudes toward ethical dilemmas, the circumstances in which the dilemmas need to be resolved, and methods for making the solution easier. Such accounts, however, do not indicate either the reasons for making a certain decision or the reasons leading to the ethical or unethical behavior (Bommer, Gratto, Gravander, & Tuttle, 1987). This state of affairs in no way diminishes the importance of ethical knowledge, nor should it relegate ethical knowledge to a secondary or unimportant area. It is crucial, therefore, that specific courses be offered that directly address applied ethics in sport management. The ability to make ethical decisions is a much needed critical skill necessitating a rational thought process. Present breaches in ethical practices within our society, as well as in sport and in sport management specifically, require that critical attention be given to ethics.

The reasons for unethical behavior in sport and other forms of this current state of affairs are attributed to many factors and are debated by philosophers of sport ethics. For example, Zeigler (1992) states that the "lack of a systematic approach to ethical understanding can be blamed on the doctrine of separation of church and state" (p. 2). Although this situation may well be partly responsible for the unethical practices and social injustices that people experience in North American society, it is not the sole reason. Social theory indicates that the capitalist nature of the North American sociopolitical system and the accompanying motivations such as profit-making have affected ethical behavior. The drive to succeed in North American society, coupled with the "winning is everything" and "win at all costs" attitudes, has misguided or misdirected individual thoughts and actions, particularly in regard to the need "to win" and be successful in sport. In addition, the commercialization of sport and the influences of the media contribute significantly to the corruptive nature of the sport setting.

Sport in Society

Understanding the reasons individuals attribute to the meaning and significance of sport in their lives may help them realize the potential that this setting has for the development of moral character and ethical behavior as well as any actions of an unethical nature. The pervasiveness of sport in North American society is well documented by sport sociologists (Eitzen 1993; Eitzen, & Sage, 1993; Leonard, 1993; McPherson, Curtis, & Loy 1989). Some form of sport, whether it be youth sport, college or university sport, professional sport, or some other form of sport participation or spectating, permeates aspects of people's lives in varying degrees and fashions. The effects of sport on individuals within North American society are monumental. Family schedules are altered to accommodate participation, and special events, such as Super Bowl Sunday, the World Series, NBA Playoffs, and other forms of sport, have great significance for many people. The concepts within sport that have gained much attention in North American society are those motivational slogans like "higher, faster, stronger," "go for the gold," and the pseudo-Lombardian expression "win at all costs." People have been conditioned to evaluate the better, more powerful individual, team, school, city, state, and country based solely on who won and who lost. The political systems of nations have even taken on certain influence and dominance as the successful sport participant(s) and medal counts bring prestige and recognition to various political systems.

Whether or not the capitalistic nature of the North American economic system is the reason for such emphases should be examined. The dilemma that amateur and professional sport in North America faces is the seriousness of its nature in relation to other issues and problems within society. It has been said that sport is too much of a business to be a game and too much of a game to be a business. Either way, when one investigates the economics of sport, there is an overwhelming relationship between sport and the money involved in this enterprise. This is especially evident when one examines the amount of money paid for televised sport advertising, rights to televise the Olympic Games, attendance at professional baseball game, professional athletes' salaries; money spent and generated in college football programs and bowl games; and the money invested in professional sport franchises.

The concept of sport as a pleasurable activity played for sheer enjoyment is in conflict with the concept of sport as work or sport in a corporate setting. Eitzen (1993) indicates that money has superseded the content as the ultimate goal of sport and that illicit tactics in various sport settings are commonplace. Expanding the possible link between the economic issue and ethical behavior in sport, Sage (1990) discusses the concept of professional leagues as cartels. Defining a cartel, Sage (1990) notes that it

> is an organization of independent firms that has as its aim some form of restrictive or monopolistic influences on the production or sale of a commodity as well as the control of wages. Obviously cartels increase the benefits for the powerful few at the expense of the many. (p. 142)

Freedman (1987) points out that sport leagues operate as cartels by (a) restricting interteam competition for players by controlling the rights of players through drafts, contracts, and trades that reduce competitive bidding between teams for player services; (b) acting in concert to admit or deny new teams and to control the location and relocation of teams; and (c) dividing local and regional media markets, as well as negotiating as a single entity national media rights fees. The concept of the professional sports league's functioning as a network of power emerges and thus places in question the ethical workings of such an organization. There are tremendous advantages to be gained in terms of power, through both its use and abuse, and in terms of the accumulation of profits within this system. Although the benefits of the sports cartel are reaped by the owners, it is the powerless laborers or athletes and consumers who encounter the more negative effects of such a system (Sage, 1990). Ethical questions abound within the myriad of economic explanations of sport in society.

Personal Beliefs

More attention must be given to the need to be ethical and just, but what must also be given undivided attention is the basis upon which our professional ethics are founded. Personal ethical behavior must be examined in people's daily lives. The emergence of personal ethics and the development of professional ethics do not occur in a vacuum, nor are they necessarily two different forms of beliefs (Beauchamp, 1988). Therefore, such study must be logically undertaken and based on sound personal and professional understanding. This venture will necessitate study from a theoretical perspective as well as an examination of applied experiences within the sport setting.

Along with examining theories of ethical behavior, a personal analysis of individual values and beliefs regarding sport and its place in North American society must occur. Included in this personal analysis must be questions, such as

- What does sport mean to individuals as players and spectators?

- What expectations do people have of the institution of organized sport and its players and coaches?

- Of what value is sport to North American society, to children, high school students, college and university students, as well as to those involved with professional sport?

Questions of this type should be considered before any general ethical analysis can be applied. Individuals live in an era of increasing consciousness and concern about a variety of social issues. Such issues are also prevalent within the institution of sport. Violence; oppression of women, racial, and ethnic minorities; and discrimination against the disabled and aged prevail in sport. These and other social injustices cannot be ignored and must be addressed because they affect individual actions in sport as players, spectators, and administrators.

There is an increase in the recognition of the need for the understanding of ethics within sport management as well as within business, medicine, and law. Gaining an understanding of how personal and professional ethics build on each other and subsequently emerge together will assist individuals in making ethical judgments. Such an emphasis cannot escape those preparing sport managers, nor can the responsibility slip away from those students preparing for careers in sport settings.

Ethical Concerns in Sport Management

Sport managers are faced with ethical decision making each day they are on the job. Moreover, those associated with sport at all levels (i.e., informal sport, organized sport, corporate sport, and pseudo or trash sport) are continually engaged in an ethical tug-of-war regarding philosophy, value, and purpose of such programs; behavior of coaches, players, and spectators; rules governing the sports; and the political and economic influences of sport. The role of sport and the behaviors it elicits within North American society need to be reevaluated by everyone in order to determine the value and importance sport currently and potentially holds.

Ethical concerns in sport management as noted cover a broad perspective. The question arises, however, as to whether the practice of fair and just ethics is more easily said than done, given the competitive nature of the sport business and its practices. For example, professional players demand and receive more monetary rewards than ever before, and NCAA violations abound in college and university athletics. Additionally, allegations of illegal practices by alumni, boosters, and coaches are in the forefront of the news. Excessive violence, cheating, and the unruly behavior of spectators continue while the cases of drug abuse and other illegal actions on the part of players mount. The actions of sport administrators, coaches, team managers, and trainers are also questioned as violations of laws regarding human rights, civil rights, and equality are alleged.

There is a void of moral and ethical examination among the participants of sport, including spectators, players, and those who manage and administer sport. In an interview with Ted Lee (1992) on sports and the ethical tug-of-war, Kretchmar notes that certain actions in sport that are morally questionable are referred to as technical competence in the execution of skills or as part of the strategy of the game. The intentional fouling of a player in the last minutes of a basketball game in order to set up an opportunity to gain possession of the ball and the excessively rough contact under the basket in the name of defensive play are but two examples of Kretchmar's reference. Unfortunately, moral and ethical questions are not posed by coaches, players, and spectators to the extent they should be when they are situated in the context of sport. It appears that society encourages this type of behavior and that the objective of sporting contests becomes how to find a better opportunity to win rather than using moral and ethical principles to guide behavior. This is not an either/or situation; both objectives can be achieved. The indicators of trends in sport are evident in the sport marketplace, but what needs to be examined is the ethos (guiding principles) underlying the actions of individuals in sport and whether that behavior is ethical or unethical.

At all levels of sport, the behaviors of those involved are being scrutinized more now than ever before. As long as the monetary value of winning permeates the sports world, the challenge of acting in an ethical manner will always be present. Yet high ethical standards in sport are upheld by individuals who do, in fact, follow rules and whose behavior is ethical, but these individuals rarely receive praise for their ethical achievements. It is situations and individuals, such as the former East German Olympic movement, Ben Johnson, Pete Rose, the multitude of NCAA violations by colleges and universities, and the more recent situation involving the Olympic ice skaters Nancy Kerrigan and Tonya Harding, which are publicized and receive greater notoriety. Certain situations in sport, such as what is at stake in the contest, may lead individuals to not necessarily play by the spirit of the rules. Some may choose to push the rules to the edge of what is allowed or legal, or blatantly and consciously ignore the rules. When individuals do push or cross over the line in this fashion, what must be determined is the action involved, the intent of the action, the ways in which others have been affected by the action, and the penalty that may ensue. The question arises as to one's desire to win versus one's internal value system.

In light of the examples above, sport managers need to develop ethical principles to guide sport and to monitor their own administrative actions in sport. Eitzen (1993) suggests the following principles that represent the obligations to sport and its participants in addition to the ideals for which sport managers should strive: (a) Athletes must be considered ends and not means; (b) competition must be fair; (c) participation, leadership, resources, and rewards must be based on achievement rather than on ascribed characteristics; and (d) the activity must provide for the relative safety of the participants (pp. 109-110). Such principles, which will be addressed in more detail in a later chapter, are certainly appropriate for the sport manager to follow. The basis of these principles is underscored by Weiss (1969), who writes that "sport should begin and be carried out with a concern for the rights of others" (p. 180).

Value in Studying Ethics Applied to Sport

Just as philosophy plays an important role in the development of personal beliefs and actions, further examination of the axiological (the study of values) realm of philosophy, specifically ethics, reveals the quality of those beliefs, decisions, and behaviors. Philosophy is considered to be profound thinking. Actually, it is profound living. One's life should be unified by a combination of logically sound, ethical thought and action. The study of ethical theory in sport is not reserved for the theoreticians and philosophers, but rather is a necessary practice for everyone, especially for someone such as the sport manager, who has responsibilities for individuals, programs, organizations, budgets, and revenues.

Familiarity with major issues in North American society and within sport from the philosophical perspective gives the sport manager an advantage in knowledge, understanding, decision making, and problem solving within the specific sport setting. In order to understand the structural roots of unethical behavior in sport, or to understand specifically why exploitation, violence, cheating, and other acts of immoral behavior occur, it is necessary to examine the structural conditions of society. According to Eitzen (1993), "the ethical problems of American sport have their roots in the political economy of society" (p. 118). Massification and commodification are cited by critical theorists, specifically Marxists, as the dominant structural conditions within capitalistic society that explain why unethical choices are made within social life. *Massification* refers to the consequence of society's increased bureaucratization, rationalization, and routinization. Hughes and Coakley (1984) explain that within sport, massification is exemplified by its specialized, technocratic, controlled-by-the-elite, and impersonal nature. Sport is said to mirror the massification of the larger society through such depictions as work, spectacle, power politics, and big business (Eitzen, 1993). Elements suggesting massification within the sport setting increase the possibility of unethical behavior by the participants. One such element is the explanation that

> as the tasks in sport become more complex and specialized, the anonymity of the participants increases. This occurs even on a single team, as in football, for example, when the offensive and defensive units practice separately and meet independently with their specialized coaches. Social contact is minimized and the norms of reciprocity that are essential to community are evaded even among teammates. (Young & Massey, 1980, p. 88)

The other element involves anonymity. Because of short-term and episodic interactions, what occurs between participants is segmented, and players rarely encounter each other in their different roles. The result of this lack of interaction is impersonal relationships, fostering in the competitive setting an attitude of "the ends justifying the means" or a "me-first" type of behavior. Thus, unethical behavior, including exploitation, excessive violence, manipulation, cheating, and fraud, may occur more frequently.

Young (1984) indicates that *commodification* "refers to the social, psychological, and cultural uses of social structures for the commercial needs of monopolies" (p. 7). Within this structure, the individual is viewed and treated as an object to be manipulated, bought, and sold. Team owners and managers of sport focus on profit maximization from this perspective, rather than on any humane concerns. The enterprise of sport tends to produce what can be sold. Spectacle is popular, for sale, and consumed by the spectator or customer. Violence is given attention as the selling point for sporting events, and both women and men are portrayed as sex objects for the sake of advertising. Sport within this reference is considered as "dis-play" and void of the value it was intended to hold for the individual. Sport as a spectacle consumed for entertainment certainly does not retain its personal value and meaning. The packaging, selling, buying, and trading of athletes for the sake of sport, subtracts from the human element that is so very vital to sport participation and perpetuates the commodification of sport for the sake of the "market." What can people expect from athletes who have been alienated from each other and manipulated by the political and economic systems? Is it any wonder that sport participants view one another as means to their ends? Does this not contribute to and perpetuate the "in-at-any-cost" attitude?

At another philosophical level, the concept of relativism tends to permeate ethical beliefs and actions. That is, no absolutes exist, and right and wrong actions are dependent on the current situation. As a result of relativism there is a loss of standards and expectations for behavior, a loss that leaves open the opportunity for rationalization. Many individuals rationalize their actions in numerous ways. One way is to evaluate the risk of being caught and the degree of the resulting penalties. Another approach of rationalization employs the expressions "everyone else is also doing it," "no one will be hurt" by the action, or both. Thus, rules for some are regarded as hurdles, rather than guidelines by which they can shape their lives. Moral bankruptcy seems to be more prevalent than actions based on sound ethical decision making.

Personal and Professional Ethics

Individuals bring to the sport management setting personal values, beliefs, and backgrounds. Behavior within a specific job depends to a certain extent on the strength of the commitment to those values that individuals hold. Honesty and integrity also play a part in one's on-the-job behavior as does the courage to uphold personal values. The overall ethical practices and environment in which the job occurs and the individuals within the organization who uphold upstanding practices also influence personal and professional ethical behavior. Because the overall responsibility for ethical or unethical behavior rests upon the strength of the individual's moral commitment within the organization, personal moral and ethical development is pertinent to responsible action. Questions arise in businesses regarding the premise that all behavior should revolve around economic criteria and subsequent gains irrespective of moral consideration. If this is the case, individuals and efforts can be dehumanized and deemphasized as a result of unethical behavior. Moral, responsible, ethical behavior would exist in the world as totally separate from business practices of the organization. The latter dichotomy is morally suspect at best and morally dangerous at worst.

The basic philosophy and traditions of the organization or business and the individuals who are responsible for its leadership set the tone for the behavior that is to be followed. Once clear expectations are set forth by leaders regarding ethical behavior on the part of employees or representatives, then individuals must assume responsibility and be accountable for their actions (Branvold, 1991).

Social Responsibility

Although social responsibility is also addressed in a later chapter, it is important at this point to be aware of the concept so that it can be considered throughout the text.

Social responsibility involves moral and legal accountability on the part of individuals for the self and others. Reliability, trustworthiness, and concern or regard for others as a part of one's behavior are characteristics of social responsibility. The emergence of social consciousness leading to a commitment of social responsibility as a personal way to behave is paramount on the part of all sport managers and administrators. The development of social responsibility is not necessarily an easy task in today's sport settings. A primary objective in today's sport world requires that attempts be made to achieve a balance between profit or success in sport, at whatever level, and the achievement of these goals in a responsible and ethical manner.

Social awareness, or the act of being socially responsible and responsive, can be built into the objectives within the process of planning in sport management.

For example, nonprofit organizations are based on an awareness of very real societal needs, thus creating the tendency whereby people lose sight of the potential positiveness and ethical considerations that the concepts of social awareness and social responsibility possess. This is not the case, however, with some or most profit-making organizations in which profit maximization is the ultimate objective.

Various populations within modern society for which sport managers must be responsible are those individuals with differing mental and physical abilities, gender, race, sexual orientation, opportunities, income levels, and class levels. It is critical to accept the social responsibility within the context of sport and not to limit participation by certain groups of individuals. The concept of social responsibility enters heavily into the offering of sport programs for all and necessitates concerns for social justice within the sport setting. Sport managers must, therefore, adopt a philosophy of equity and inclusion rather than one of exclusion (DeSensi, 1990).

Questions must be raised by those involved as to the social responsibility leaders must take regarding the organization, management of funds, treatment of players and spectators, and basic integrity in sport. Within the school setting, they must question the value and contribution of athletic programs to the college or university and acknowledge that such programs are a primary public relations tool of the institution. This leads to the question of who the primary beneficiary is in this case: the institution of higher learning or the athlete? Departments of athletics attempt to please various social groups, including alumni, university and athletic administrators, media, university faculty, athletes' families, corporate sponsors, boosters, the NCAA, and the community as a whole, while attempting to act responsibly to each individual athlete. In many cases, they do not ensure that athletes are treated equitably and receive an education during their eligibility with the college or university. Further, what must be maintained is the academic integrity, financial integrity, and overall commitment to equity within these school sport programs.

In professional sport, the concept of accruing profit takes precedence. The economic impact generated by professional teams is not to be slighted. "The pursuit of profit maximization has taken first place while sport management and labor have forsaken the public interest in favor of monetary self-interest" (Hemphill, 1983, p. 2). It is precisely this point, which needs to be reckoned with social responsibility, that the sport manager must consider in her position. The public interest in sport, revenue- generation potential, and social responsibility of the team owner to the community must be weighed. Taking into consideration what meaning the franchise holds for a community is also vital. Although a particular city depends on the revenue that is generated by a professional sport franchise, the fans who identify strongly with home teams and affect revenue must be recognized. In addition, franchise location stability, team performance quality, and the unpredictability of performance outcome are obligations the sport team owner has to a community. The mutual obligations and responsibilities of owners, managers, cities, and fans have a great impact on the success of a particular professional team. Those who realize these responsibilities and direct actions and behavior toward meeting social responsibilities ensure that the needs of the community are met. Through such actions, all facets of the franchise and community mutually benefit.

Unfortunately and often, the cartel-like nature of professional sport and its power structures take over, and the idea of being responsible for or to a particular community is neglected. In a study by Flint and Eitzen (1987), this point is substantiated:

> Because sport is still categorized as simple play, the power of wealthy capitalist owners can be overlooked as simple aberration or eccentric pastime. Although the meritocratic recruitment arguments are held high by the owners as well as the participants (players or consumers), little attention is given to the contradictory fact that owning a team is not based on merit but on enormous wealth. (p. 25)

To elaborate further, the concept of ownership comprises the entrepreneurial freedom of operation, the refined security of monopoly capitalism, the independent pursuit of self-interest, and the control of market exigencies by corporate directorates. Too often professional sport franchises breach their commitments to the community and behave in morally objectionable ways.

Socially responsible sport franchises can emerge if responsible individuals make changes that enhance the long-term operation of the professional sport franchise rather than sacrifice public interests for monetary gains. Once again, the question of ethics is brought to the forefront as the basis for responsible decisions made for and in sport.

The breadth of ethical concerns for sport managers keeps expanding as all facets of the responsibilities associated with this profession are examined. It is a tremendous undertaking to assure that sport retain its integrity in regard to individuals, resources, and rewards as we consider its purpose and value in North American society.

Summary

This chapter presented an introduction to the ethical concerns associated with sport management. The value in studying ethics, an overview of sport in society and associated ethical issues, the need for personal and professional ethics, and the concept of social responsibility were presented to set the stage for what is to come in the next chapters. The value of sport in our society is pointed out in an effort to evoke self- reflection on the part of sport managers in order to examine the meaning and value they give to sport and in order to discover the potential roots of unethical behavior in sport settings.

This introduction is only a beginning to the numerous questions that are raised regarding ethics and sport managers. As the theory and application of ethics are pursued within this text, personal and professional ethics, models and codes of ethics, and the future of sport management ethics will also be addressed in an effort to help sport managers gain a better understanding of their responsibilities and obligations to sport and the individuals associated with sport.

Questions for Consideration

1. How are ethics for the sport manager defined?
2. What is the value of studying ethics in sport?
3. How is social responsibility incorporated into the concept of ethics?
4. What are the potential roots of unethical behavior in sport?
5. Of what value is sport in our society, and why do we place such value on sport?

References

Beauchamp, T. L. (1988). Ethical theory and its application to business. In T. L. Beauchamp & N. E. Bowie (Eds.), *Ethical theory and business* (3rd ed., pp. 1-55). Englewood Cliffs, NJ: Prentice-Hall.

Bommer, M., Gratto, C., Gravander, J., & Tuttle, M. (1987). A behavior model of ethical and unethical decision making. *Journal of Business Ethics, 6,* 265-280.

Branvold, S. (1991). Ethics. In B.L. Parkhouse (Ed.), *The management of sport its foundation and application* (pp. 365-378). St. Louis, MO: Mosby-Yearbook, Inc.

DeSensi, J.T. (1990). Philosophy and social responsibility. In J. Parks & B. Zanger (Eds.), *Sport and fitness management: Career strategies and professional content* (pp. 223-231). Champaign, IL: Human Kinetics.

Eitzen, D.S. (1993). Ethical dilemmas in sport. In D.S. Eitzen (Ed.), *Sport in contemporary society: An anthology* (4th ed., pp. 109-122). NY: St. Martin's Press.

Eitzen, D.S., & Sage, G.H. (1993). *Sociology of North American sport* (5th ed.). Dubuque, IA: Brown & Benchmark.

Flint, W.C., & Eitzen, S. (1987). Professional sports team ownership and entrepreneurial capitalism. *Sociology of Sport Journal, 4,* 17-27.

Freedman, W. (1987). *Professional sports and antitrust.* NY: Quorum Books.

Hemphill, D. (1983). *Social responsibility of a professional sport franchise to a community.* Unpublished manuscript, University of Tennessee, Knoxville.

Hughes, R., & Coakley, J. (1984). Mass society and the commercialization of sport. *Sociology of Sport Journal, 1,* 57-63.

Lee, T. (1992). Sports and the ethical tug-of-war. *Ethics: Easier Said Than Done, 16,* 30-39.

Leonard, W.M., II. (1993). *A sociological perspecitve of sport* (4th ed.). NY: Macmillan.

McPherson, B.D., Curtis, J.E., & Loy, J.W. (1989). *The social significance of sport: An introduction to the sociology of sport.* Champaign, IL: Human Kinetics.

Morgan, W.J., & Meier, K.V. (Eds.). (1988). *Philosophic inquiry in sport.* Champaign, IL: Human Kinetics.

Sage, G. (1990). *Power and ideology in American sport: A critical perspective.* Champaign, IL: Human Kinetics.

Stieber, J. (1992). The behavior of the NCAA: A question of ethics. *Ethics: Easier Said Than Done, 16,* 50-53.

Vander Velden, L. (Ed.). (1993, Winter). *NASSS Newsletter,* University of Maryland.

Weiss, P. (1969). *Sport: A philosophic inquiry.* Carbondale, IL: Southern Illinois University Press.

Young, T.R. (1984, November). The sociology of sport: A critical overview. *Arena Review, 8,* 1-14.

Young, T.R., & Massey, G. (1980). The dramaturgical society: A macro-analytic approach to dramaturgical analysis. *Qualitative Sociology, 1,* 78-98.

Zeigler, E.F. (1992). *Professional ethics for sport managers* Monograph. Champaign, IL: Stipes.

CHAPTER 2

BASIC CONCEPTS AND PROBLEMS IN ETHICAL DISCOURSE

Chapter Objectives

- to become familiar with the concepts of values (axiology) and to understand the nature of definitions and clarity in language
- to comprehend the nature of ethics
- to differentiate between ethics and morality
- to consider various ideas on moral development and moral reasoning
- to know the meaning of ethical conduct and what constitutes misconduct

---

This text seeks to discuss the ethical dimensions of sport management practices from an applied perspective. That is, in the course of everyday experiences within various sport management settings, there inevitably arise moments when ethical concerns have to be addressed. Questions of honesty, cheating, responsibility, fairness, justice, personal rights, and the like cannot be avoided in most working environments, and sport management is no exception. However, the mere identification of ethical considerations in the workplace is not enough.

Sport managers must make concrete moral decisions, often under circumstances that are unclear. For example, one might ask, are individuals ethically responsible when events and the actions of others are beyond their control? Where does this responsibility begin, and where does it end? When is common sense a factor in demonstrating responsibility, and when is one obligated to assume responsibility? How responsible should one be? These, and certainly numerous other ethical questions, indicate that sport managers must be concerned with issues of a substantially different nature than the technical problems they face on a daily basis.

This chapter will lay a foundation of some of the basic concepts, terminology, and problems in ethics toward understanding the nature of ethical judgments in sport management. Becoming familiar with the language and concerns of ethics at this point will assist readers in their understanding of ethical dilemmas. Readers will also acquire enough basic knowledge of ethics to adequately arrive at sound moral decisions when confronted with ethical difficulties. The latter will be taken up specifically in sport management in the applied chapters of the text.

The subsection topics below do not exhaust the terms and issues found in ethics, and they are not treated extensively, but they do provide an adequate starting point for consideration. In addition to the introduction of ethical terms and problems, specific sport and sport management examples and illustrations will be provided to underscore the meaning of concepts.

Axiological Concerns and Definitional Efforts

According to *Webster's New Collegiate Dictionary* (1977), the word *axiology* refers to "the study of the nature, types, and criteria of values and of value judgments esp. in ethics" (p. 79). Already then there is a clue as to the content of ethics, namely, that it will involve an examination of some aspect of values. However, before the concept of ethics and other important terms are considered, an introduction to axiological concerns and definitional efforts in general seems in order.

Axiology is usually considered a branch of philosophy that investigates a broad range of areas where value issues arise. For example, one might value a certain belief or opinion, a way of life, a type of individual character, a particular action, a certain physical object, and the like. In general, the things people value and what counts as a value are numerous. They can include abstract notions and also concrete entities. Values can be expressed overtly in what one says and does, as well as covertly in individual thinking and feeling patterns. So one may say that he prefers competitive games and sports rather than fitness and jogging sessions because he finds the latter less challenging, or one may behave differently toward female athletes because he holds the belief that it is unbecoming for females to engage in athletic contests and sees their social role as mainly a domestic one. Despite these variations in expression, a *value* is typically anything we assess to be worthwhile, interesting, excellent, desirable, and important.

One serious difficulty that arises when discussing values is determining which values to adopt and express. On what evidence does one accept certain values and reject others? Is there a way to rationally justify some values and not others, or should values and what people value be left to personal preference? These are samples of long-standing and vexing questions that we can address only in a cursory manner in this section. They do, however, indicate to some degree the complexity of axiological concerns.

Although the study of values has been part of Western intellectual history for over 2,000 years, beginning with the Greeks, the term axiology was introduced at the start of this century (Findlay, 1970). In its modern usage it can refer to a strand of ethics or a general notion that deals with *value-theory* or *theories of value*. These expressions can include theories about what is good, what is an obligation, what is a virtue, what is truth, what is beautiful, what is right, and the like. These theories would consider such topics in terms of the worthwhileness of various specific subject matters. In this sense, axiology is a field of study with the aim of leading to concrete resolutions of issues that involve value concerns. For example, in a health club setting, the question of serving alcohol can be considered from a value-theory perspective. Would the sale of alcoholic beverages comply with the purpose and mission of a health club? Should the provision of such an amenity be guided by principles of profit or by the welfare of health club patrons, or perhaps by both?

The preceding questions point to the general value of the health club itself, to economic value, and to social and health values held by members and potential members. By raising such questions, the health club manager or owner might consider whether it would be worthwhile to provide alcoholic drinks on the premises. These are only some of the value elements for consideration here, and there certainly could be more. Further, this application of value-theory to a specific case may or may not contain any moral imperative, in the sense of prescribing what one ought to do. In general, though, many current value issues include some prescriptive element.

Because the latter is usually the case, let us briefly examine the variety or kinds of values there are in order to distinguish between moral and nonmoral values. For many people, statements of facts and values are difficult to discern because we fail to be objective and honest about our opinions and beliefs. One's own prejudices and biases often color the way one assesses certain objects, human actions, and situations. Sometimes it is the social context and historical period in which a person lives that shape the attitudes he or she possesses and hence the claims a person makes. Often, vague language and unclear usage of words confuse meanings so that fact and value claims are not distinct. Nevertheless, it is imperative that factual propositions be distinguished from value statements. Usually the former can be independently verified, whereas the latter are open matters for discussion (Billington, 1988). For example, to say there has been a steady rate of growth in attendance at the SkyDome in Toronto for baseball games is an empirical or a factual matter. On the other hand, to claim that it is fun going to live baseball games is a value judgment. Some people simply despise or ignore sports and place little or no value on them. Debatable statements then often point out areas where judgments are based on one's values rather than on what can be conclusively verified.

Once value statements are identified, another classification can be proposed to distinguish between values that have a moral (prescriptive) content and those that do not have any moral implications. Making this distinction is often difficult because it usually relies on what an individual means by good. There are numerous definitions and usages of the word good, and this adds to the problem of sorting out various moral and nonmoral values. However, the term good as a value-laden expression may not only refer to something that is good, but it may be also used to describe the goodness of something or something that has the property of being good (Frankena, 1973). These are two different senses of good. Moreover, a general use of the term good often implies a desire to see such a good come into existence or implies the suggestion that one ought to pursue a particular good, but this need not be so. We sometimes use good without moral intent or a moral foundation. Therefore saying something is good need not imply a prescription to bring about a particular good or any moral grounds for making such a claim. Some examples will help clarify this point.

To say "this is a good bat" and "this is a good mitt" can refer primarily to the *usefulness* of these objects. Here, the purpose of each object may be the most important consideration, without suggesting to someone that she should go and purchase the same bat and mitt. This sense of good is based on whether the purpose is good or not. The claim "it is a good idea to buy sports equipment when they are on sale" points to an *extrinsic* or *instrumental* sense of good, or when good is considered *as a means*. Here, one would be a careful and prudent equipment manager to make purchases when costs are lower. To exclaim "that was a good hit" may indicate that one had a rewarding experience while watching a batter make a solid connection on a pitch. A fine hit, catch, or save may have *inherent* goodness because each evokes a worthwhile experience. Unrelated to the last two nonmoral senses of good, some things may be given the attribute good to indicate they are good when one experiences them. To say "skiing or sailing is good" may mean that they are good for their *intrinsic properties*. That is, they are good because they are enjoyable in and of themselves. Finally, one might say, "A world without sports in it would not be a good one." The meaning here might be that sport *contributes* to what some might call the good or happy life. The latter may be understood in a nonmoral sense where again no prescriptive or "ought" claims are being advanced. It is not that one wishes everyone to help create a world with sports in it, but that sports, for some, is part of what makes life worthwhile (Frankena, 1973).

The preceding discussion then identifies a number of nonmoral values to contrast moral values ("ought" statements) and explains how the notion of good can be used in a variety of senses. These nonmoral values can be summarized as utility values, extrinsic values, inherent values, intrinsic values and contributory values. Some of these values can be further divided into those that serve as a means and those that serve as an end, although in some circumstances even this distinction is difficult to ascertain. Because there are a number of differing types of values, it is also sometimes difficult to sort out what particular value one is addressing. Is one speaking about an inherent or an intrinsic nonmoral value or perhaps even a moral value? Despite the confusing nature of the various terms introduced here, it is still essential to identify and distinguish between these various expressions and their meanings.

There are other characterizations of values that can be considered. First, any discussion of values implies their contrary, or *disvalues*. So if one uses the terms good, right, just, responsible, etc., these will all have their opposite corresponding expressions, such as bad, wrong, unjust, irresponsible. In this sense, values may be characterized by being either positive or negative. Second, values can usually be ranked in some type of hierarchy in which there are lower and higher values. Finally, values are connected to a particular and distinct content, even if that content is an abstraction. The values of holiness and beauty still refer to separate things that people respond to in concrete ways (Marias, 1941/1967). These points are made in order not to lose sight of the many ways in which values (or disvalues) can indicate what one considers desirable, worthwhile, significant, and the like. It further indicates the degree to which axiological matters involve complicated issues and distinctions.

Part of the preceding discussion touched on the difficulties associated with defining the term good. A number of different meanings were presented, and it was pointed out that confusion could arise if one did not clearly define the word good. Everyone has likely experienced breakdowns in conversation because certain terms used were vague or ambiguous. In many cases, expressions that are not clearly defined lead to a lack of understanding and sometimes misunderstanding. Clarity in language then often hinges on the appropriate definition of words. Analyses and decisions in ethics also involve the clear comprehension of terms, and so it would be useful to briefly examine the area of definitions.

The topic of definitions can be found in many logic textbooks, because the construction and meaning of arguments often rest on the use and comprehension of language. We will only consider some of the main purposes and types of definitions as discussed by Copi (1982).

Why does one bother defining words? A simple and immediate answer might be to make oneself better understood in the use of language. Yet the learning of language is a complicated process. It usually begins through observation and imitation. It is also an accumulative process. That is, one builds a store of words, the meanings of which are readily available, and one learns how to use such words in appropriate contexts. But the observation or imitation approach (and perhaps the use of examples and descriptions) reaches a limit until a more formal method for understanding words and increasing one's store of words is required. At some point, when one hears or reads a new word, only a formal, explicit explanation or definition will suffice—like turning to the dictionary. One particular purpose of definitions then is to increase one's vocabulary.

Words that have two or more distinct meanings have the potential to be used in ambiguous ways. The word good discussed earlier is a classic example of an ambiguous term. How often does one know precisely how good something is or when something or someone is good? Words are often ambiguous when their meaning in a particular context or sentence is unclear. For example, "would you like a punch?," "my sister is mad," and "Marx's *Capital* is a very heavy book" are three statements that include ambiguous words. Without further information, the meanings of these statements are unclear.

When ambiguous terms and phrases and their various senses are used more than once in discussions, arguments, or essays, shifts in meaning can lead to *equivocations*. For instance, "Only man is rational. No woman is a man. Therefore no woman is rational." commits what is known as the *fallacy of equivocation* (Freeman, 1988, p. 119). This argument makes use of two different definitions of man, and the reasoning and conclusion here are obviously incorrect. Sometimes entire sentences are ambiguous because their structure leads to confusion. "He has two grown sons and a daughter in a nunnery" could leave the impression that his sons are also in a nunnery. A comma after "sons" would correct what is known as an *amphiboly*, a structurally flawed ambiguous sentence (Salmon, 1989, p. 325).

Relative terms, such as small, large, heavy, light, are sometimes used in speech and in writing in unclear ways. A light elephant is not a light animal. A small mountain is not a small land mass. A change of emphasis or *accent* can also alter the way terms are used and the meaning of expressions. So, the statement "all men are not liars" can mean that some men are not liars or that indeed each and every man is not a liar. The first meaning is suggested if the emphasis is placed on "all," whereas the second meaning is implied when the accent is place on "not." In these and in most cases of ambiguity, the context of the words and statements can sometimes provide a clue as to their intended meaning. Although many instances of ambiguity should be avoided in language, ambiguity has an important place in literature, poetry, and humor. In general, however, language discrepancies related to multiple meanings identify a second purpose of definitions, which is to eliminate ambiguity.

Definitions of terms are often required when words are vague. Vagueness refers to expressions that require further clarification as to their meaning. Vague terms generally arise when "borderline cases" are discussed. In such instances, it becomes difficult to understand a vague word without specifying more precisely its meaning. Terms like happy, bald, democracy, old, obscene, maturity, and death are considered vague. Most color words are vague. How red does something have to be to be called red? How bald does someone have to be to be called bald? When is a person mature, or old, or happy?

In many circumstances, definitions can clarify the meaning of these vague expressions. Sometimes authoritative bodies, the judiciary or government, legally define vague words like obscene, person, and living. In other contexts, vague expressions, such as "see you later" or "take care," have a place in our use of language. Some words are both vague and ambiguous. Heavy is vague in the sense of how heavy is heavy? It can be ambiguous by referring either to weight or seriousness. A vague expression, however, lacks meaning not because there are two or more distinct meanings attached to it, but because it does not contain enough information in the meaning one intends to convey. The preceding discussion then suggests a third purpose for definitions and that is to eliminate vagueness.

Two other purposes for definitions are offered by Copi (1982). In the sciences, many words are given precise definitions to make various theoretical claims. Although vagueness and ambiguity may be avoided by providing such technical definitions, these are not the primary reasons for employing such definitions. A chemist may define an acid in principle to distinguish it from other substances, and this may have little to do with others, such as cooks and sheet-metal workers, who make use of acids (Copi, 1982, p. 142). So, definitions can serve a theoretical purpose. Finally, definitions are sometimes used to influence the attitude of others. Words are sometimes defined to elicit an emotional response or to serve as a rhetorical device. Emotive value is usually attached to words like abortion, euthanasia, racist, rapist, and molester. Sometimes one defines such words not to provide an explanation of their meaning, but to arouse certain feelings in others or to alter the views or beliefs of others.

The various purposes of definitions imply there are several types of definitions. *Ostensive* definitions are the most rudimentary type of definition. Here, one merely points to an object, action, or situation and assigns it a name. Parents use such definitions with infants and young children by pointing to things and repeating the names of those objects. There are at least two limitations of ostensive definitions. Sometimes children associate the name of an object with something other than the object being pointed out. For example, one's finger, rather than the protrusion on the side of the head, is identified as the ear. Second, if no object is available, then this type of definition cannot be employed. Abstract entities cannot be defined ostensively, nor can waterfalls or caves if photos are unavailable (Salmon, 1989).

Stipulative definitions are those that introduce a new term into a language. As new products and technologies are created, new names also are created to assign meanings to such advances. Computer language today has its own vocabulary with many newly invented words like *byte, disk, download, boot*. There are usually two requirements for stipulative definitions. A new term should not already have a widely accepted meaning, and it should provide a useful addition to language (Salmon, 1989). A stipulative definition is not necessarily true or false; instead, it is offered as a proposed new meaning of a term that will be accepted within a specific context.

A *lexical* definition, in contrast, refers to an accepted meaning of a word that is either true or false and that is usually offered as a way to reduce ambiguity. Lexical definitions must conform to standard or conventional meanings and usages of words, and based on this, it can be determined whether or not someone uses a term correctly or incorrectly (Copi, 1982). Dictionary definitions are considered lexical definitions.

The latter two types of definitions do not reduce vagueness, but *precising* definitions do (Salmon, 1989). Because vagueness involves "real" borderline cases, new meanings cannot clarify vague expressions. *Precising* definitions utilize meanings already established, but they go beyond an appeal to ordinary meanings to reduce confusion in particular circumstances. Such definitions are often employed in the legal system when new and difficult cases arise. For example, some women today act as paid surrogates for those unable to carry a pregnancy to term. The question of who is the "actual" mother of the newborn might require a *precising* definition.

A fourth type of definition is a *theoretical* definition. Such definitions are connected to the proposal of new theories, and because most theories can be questioned, so too are the definitions they introduce. Theoretical definitions seek to provide meanings that can be accepted in principle. They do not necessarily appeal to common usages of terms, though they can be considered correct or incorrect, and they do not propose completely new meanings. Instead, a theoretical definition serves to clarify an expression used when proposing a new theory. Its acceptance is intimately bound to the acceptance of the theory itself.

Finally, there are *persuasive* definitions. These make use of emotive and expressive language to influence attitudes. Many words can be defined in rhetorical language and thereby act as devices of *persuasion*. Terms like *abortion*, *homosexual*, *communism*, and the like can be defined negatively or positively. In intercollegiate sports, many women's team names carry the prefix "lady" (e.g., Lady Vols or Lady Badgers), and for some, this conveys the meaning that women's sport is inferior to men's sport. Although persuasive definitions are not always derogatory—they may even be humorous—one must be sensitive to the expressive ways in which words are defined.

Far more could be said about definitional efforts and the general area of meaning. However, by recognizing some of the main purposes and types of definitions, one gains an added sense and appreciation for the nuances of language and the varied usage of words. This sensitivity will become invaluable as we proceed to examine other concepts in this chapter and other topics in this text.

KEY CONCEPTS

axiology	value	value-theory	extrinsic
intrinsic	disvalues	equivocation	fallacy
accent	amphiboly	ambiguity	vagueness
ostensive	stipulative	lexical	precising

Ethics

Many people rarely consider the area of ethics, at least from a formal and rigorous perspective, and yet all people frequently engage in making ethical decisions. How often does a person declare someone else's behavior to be right or wrong, good or bad, worthy or unworthy, and the like? How frequently does one say someone ought to do this or should not do that? How many times does one assert that this is worth pursuing and that is worth avoiding? But on what rational or reasoned grounds do individuals make such claims? If, broadly speaking, ethics involves principles used to assess human actions and concerns in terms of right or wrong, good or bad, then many ethical judgments are arrived at through conventional wisdom, intuition, reliance on some authority, or by some other readily available means. Few people then engage in serious inquiry into the theories and axioms underlying ethical judgments, yet it would be useful to have a basic understanding of some of these notions. In this section, we will examine the nature of ethics by introducing some of its main themes and ideas.

As mentioned in the previous section, ethics or *moral philosophy* is concerned with value issues and decisions. Matters of value can be either described as *normative* or *nonnormative*. In the latter case, ethics does not address a particular moral position (e.g., opposing boxing because it is predicated on violence), but is instead concerned with descriptive features of ethics or the meanings of ethical terms and expressions. Normative ethics, on the other hand, involves defending certain ethical principles and standards or virtues in a systematic way or demonstrating the applicability of such systems in an area like sport management (Beauchamp, 1991). This text will be primarily concerned with normative ethics in the latter applied sense.

In most instances, the main task of ethics is to evaluate the standards of right or wrong that people assign to behavior, motives, intentions, and persons (Cornman & Lehrer, 1974). Without the moral quality of good or bad attached to such an assessment, then, it is unlikely that ethical decisions are involved. For example, one could say to a tennis player, "After your opponent hits down the line and approaches the net, you should return with a cross court." Although the term *should* is used, the preceding has no moral relevance but is strategic or tactical advice. In contrast, to say a player should not call a fault when he or she knows the ball touched the line indicates that it would be wrong to do so. Ethics is primarily concerned with the latter type of instances.

There are generally two types of ethical judgments. As indicated in some of the questions raised in the opening paragraph of this section, ethical decisions may relate to a person's conduct in terms of what an individual should or should not do, or to something that is either valued or not valued. Frankena (1973) calls ethical judgments related to human actions *judgments of moral obligation*. Words like ought and should, right and wrong to describe particular and general behavior are included in this category. He calls ethical decisions concerned with intentions, motives, and the character of individuals, *judgments of moral value*. Expressions like good, bad, praiseworthy, reprehensible, and virtuous can describe the state or condition of one's character, motives, or intentions in particular and general ways. Again, there are also judgments of nonmoral value, discussed in the previous section, which are not strictly speaking part of ethical considerations, though they are part of axiology.

Ethical judgments contain a moral component as related to conduct or values, yet morals and ethics can differ. Ethics is considered on the level of theory or principles, whereas morals are observed on the level of practice (Billington, 1988).

In ethics, one appeals to rules or maxims as a way to justify certain moral decisions, irrespective of whether those decisions are right or wrong (there are good and bad ethics). On the other hand, morals usually describe a personal set of values expressed in individual actions in concrete situations. So the morals of a sport director would matter to one's family and friends, and this might differ from the ethical principles she applies to refrain from "padding" the budget. In most cases, the adjective *ethical* is synonymous with *moral*. That is, the ethical or moral thing to do is considered the right or good thing to do.

Billington (1988) identifies six features of ethical or moral questions to differentiate them from questions raised in other disciplines and areas of study:

1. *No one can avoid dealing with moral questions.* People can live without being concerned or having knowledge about many things. But as long as one lives with and alongside others, or is remotely influenced by others, one encounters moral issues and makes ethical decisions.

2. *Moral decisions involve other people.* There is no such thing as a private ethics. Individuals sometime feel that certain personal decisions do not affect others, but on closer examination they do. The decision to solo mountain climb on a dangerous cliff seems quite personal and would harm no one else. Yet, should one die from such a venture, others would be deprived from such a loss.

3. *Moral decisions are reserved for things that matter most.* Many disciplines serve to enable others to reach a level of happiness and self-fulfillment in their lives. This is certainly true of education. However, it is probably not that important which pedagogical method one employs to enjoy success as a teacher. On the other hand, deep divisions might exist between teachers over issues like honesty, cheating, bigotry, racism, sexism, and the like. Technical or strategic judgments are usually less pressing and are qualitatively different from moral ones.

4. *Ethical decisions offer no final answers.* Although many groups of people in society like doctors, lawyers, legislators, and religious leaders, espouse "clear" solutions to moral questions, philosophers usually provide no definitive right or wrong answers. Some ethical theories and behavior may be shown to be more reasonable and correct than others, but to offer a completely satisfactory answer to a moral problem is too ambitious a goal. Although this might frustrate many people, thinking clearly and rigorously about moral issues is in itself challenging without arriving at a final answer.

5. *Choice is a central element of morality.* If someone is forced to act in a way that is morally despicable, one would not generally hold that person blameworthy. The difficulty of course is determining how much and what kind of "force" did the individual experience to deny him a choice. Are there life situations where choice is impossible? Perhaps issues like

blameworthiness can only be dealt with in degrees? If so, then moral decisions might always include choice. One thing is certain, however. Trying to avoid a moral problem is also a choice. In this sense, no one can remain neutral about ethical concerns.

6. *The aim of moral reasoning is to discover right or correct forms of behavior.* Seeking some kind of truth is the aim of most disciplines, like in the sciences where there are accepted methods to verify truths. But this must be precluded when making ethical decisions. Because there are numerous competing ethical theories, all containing some weaknesses, and no singular method for arriving at ethical solutions, no action can be declared absolutely correct or incorrect. But this does not mean that no right or correct behavior can be recommended through moral analysis. Certain conduct might be more justified (and hence right or correct) than others, and an appeal to ethical principles might reveal these differences. Ethical discourse can at least try to ensure and encourage honest, open debates about controversial moral issues.

These distinguishing features provide an adequate overview of the nature of ethics. But there is another approach toward identifying other characteristics about ethics, and that is to describe what ethics is not. This is a method employed by White (1988) and one we shall now consider by following his lead.

Ethical decisions have little to do with the way one feels, but rather with the way one thinks or reasons. Statements of feeling are usually personal expressions of one's emotive state, and they often cannot be seriously challenged. If someone feels happiness or grief or is in pain, it is almost absurd to question such feelings or to recommend that one ought not to have such feelings. One mainly accepts other people's feelings at face value.

The same is not true of ethical judgments of the normative variety with which we are concerned. Questioning these decisions is most appropriate for it usually means one is asking for some sort of justification for a stance on a moral issue: Why do you oppose the "good foul" in sport, or why are you in favor of transferring greater funds to men's intercollegiate sport rather than to comparable women's sports? To answer these questions requires an appeal to sound reasons, principles, rational arguments, and the like. One will rely mostly on thinking carefully about these issues.

In fact, emotions would likely hinder or possibly create a bias toward a clear, well-reasoned response to these concerns. If one were to simply answer, "I get upset when I watch a 'good foul'," and "I just feel women's sport is less worthy than men's" and leave it at that, then there is no attempt here to defend one's moral decision, nor would there be any point to challenge these positions. But at least two of the features of ethics mentioned earlier indicate why these reactions are unsatisfactory from a moral point of view. Recall, there is no such thing as private ethics, and others are affected by one's moral decisions. Ethics is situated in the public domain.

Because of these characteristics, when making ethical judgments one is obligated to recommend one's moral decisions to others. Consider if an individual decided that cheating on exams was fine for him, but not for others. If reciprocity cannot be granted for one's ethical judgments, it places suspicion on the strength of one's moral convictions. Further, people generally want others to respect their ethical decisions, and at times people want to convince others of the correctness of their judgments. These goals can only be accomplished through critical thinking and by accepting the challenges of others, not merely by expressing one's feelings.

Moreover, feelings can and often do change for no apparent reason. One can feel sincere or guilty over certain issues one day and feel just the opposite the next day. People sometimes then arbitrarily have and express their feelings. Further, it would hardly be appropriate to rely on the strength of emotions as a guide for moral conduct. Feeling sincere about racist causes does not make an assault on a member of a minority group right. Although an examination of one's feelings may reveal certain reasons for making ethical decisions, relying foremost on one's feelings is not part of most ethical considerations.

Ethics is also not about relying on authoritative voices or bodies to tell us what is right or wrong, good or bad, and the like. This is a posture one assumes for any type of philosophical inquiry. Everyone must ultimately arrive at ethical decisions independently of what others have to say. This does not mean that others do not influence a person's moral judgments, but what counts most in the end is what that person thinks.

Parents, teachers, government and religious leaders, and the like may insist that the individual accept their word as final, not because they have put forth good reasons for accepting their views, but because they are in a position of authority. They may even tempt the individual with various rewards. But manipulation, threats, and coercion have no place in moral discourse. Dialogue on ethical matters must be built on a foundation where people's reasons and rational arguments can be freely offered and rejected, and where one can decide for oneself whether to accept or oppose moral positions.

Placing importance on individual thinking, however, should not lead to the idea that ethics is, therefore, dependent on absolute personal authority. Individuality referred to above stresses the point that moral decisions cannot be made for a person, and that to a large extent each person is responsible for the moral position she or he assumes. If morality were based strictly on the authority of individuals, whose ethics would people claim is superior and would they want to follow? In fact, such questions could not even be raised on such a view. But people do pose such queries when it comes to moral issues, and this reveals something important.

The ability to distinguish between right and wrong, good and bad, compels one to raise questions about the relative worth of moral judgments and the actions guided by such decisions. Because these are comparative matters, they necessarily involve considerations beyond one's private domain. Moral disagreements are between people. One cannot claim a moral decision is correct unless it is held up against someone else's alternative view that might oppose it. This is partly how the scientific method works to verify truths, and this feature has a place in ethics. It ensures that no single person has a monopoly on what is morally right (otherwise slavery and torture could be justified) and that moral views can change (one can convince someone else that capital punishment is right or wrong). Although individuals must make up their own minds about moral dilemmas—that is, they have to live with and be largely responsible for their ethical decisions—no person can claim to be an absolute authority on moral issues.

Although no one individual is a moral authority, some people equate what is ethical with what is legal. In other words, nothing is deemed morally wrong if it conforms with the law. But are ethics and the law the same?

At first glance, many laws do seem to prohibit and punish actions considered morally unacceptable like murder, theft, molestation, fraud, embezzlement and the like. But as a bearer of high moral standards and as a moral authority, the law is questionable. As White (1988) points out:

> But there are problems with making the law an ultimate standard of right and wrong. The law allows many actions that are morally offensive (manipulating people or lying to your friends). It prohibits things that might be morally neutral or even good (certain sexual practices). And it is changeable and contradictory. (p. 15)

Laws in the United States once permitted slavery, laws in Nazi Germany gave sanction to antisemitism, and laws in the former USSR denied basic human freedoms. In each case, the laws were abandoned, but only after much bloodshed. Other practices like capital punishment, abortion, euthanasia, pornography, prostitution and so on are illegal in some countries but legal in others. Even within one's own country, laws change or are different with regard to some of these moral issues. Prostitution is legal in Nevada but not in other states. Does this make prostitution right or wrong?

In any nation, the law may serve to please the majority of its people, a particular political party, or some dictator, and this would have very little to do with the establishment of what is ethical. Even a majority view can condone immoral practices. Moreover, the authority of law can be coercive in many practical instances, whereas ethical principles are held open to be scrutinized and accepted or rejected freely. Ethics, therefore, is unlike the law in many respects when it comes to moral concerns.

Finally, there is one area many people subscribe to as a moral authority and for moral guidance: religion. In fact, some people claim that without religion there can be no morality at all. Because religion is mostly concerned with how we lead our lives, it has much to say about living a moral life. Many people turn to religious teachings and authorities in times of moral crises and do find acceptable, sound answers. But there are differences between religious ethics and philosophical ethics.

White (1988) identifies three main distinctions. Religious ethics focuses on one's spiritual sensitivities and needs, whereas philosophical ethics appeals primarily to one's intellect and reasoning abilities. Second, religious ethics is often expressed in authoritative and emotive terms, and this mode of expression takes religious ethics beyond public and philosophical debate. Finally, those who deny religion altogether (atheists) can still engage in moral discourse as rational human beings and also live decent lives.

Religion is not being denied here as an area where there are answers to moral questions. However, one must recognize that the tasks and objectives of religion are different from those of philosophical ethics. What is sometimes more surprising is to learn about the common moral grounds and solutions they share. Despite the occasional overlap, religious ethics and philosophical ethics are not equivalent.

This section has provided an overview of the nature of ethics by indicating the kinds of value issues taken up by moral judgments and by discussing what ethics is and is not. In the following, we will discuss the characteristics of morality, which is related to the concept taken up here.

KEY CONCEPTS

normative	nonnormative
judgments of moral value	differentiation of ethical questions
ethics and authority	ethics and the law
ethics and religion	judgments of moral obligation

Morality

There are important connections and differences between ethics and morality; the latter can be considered the subject area of the former. That is, the principles and theories of ethics derive from or explain the way of life, beliefs, attitudes, intentions, and motives that are judged to possess moral qualities. The term *morality* usually encompasses all facets of life in which moral questions can arise. For this reason, religion and morality are closely linked as indicated above.

Beauchamp (1991) describes morality as "a social institution with a code of learnable rules" (p. 6). The social nature of morality, its application of certain rules, and its expansive concerns separate it from ethics, which has a primary theoretical interest. Morality then is grounded in practical affairs of social life, and this will be the focus of our examination here.

Most social rules are already established and given, and so morality exists prior to any one person. People inherit and appropriate morality at a young age when they are told what to do and what not to do: "Brush your teeth after every meal," "don't run too fast or you might fall," and "don't go into the pool alone" are all familiar "do" and "don't" expressions. Such rules involve self-interest and teach young people to act in a prudent manner.

On the other hand, "leave your sister's toys alone," "don't cheat when you play soccer," "always tell the truth," "honor your mother and father," and the like are considered moral rules. These rules take into account the interests of others, their rights, and the respect they are due as human beings. These rules teach one how to behave with others and what is expected in one's conduct in relation to others. In most instances, morality is other-regarding and is the foundation of every society (though some challenge this view). Morality, more properly speaking then, is concerned with behavior and rules in this social and morally relevant sense (Velasquez, 1992).

According to Frankena (1973), morality is both similar to and different from some aspects of law and certain features of social customs and etiquette. People are introduced and taught about morality and society's conventions through similar patterns of development. However, morality, like law and unlike customs, is not overly concerned with matters of taste and appearance. On the other hand, morality, like conventions and unlike law, does not rely on an authoritative body that might be manipulative and coercive. Some go beyond the realms of law and convention to say that morality is whatever is guided by pure intentions, like benevolence or doing what is right for its own sake. The latter can be important in the exercise of morality, something one would not entirely rule out, but more important, morality differs from prudent behavior, personal or social taste, and threatening actions.

That morality as a social institution serves to guide individual conduct does not necessarily mean that people merely act according to social norms and standards. Society's moral system does indicate what is forbidden and what is permitted in many areas. However, one also learns to take an individual moral perspective on many distinct issues where society's rules may not be very helpful. That is, morality teaches people to understand and apply standards from a personal moral point of view, as well as to adopt norms from society at large (Frankena, 1973).

As well as examining the social institution thesis, Beauchamp (1991) identifies four distinguishing marks of morality. Reference has been made to some of these features already, but a short review of each will better establish the nature of morality.

1. *Morality is concerned with moral ideals that are accepted as "supremely authoritative or overriding" guides for behavior* (p. 16). This means that issues of self-interest, personal politics, religious influences, and the like cannot supersede a moral principle, but granting such high significance to ideals simply because they are moral may be inadequate. Such principles would require moral justification to be granted an overriding status. But then the entire question of moral weight, competing demands, and moral justification could also lead to a circular argument (a chicken-egg-type dilemma). Moreover, people often behave without placing moral ideals at the top of their list of concerns, especially when involved in activities with

alternative demands (e.g., when playing sports). The supremacy of moral principles may be a sufficient, but not always a necessary, condition of morality.

2. *Morality contains a prescriptive character.* Morality guides human action by recommending that one act or refrain from acting in certain ways. Sometimes this is explicitly understood by using words like "ought" and "should not," but at other times, expressions that appear to be moral may contain a vague or no prescriptive sense. To say "that was a noble gesture" or "she displays virtue" can tell us relatively little or nothing at all in terms of how we should act. While recognizing this weakness, morality usually prescribes actions for us, and in many instances this is considered the hallmark of morality.

3. *Universalizability is a distinguishing feature of morality.* This component was briefly mentioned in earlier discussions, but it refers to the notion that moral judgments must be held the same for all people in relevantly similar situations. In principle, this element of morality is quite rational and credible. In practice, however, universalizability has at least three problems. First, there could be serious disagreements as to what counts as "relevantly similar situations." Second, this characteristic suggests that moral ideals and principles can be theoretically deduced for all people without any consideration of cultural differences and the real choices people have when making moral decisions. Universalizability is also not applicable to supererogatory acts, behavior beyond acceptable standards, such as giving charity or acting heroic. This criterion is a foundational element of morality for many people, and in many circumstances it is an exceedingly important criterion, but it has its weaknesses as well.

4. *Morality has to have a central concern for the well being of others.* It must consider both harms and benefits to others, and guide people toward the general enhancement of human beings. Certain virtues like generosity, empathy, justice, compassion, and the like might be expressed to show one's interest in the welfare of others. Unfortunately, these virtues are sometimes manifested in prejudicial ways in terms of favoring one class or group of people. For example, scholarship athletes and athletic "perks" might indicate inequitable treatment between college athletes and the average college student. Maintaining consistency when expressing such virtues can be a problem. Simply applying action-guiding codes based on this criterion might also display a bias, for instance, in the area of affirmative action and charges of reverse discrimination. Although concern for others is a central element of morality, how morality and the welfare of others are linked must be clear and unequivocal.

One can see that each of these four distinguishing marks of morality is deficient to some extent and that it would be difficult to arrive at a satisfactory set of sufficient and necessary conditions for morality. Beauchamp (1991), therefore, considers a pluralistic approach to determine what counts as morality. Perhaps no single unitary definition or set of features can characterize the moral. On the other hand, there may be some characteristics of morality that, if present, adequately tell people that they are dealing with a moral principle or ideal.

After presenting several combinations of the above marks, Beauchamp concludes by saying that different combinations may apply to various behaviors or events, and in each case one could sufficiently determine what counts as morality. This approach is perhaps the most reasonable way to view morality because it accounts for the dominant marks of morality and it is also linked to specific situations and actions.

Besides addressing the question of what morality is, three other features of morality deserve our attention: the idea of a moral position, the object of morality, and the motives for moral behavior (Beauchamp, 1991). It has already been stated that sport management ethics is an applied area of moral philosophy. Ethical theories and principles would be applied to try to understand, examine, and resolve particular moral dilemmas in sport management. As we shall see immediately below, sport management practices can be, and are, defended by appealing to moral positions.

These positions are usually some important, unquestioned underlying moral stances, free of prejudice, emotional reactions, and personal preference, which are taken up to defend certain behavior. But a genuine moral position is difficult to identify. A sports section editor might defend the lack of female sports coverage in the newspaper by saying "but everyone knows female sports is boring." A sports promoter might defend a certain questionable marketing campaign by claiming, "What they don't know can't hurt them." An athletic director might ignore the fact that athletic department student interns are providing college tours for potential scholarship athletes during prohibited times of the year by claiming, "Any student can show a prospective student the campus." In each case actions are defended by appealing to a moral position. But in these instances each view may be biased or prejudicial.

People express moral positions about many issues and over many types of behavior, but they rarely state their moral positions so clearly that these positions are free from some sort of rationalization. It may also be unsatisfactory to state one's moral position in such general terms that the connection to morality cannot be clearly acknowledged (Beauchamp, 1991). These difficulties can surface because moral positions usually require the articulation of sound, reasoned ethical principles and ideals, which are hardly ever considered on a day-to-day basis. One should, therefore, remain suspect when moral positions are supplied as reasons to explain various actions and situations.

Like the question of moral positions, the object of morality can also be unclear, yet important toward understanding the parameters of morality. What is one attempting to achieve by morality? What purpose does morality serve? We have already discussed social and personal themes related to morality, but these were just general observations. These questions should not cause much despair because many philosophers have left the question of morality's purpose or function vague.

Some have suggested that morality can lead to a happy life; others have stressed a "good will" might guide one's moral decisions. Still others claim that morality serves to combat deteriorating social relationships. In this view, human relations degenerate because there are limits to resources, sympathy, and information (Beauchamp 1991). Examples of this deterioration include all kinds of physical and psychological violence, various forms of intolerance and injustice, business and government scandals, and a host of other problems of an interpersonal nature. Morality tends to diminish one's limits of sympathy, for example, so one recognizes and is sensitive to these impaired social relations and ultimately acts to better this state of affairs. But who can really say what *the* object of morality is?

Morality can point toward a number of goals and purposes like the ones just mentioned. Morality is concerned with human rights, freedoms, and needs. It also censures selfish and harmful acts toward others so people get along in society. By leading a moral life, it is likely that many people can attain a modicum of happiness and perhaps possess the character to make sound moral decisions and "do the right thing." It might be more reasonable then to look for several purposes and functions of morality rather than one all-encompassing object.

Finally, what motives does one have for acting in moral ways? What compels one to follow societal rules that constitute morality? Nowell-Smith (1967) suggests there are three basic motives. *Enlightened self-interest* might make us fearful to act in ways that go against our moral duties and obligations. Few people would want to feel socially isolated because they failed to follow certain moral rules. In some cases, some type of punishment is meted out for violating the tenets of moral codes. Still, most people realize that in the long run adhering to societal rules has social and personal advantages.

Respect for rules is another motive. We are taught at an early age how to follow rules and what rules to follow. Consider going to a foreign country and learning its customs and laws. One might encounter different mannerisms, etiquette, procedures, and regulations that guide all facets of life in a relatively new way. One would also likely be made aware how many of one's own cultural rules are different and go unquestioned. Sometimes one is unable to account for why one does certain things, and one claims "that's just the way it's done." Social rules can be deeply ingrained in this sense. At other times people fail to question not only the rule but also the source or author of a rule. An extreme case of this might be following the rules of cult leaders, who seem to have an incredible hold on their followers. In a milder form, most bureaucratic rules are rarely disputed and are uncritically accepted by most people. Being accustomed to obey rules then is another motive for morality.

Finally, *other-regarding* motives create in people a commitment to morality. Care, trust, compassion, benevolence, respect for persons are some of these motives. People often act in moral ways simply because they possess a deep concern for others. This motive is sometimes difficult to identify because the same act might also be compelled by a rule. Nevertheless, people should recognize that genuine instances of selflessness do occur and can serve as a motive for morality.

The discussion of ethics and morality to this point has covered a fair number of themes and ideas. Both areas are closely related, but they can be distinguished. In general, ethics refers to the theoretical aspects of moral philosophy, its standards and principles, whereas morality inquires into the social implications and expressions of ethical judgments. To better understand the nature of morality we briefly considered the way societal rules are taught and apprehended. We will examine this process further in the next section, which deals with the interrelated topics of moral reasoning and moral development.

KEY CONCEPTS

prudent other-regarding	morality as overriding concern	
prescriptive	universalizability	well-being of others
moral positions	enlightened self-interest	
respect for rules	moral objects	

Moral Development and Moral Reasoning

People begin to learn about morality at a young age, as mentioned above, but questions like how does one come to know right from wrong, how does one recognize a moral problem and how are moral decisions arrived at as one matures require more detailed answers. Moral reasoning and development consider these and other similar questions.

For most people, the identification and application of moral standards start in the home. Parents and guardians are usually the first teachers of morality, and the lessons and values they try to instill are extremely varied. They not only provide moral instruction in terms of resolving any number of important and sometimes trivial problems, but they are also instrumental in shaping the moral character of children.

Some of one's early moral education occurs explicitly. At about the time a child can begin to understand language, parents bombard children with all kinds of rules to follow: People admonish children for not doing this or doing that, praise children for appropriate behavior, and tell children to trust and cooperate with others, and occasionally, to be suspicious of some people. In other instances, moral lessons are learned implicitly. Adults use facial expressions, a look, gestures, or body language to convey approval or disapproval over a child's moral behavior. Through one's immediate family, and especially from one's parents, a wealth of moral values, rules, and standards is appropriated.

Parental figures are certainly not the only moral teachers of children, and the home is not the only place where moral education occurs. Children learn about morality from day-care personnel, school teachers, coaches, relatives, other parents, and other children. They also find themselves in different environments like in front of the television, at a friend's home, in public places, or at the day-care center, school, and the playground where ethical problems arise. Despite the many situations they find themselves in and the numerous people they come in contact with, children learn to develop the capacity to deal with moral issues

The important word in the last sentence is *learn*. No one is born with the ability to reason about moral concerns. Morality, moral standards, and rules are inherited. We are first exposed to morality, and only later do we acquire the capacity to think critically about moral issues. Most children then cannot utilize moral reasoning until they possess some language skills, become socialized to some extent, and have sufficient life experiences. This indicates that moral reasoning is acquired in a developmental way, a view that has been recognized throughout Western history. Just as our physical development can be traced, so too can our moral development. Contemporary research on moral development has been most prominently advanced by Lawrence Kohlberg, and it is to his work that we will now turn to discuss this process and the notion of moral reasoning.

Building on Jean Piaget's ideas of moral development, Kohlberg (1987) believes, unlike Piaget, that children and adolescents move through distinct moral stages in which different levels of moral judgments can be identified. Kohlberg's model consists of three levels, the preconventional, the conventional, and the postconventional. Those generally under the age of nine, and perhaps adolescent and adult criminals are at the preconventional level. The conventional level refers to the acceptance and conformity to society's laws, rules, conventions and norms by most adolescents and adults. Finally, the postconventional level includes those above the age of 20 who can apply moral principles to social rules, and who accept the latter based on such principles and not on conventions.

Kohlberg (1987) sees these levels of moral development in terms of the relationship between the individual and society's rules and expectations. Consequently, Level I is characterized by a separation between conventions and the individual. The person here sees social rules as external to the self. A Level II individual closely identifies with society's rules and expectations, while a Level III person has identified his or her values independently of social norms, and in some cases the two may conflict, based on ethical principles.

In each of these levels, there are two moral stages, one more advanced than the other. Kohlberg (1987) elaborates on each of these stages by considering three areas: (a) what is right, (b) the reasons for doing right, and (c) the social perspective behind each stage. Let's turn to examine his model in greater detail (Kohlberg, 1987, pp. 284-286).

Level I: Preconventional

Stage 1—Heteronomous morality. What is right is not to break rules that have punishments attached to them, to be obedient for the sake of obedience and not to cause physical harm to others and property. Avoiding punishment and recognizing the power of the authority who sets the rules are the reasons for doing right. From a social perspective, morality is viewed as egocentric. Individuals do not account for the interests of others; they recognize only the physicality of actions, not their psychological aspects, and they cannot differentiate between their point of view and that of an authority.

Stage 2—Individualism, instrumental purpose, and exchange. What is right is to follow rules to achieve one's own interests, to let others do the same, and to deem as fair what is an equal exchange, deal, or arrangement. Reasons for doing right are to serve one's interests while realizing others are fulfilling their interests. Socially speaking, this stage expresses a concrete individualistic point of view. Each person has his or her own interests to pursue, making each right in a relativistic sense.

Level II: Conventional

Stage 3—Mutual interpersonal expectations, relationships, and interpersonal conformity. What is right is to live up to the expectations of those who are in one's immediate sphere of influence, to be good by displaying proper motives and concern for others, to keep mutual relations with others through loyalty, trust, confidence, respect, and gratitude. Reasons for doing right include the desire to be good, to have others recognize this goodness, to show concern for others, to follow the Golden Rule, and to adhere to rules and authority that support general good behavior. Relationships between individuals is the main social perspective here. One becomes aware of the feelings and expectations of others beyond self-interest, can apply the Golden Rule, and assume another point of view, but does not yet fully recognize the larger social context and system.

Stage 4—Social system and conscience. Doing right involves fulfilling agreed-upon duties, adhering to laws except in extreme cases, and contributing to groups, institutions, and society. The reasons for doing right include ensuring the maintenance of institutions and society, preventing their erosion, and letting one's conscience guide the fulfillment of obligations. One is aware one is a member of society, yet is able to differentiate society's perspective from interpersonal agreements and motives by recognizing roles and rules in the social system and identifying the place of the individual in the social system.

Level III: Postconventional, or Principled

Stage 5—Social contract or utility and individual rights. What is right is being aware that others and individual groups hold different and relative values and rules, accepting these differences by reason of a social contract (to ensure the impartial interest of all), and upholding basic fundamental values, like life and liberty, above any relative values. The reasons for doing right include recognition that abiding by laws preserves and protects the rights and interests of others, security in the knowledge that others enter into the social contract freely and with commitment, and rational acknowledgment of the utility of a contractual social arrangement. This stage is called the prior-to-society perspective because the individual is aware that values and rights are independent of social agreements.

The person tries to integrate various perspectives through formal procedures to arrive at contracts and agreements that maintain impartiality and follow due process. He or she also considers moral and legal matters noting that they are sometimes in conflict and difficult to integrate.

Stage 6—Universal ethical principles. What is right are self-chosen ethical principles that are the foundation for justifying laws and particular social agreements. When laws and these principles are in discord, one follows the principles. Such universal principles include justice, equality of human rights, and respect for the dignity of individuals. The reasons for doing right are the beliefs that these principles are valid for the rational person and that one has a personal commitment to uphold them. One takes a moral point of view at this stage, and all social attachments derive from this perspective. Persons are recognized as ends in themselves and must be treated as such, and it is acknowledged that rational people understand the nature of morality.

Kohlberg's model and analysis certainly offer or provide a useful way to understand the stages of moral growth and differences in moral reasoning. As a cognitive-developmental approach, the stages are ranked in a hierarchy, and so there are higher and lower stages. Kohlberg (1987) is careful to point out, however, that higher stages are not morally better than lower ones and that individuals at higher stages are not morally superior to those at lower stages. The ranking of moral stages is primarily to indicate that people have a better capacity to solve moral problems at higher stages, especially when issues of justice are considered.

Kohlberg has tried to demonstrate that his developmental model is universal by developing testing instruments to measure the moral stages, by conducting cross-cultural and gender-difference studies, and by finding relevant connections to personality, cognitive, and socialization theories. In many of these efforts, Kohlberg maintains that justice claims most clearly reveal different levels and patterns of moral reasoning and that the principle of justice has a central place in moral and social philosophy. This view is not shared by everyone.

Velasquez (1992) discusses the work of Gilligan, who agrees with Kohlberg's moral levels and stages, but she claims that Kohlberg neglects to account for the moral development of girls and women because his studies investigate mostly male subjects. In her own research, Gilligan (1982) has tried to show that males employ impersonal, impartial, and abstract moral rules and rely on principles of justice and rights to deal with moral problems as expressed at the postconventional stage. By contrast, women view moral issues in terms of caring for others and feeling responsible for the maintenance of relationships. In the early stages, the preconventional ones, this care and responsibility are primarily to oneself. At the conventional level, women internalize the social conventions of caring for others to the point of neglecting themselves. At the mature or postconventional level, women take a critical stance and strike a balance between caring for others and for themselves.

Although there are studies to indicate there are no gender differences in moral development, Gilligan's work provides an alternative approach toward understanding moral growth and reasoning. Kohlberg (1987) has responded to Gilligan's criticisms and acknowledges that males may focus more on justice and females more on care, and that there might be a two-track approach to moral development, even though significant differences between the genders may not be evident. He, therefore, concedes there may be a stage-type development based on care. He notes that particular moral situations may elicit a justice or a care response, and so the type of moral dilemmas one presents to research subjects can result in different findings. He also believes that caring and sympathy toward others are presupposed by any theory of justice, so there are linkages between caring and justice.

The important point of the preceding discussion is to recognize the areas of agreement between Kohlberg and Gilligan. Each considers moral development to occur in stages, moving from preconventional to conventional to postconventional levels. These stages are sequential; that is, one moves from a lower stage to a higher one. But this does not necessarily mean that everyone reaches Stages 5 and 6. In fact, Kohlberg believes most adults remain at the conventional level. Finally, Gilligan and Kohlberg both assert that moral development and reasoning lead to greater critical awareness about issues of right and wrong, and this motivates some to aspire to the postconventional level in which rational, open dialogue can lead to resolutions of moral conflicts (Velasquez, 1992).

Because most of the preceding discussion focused on moral development, let us now turn to examine the nature of moral reasoning. Some of the following points have been mentioned previously, but they are worth noting again in the present context.

Moral reasoning involves the cognitive procedures people employ to arrive at moral decisions and judgments. There, of course, is no one infallible process to follow. But in general, two important considerations are part of moral reasoning: (a) an understanding of what moral standards require or prohibit and (b) evidence to indicate that a policy, organization, or particular conduct contains features that apply to (a) (Velasquez, 1992). For example, "the killing of innocent people is wrong" might be a moral standard. If during a war it was known that there were stranded civilians in a village, then it would be morally wrong to order the village destroyed. In sport management, "the exploitation of others is wrong" might be a moral standard. An athletic director who compelled scholarship athletes to run errands for him and maintain the upkeep of his home would be committing a morally wrong offense.

As one can readily tell, three elements are involved in moral reasoning: moral standards, evidence, and moral judgments. Each component is essential in order to justify moral decisions taken by an institution or individual, or the moral directives of a policy. Although each feature is significant, one or the other may not be explicitly stated or given. In the wartime example above, the moral standard could have been omitted, and the reasoning would have remained intact.

In the case of the athletic director, the moral decision about his behavior could have been unstated, and the example would have made reasonable sense. Similarly, there may be evidence that is widely known and accepted that would not require mention (e.g., there is about the same number of men and women in North American society). Still, in reasoning coherently and clearly about ethical matters it is recommended one be explicit about each component to avoid making weak moral arguments and poorly reasoned decisions.

This approach is suggested because too often people fail to make use of sufficient and appropriate evidence to support moral claims; or their decisions, evidence, and moral standards are not relevant to one another. It is also the case that there may be general agreement about moral principles, but some would attach certain qualifications or modifications to them. By doing this people find exceptions to alter some judgments that follow from a standard (Cornman & Lehrer, 1974). For instance, some who oppose abortion might find this option acceptable in cases of incest and rape. It is also difficult sometimes to distinguish between evidence and a moral standard, especially in practice when one occasionally thinks facts speak for themselves. So finding that fewer women are in positions of authority may not, in and of itself, support the standard that any society that treats men and women as unequal is unjust. Clearly the components of moral issues are much more complex than this, yet in the main, the three elements discussed here are critical parts of moral reasoning.

Now that the constituent features of moral reasoning have been considered, it would be useful to examine next how one evaluates moral reasoning. Terms like *standards, justification, reasons,* and *decisions,* introduced in the above discussion, sound very much like expressions used in constructing logical arguments. In fact, moral arguments do rely to a large extent on the criteria of logic. Although logic seems to provide an almost foolproof way toward assessing the strength and weaknesses of arguments, its precision as a method of evaluation is not always ideal when considering moral issues.

Moral dilemmas often appeal to one's intuitive sense about whether something or someone's behavior is right or wrong. In some instances, we tend to distinguish between good and bad intuitively. Although many people would generally claim lying is wrong, who could rely on this principle if a known killer asked you the whereabouts of his next likely victim? Intuitive feelings and opinions do have a place in moral reasoning, yet total reliance on these would create enormous difficulties. For one thing, whose intuitions and opinions would one judge most acceptable? In addition to the limited value of the individual's intuitive sense, people must also recognize that moral reasoning is not an "exact science" like mathematics. Any analysis dealing with moral concerns cannot possibly expect to treat particular problems with complete certainty. This is not to say that clear thinking about moral matters is impossible but to point out that one is not dealing with mathematical absolutes and immutable formulae.

Now that we have stated these qualifications, let us consider three general criteria of good moral reasoning as suggested by Simon (1991). First, moral reasoning must remain impartial. One must not take a self-interested perspective when making moral judgments. That is, it would be morally incorrect if one were to formulate ethical principles tailored to meet personal desires, interests, and needs. This is not acceptable in moral discourse because it arbitrarily excludes others from such deliberations and places oneself in a morally superior position. No one can justifiably claim the latter. But one quickly learns that taking an impartial position is not always easy because it requires one to consider the perspectives of others and to ignore any individual privileges and advantages.

A second criterion of moral reasoning is to take a position that is systematically consistent. For example, if one's moral viewpoint is generally to refrain from harming others, then it would be inconsistent to claim that harming others is acceptable in certain situations, unless the circumstances in each instance could be shown to be relevantly dissimilar. So, the principle of not harming others should equally apply in various public situations and places, but likely not on the front line during a war. The issue of violence in sport hinges on this criterion because some contend a sport environment is relevantly dissimilar to other circumstances, and therefore, certain practices are permitted in sport whereas they would not be in other situations (e.g., one might go to jail for slashing one's neighbor with a stick, yet in ice hockey one would get a 2-minute penalty for doing the same thing, if one were caught!). If no relevantly dissimilar features can be found between two situations, then holding the same moral position in each case would lead to a contradiction. That is, if community living and ice hockey are similar, one cannot say that not harming others applies to the first situation and not the second. To do so would be inconsistent.

Finally, in addition to impartiality and consistency, moral reasoning must "account for reflective judgments about clear moral examples" (Simon, 1991, p. 11). This means that moral standards must be analyzed together with particular cases to reveal the extent of their moral worth. Critically, reflectively challenging and refining moral principles, free from cultural biases and other prejudices, can ensure that dialogue about moral issues continues in an open and uncoercive manner. Moral standards should be tested in the real world, and even on a hypothetical plane (e.g., through counter examples), if such principles are to be considered more than mere abstractions. In this way, principles are linked to actions and possible actions, a kind of test for coherence in practice.

It is rather plain to see that to refute a moral argument or position, one would have to demonstrate in it a lack of impartiality, consistency or practical moral worth, or all three. Yet even by adhering to these criteria, there is still no guarantee that a single line of moral reasoning is flawless. It may also turn out that several moral viewpoints are reasonable. What the aforementioned criteria provide are guidelines to judge whether some moral standards, arguments, and judgments are better justified than others when rationally evaluated. In many instances, this is the best one can do when one reasons about moral issues. (It has been and will be assumed in this text that ethical concerns can be rationally scrutinized and that moral positions and decisions can be assessed and justified through reason. *Relativism* is a view that opposes these tenets of morality. A presentation and critique of relativism will not be offered here, but interested readers can consult Rachels (1986) for an informative examination of this line of thought.)

Because the last criterion of moral reasoning referred to actions or possible ones taken as a consequence of ethical deliberations, the next section will examine the character of ethical conduct.

KEY CONCEPTS

parental/guardian influences	social influences	
Kohlberg's 3 levels of moral development		
Gilligan's ethic of care	moral standards	evidence
moral judgements	impartiality	consistency
coherence in practice		

Ethical Conduct

Without ethical behavior, all the moral reasoning in the world would seem pointless. Ethical principles and moral standards must at some stage take expression in the form of human conduct. Just as these axioms may be questioned, their corresponding and recommended actions are often judged to be good or bad, right or wrong, justified or unjustified. In fact, many consider the main enterprise of ethics is to define and serve as a guide for moral behavior. As Pepper (1960) states, "the term *conduct* in ethical tradition has generally meant voluntary acts of choice which necessarily involve criteria for deciding whether the choices are good or bad" (p. 4). A serious difficulty, however, is identifying the parameters by which conduct can be determined as ethical or not.

To begin, one needs to establish the domain of moral behavior. What counts as action that complies with or can be linked to moral standards? As suggested above, ethical conduct has to be voluntary. An action that results from compulsion, coercion, or even force usually cannot be characterized as moral behavior. There would be no grounds for holding people responsible for or commending their actions if they did not act with some measure of freedom. But a reasonable question is, how much freedom is required to claim behavior is indeed voluntary? Is the soldier who kills innocent civilians in cold blood merely following orders and therefore not acting freely? Is the behavior of habitual criminals a consequence of their unstable personal backgrounds and the impoverished environment in which they were reared? Is the athlete who is told by the coach to harm opposing players simply following directions and doing what is best for the team? These questions are part of a philosophical debate between two concepts, *determinism and free will*, and these ideas have an important bearing on ethical conduct.

Briefly, determinism maintains that there is a cause for everything in the universe. Because all occurrences necessarily have causes, if one can specify a set of conditions, one can predict future events, or the effects of such conditions, each and every time. To a large degree modern science subscribes to this view.

But determinism goes one step further by claiming that cause-and-effect relationships also apply to human beings. Everything about humanity is caused. Because this is the case, human beings possess neither free will nor the capacity to act in a voluntary manner. Their choices and behavior are determined. They are determined by personality, upbringing, past experiences, and training. Humans do not have the ability to do otherwise than what they do, and everything they do has a causal explanation. This, of course, means that people cannot be held morally responsible or culpable (Minton & Shipka, 1990).

However, in many instances humans do feel a sense of freedom in their choices and in their conduct. Proponents of free will, or what is also known as *libertarianism* or *indeterminism*, point out that creative and expressive behavior in the arts, for example, is rooted in freedom. Interpretation and selection are central means by which painters, sculptors, writers, musicians, composers, dancers, and even some athletes engage in the creation of art. Some claim that art provides the most radical context for the expression of free will and freedom.

Aside from the arts, it would be hard to imagine having no alternatives or control in human lives, but this would be the case if people lived in a deterministic world. It would also mean that people could neither feel proud of their accomplishments nor feel regret about any possible achievements, because who one is, what one becomes, and what one does are caused. That is, people are not responsible for any of their successes or for their failures, even those associated with moral behavior.

One's experiences, however, tell one otherwise. One does hold people morally responsible when their conduct breaches moral standards, and one even goes so far as to punish them when they violate morally binding laws. In these instances, one accepts the notion that in general people's actions are voluntary and they are accountable for what they do and sometimes do not do.

But are determinism and indeterminism the only options? In fact, there is a third view. *Soft-determinism* takes a moderate approach between the latter positions and claims they are compatible. Rather than denying causality altogether as radical libertarians would suggest, soft-determinists say that for moral responsibility to exist, some causal determinants are required (Minton & Shipka, 1990). Human decisions and behavior cannot be completely devoid of some causes. Aspects of personality and past experiences do influence one's identity, one's interests, and one's conduct. Freedom cannot be totally separated from causes, but is connected to certain types of causes, like one's personality. By appealing to specific select causes, explanations can be given about one's behavior, reforms can be made in one's conduct, and genuine instances of freedom, those not caused, can be identified. Soft-determinism points out that freedom really means being free from external restrictions when deciding to act and when acting, rather than acting without any antecedent causes.

So, is ethical conduct really voluntary? Yes and no. Perhaps the best way to approach the matter is to speak about variability (Shirk, 1965). The voluntary aspects of moral behavior come in different degrees. Good and bad habits, for example, may be construed as having less of a voluntary quality than that found in other practices. But the acquisition and perhaps alteration of habits stem from voluntary acts that are under human control. This is to say that even habits are not entirely determined. On the other hand, acts of kindness, charity or love seem to possess a greater voluntary character. Despite the voluntary nature and particular forms of benevolent action, to some degree these are influenced by external constraints.

Moreover, we have not touched on situational factors that would certainly influence the nature of ethical conduct. In some circumstances certain actions are morally neutral whereas the same conduct in a different situation would lend itself to moral evaluation. Tying one's shoelace is usually a morally indifferent act, yet to do so deliberately in a tennis match as a delaying tactic to irritate one's opponent may be ethically questionable. The extent to which actions are considered voluntary may be also traced over time. We generally hold that children have less capacity to act in voluntary ways than do adolescents and adults. So the scope of voluntary actions expands through growth and maturation. An important point being made here is that one has to have the ability and opportunity to act in an ethical manner. In addition to the question of determinism and free will, possessing the personal capacity and being in appropriate circumstances for moral behavior are also important elements in the notion of variability in ethical conduct (Shirk, 1965).

Part of the above discussion mentioned another feature of moral behavior—responsibility. Ethical conduct would likely be vacuous if it carried no sense of responsibility with it. This characteristic is significant not only from the perspective of identification but also from the standpoint of accountability. What is it that one is responsible for? For a mature, rational adult, one might say, in a cavalier way, everything that is part of and constitutes one's life. This means the sum total of one's adult experiences. Because almost every aspect of people's lives can be couched in normative (valuative) terms, their ethical conduct and responsibility can extend to vast personal spheres. Feibleman (1967) put it this way: "An adult who is in a state of health is responsible for all of his actions" (p. 81).

This is something that goes unrecognized by many people. They often fail to acknowledge the moral implications of their conduct and too easily dismiss accepting responsibility for the things they do and say. Even if people's behavior is involuntary, carried out under compulsion, or beyond their awareness, moral consequences and effects may still arise from such conduct. People are responsible even for the unforeseen results of their behavior. Therefore, responsibility runs deep in almost everything people do.

The voluntary nature of ethical conduct leads naturally then to the notion of being responsible for one's moral actions. Just as there is variability of freedom and constraints as related to behavior, so too are there differing degrees of responsibility. Adults are held to be more responsible for their actions than are children. People who are senile, insane, or who have some type of personality disorder are generally absolved of some or all responsibility for their behavior. This is why a more complete sense of moral responsibility is usually reserved for adults who are healthy, rational, and mature.

However, the last statement poses a difficulty because it is not always clear what one means by or what counts as being healthy, rational, and mature. Should these considerations include attitudes, emotions, instincts, level of intelligence, etc.? Are feelings reliable yardsticks by which to make ethical judgments, or should only reason prevail? No single pat answer can satisfy these questions. It would likely be more useful to consider such issues on a case to case basis. Defining these terms categorically would probably discount relevant areas that must be considered when making ethical decisions. Although each person can characterize a typical "healthy, rational, and mature" individual, in some particular cases, mostly the difficult ones, a clearer comprehension of these expressions might be necessary. Once this is done in a satisfactory manner, the type and level of moral responsibility attached to specific behavior can be reasonably determined.

Another significant feature of ethical conduct briefly mentioned above refers to its unintended consequences. People often think, or would like to think, that their moral behavior is a result of carefully thought-out and reasoned deliberations. That is, one is conscious of one's ethical judgments; one acts from reflection and has considered the implications of one's actions (Shirk,1965). But as stated earlier in this chapter, many moral rules are accepted and followed through habit. People sometimes know what is customary and expected, and little or no thought is given to their actions. Ethical conduct can, therefore, include behavior that is unconsciously carried out.

If this is so, then in some instances people are unaware of the effects of their behavior. They might be unconscious about their decision to act and also the ramifications of their actions. Yet these unintended results may be evaluated and assessed in terms of right or wrong, good or bad. They may have an influence on the environment or on others, influence that is morally relevant. So whether one acts wittingly or not, one's actions can carry moral weight, and one may not even realize the extent of that weight.

Related to the idea of consequences is the notion of "inaction or refraining from action," which is also an element of ethical conduct (Shirk, 1965, p. 26). Acts of omission are sometimes more difficult to detect because the premise here is that one decides not to act or to act alternatively. But the effects of doing nothing, or of consciously removing oneself from a situation, can be powerful. Gandhi and Martin Luther King, Jr., for example, advocated what is known as "passive resistance." Their movements not only created enormous social and political changes but they were also built on a moral foundation. A workers' strike is another example in which choosing not to fulfill one's role as a laborer carries ethical implications. The consequences of some strikes, especially by groups like physicians and teachers, can have far-reaching moral effects. To some avid spectators, a players' strike in professional sports is a moral issue. Boycotting a product or refusing to travel to a country that violates human rights is a moral expression. In each of these cases, doing other than expected, being passive, or doing nothing at all is an instance of moral behavior.

Finally, ethical conduct is characterized by involving others. This goes back to the idea that there is no such thing as private ethics. But the sense of involvement here is extensive. It not only considers direct, interactive moral behavior between people, such as telling the truth or treating others with fairness, but also those private moments when one sometimes catches oneself acting in an ethically suspect manner. When questioning one's behavior in these seemingly solitary instances, one is likely reacting to or reflecting on some moral standard that indirectly involves others. No such thought would ever arise otherwise.

The meaning of *others* is necessarily broad here and might include one's parents, teachers, coaches, clergy, or society-at-large. Moral rules and sensitivities are learned and acquired from such others. So at times, one's own ethical judgments might reflect their influence even when one is alone. Ethical conduct implicates others in two directions then. In one instance, one's moral behavior has a direct impact on others as far as moving out toward them and penetrating their sphere of influence. This may be performed in a clear, unambiguous fashion or in a subtle, unassuming manner. In the second instance, others have some bearing on one's moral sense that can be expressed explicitly, or occasionally, in moments of privacy. Because the ethical conduct we are speaking about is expansive, the social implications of such behavior is similarly sweeping.

Implicit in the discussion in this section is the way in which ethical conduct is understood. It usually means and includes behavior that is good, right, correct, just, commendable, and the like. To say "she displays ethical conduct in her work" is to mean that she carries out her tasks in exemplary fashion, morally speaking. So the expression *ethical conduct* generally distinguishes actions that are already virtuous. If this is so, we need to examine the nature of behavior excluded from the domain of ethical conduct.

KEY CONCEPTS

volunteerism	determinism or free will	libertarianism or indeterminism
soft-determinism	responsibility	involvement of others
unintended consequences	acts of omission	

Misconduct

Three definitions of misconduct are provided by *Webster's New Collegiate Dictionary* (1977). One refers to "mismanagement," another to "intentional wrongdoing," and a third to "improper behavior" (p. 734). All three meanings are relevant to the discussion of ethics in this text, and each will be taken up separately in this section.

The most general of the three senses is to claim that misconduct is a form of improper behavior. This is a broad category that can involve everything from transgressions of etiquette and customs to violations of morally binding laws. So, talking with one's mouth full of food, spitting at someone, and pushing oneself to the front of a queue at the grocery store are usually examples of poor, not to mention boorish, manners. Rape, incest, and molestation are criminal acts that are morally reprehensible. But take the case of adultery. In many societies it is morally unacceptable, or at least seriously frowned upon, whereas in other cultures having lovers and being married to someone else is socially permissible, or at least tolerated with no stigma attached to it. The same can be said about polygamy.

These examples indicate that improper behavior can be manifested in both serious and mild forms, and can be closely linked to one's social conditions. Impolite conduct may be easily identified and corrected. People do this constantly with children, with a fair measure of success. In going to a foreign country, one can be taught the proper way to do certain things to avoid embarrassment. Even in sports, there are specific actions that are traditionally unacceptable. For instance, when an offside is called in ice hockey, it would be improper for the player with the puck to shoot at the goal.

More serious improprieties are either construed as criminal or as being so repugnant they are morally censured by society. Criminal activities are the more obvious and readily identifiable cases. But in instances of adultery, note the following. How many political figures have had or almost had their careers destroyed or tainted by scandals involving adultery? North American society clearly considers adultery to be improper behavior, even though some politicians are able to circumvent the issue and survive. Improper behavior then includes a wide range of various kinds of conduct, and most are easily recognized.

The second meaning of misconduct refers to intentional wrongdoing. In one sense, one could claim that forms of conduct here are similar to those categorized as improper behavior, and in numerous instances this would be true. Many criminal activities as well as actions deemed morally repugnant are deliberate acts. But in some situations, improper behavior can be differentiated from acts of intentional wrongdoing.

The insanity plea is still accepted in criminal cases, and although the actual crime is considered improper, a willful posture was not present when the crime was being committed. In fact, in such cases, the defense tries to establish that the defendant did not have the mental capacity to distinguish between right and wrong, and therefore could not have deliberately set out to do wrong. Similarly, breaches of etiquette may not involve conscious, voluntary actions. Traditional social customs and mores can develop into habits, and certain behavioral patterns are performed with little or no thought to them. The same can be said for poor habits some might judge to be examples of misconduct. These instances then indicate that we must seek a more precise understanding of intentional wrongdoing.

Let us approach this expression by examining each of its components. The idea of intention and its connection to action is and has been a difficult problem in philosophy, and so we can provide only a cursory treatment of this issue. To carry out an action with intent at least means that one is free and has the ability to act, one adequately knows what one is about to do, and one is sufficiently aware of the possible consequences and implications of one's actions. To perform an action with intent has traditionally meant that a person acts from some inner desire and with volition, as a sort of antecedent cause of some bodily movement. That is, intent has to do with the power each person possesses to knowingly initiate action (D'Arcy, 1963).

Of course, serious problems can arise from such a view. For example, one can intend one thing and for some reason, a situational factor perhaps, perform an action that was unintended. One hears pleas such as "I only meant to hurt him, not to kill him," and so the intent may have been different from the outcome. For our purposes here, *intentional* will refer to sufficiently anticipating and planning in advance what actions one is about to take, being reasonably sure one can execute said actions, and realizing the corresponding implications of such actions.

This definition suggests that one must be free and have the ability to act (Velasquez, 1992). If this freedom and ability did not exist or were seriously curtailed due to a lack of power, control, access to resources or to pressure, coercion, mental disability, and the like, then one might be excused from responsibility for wrongful acts. But to intend something that is wrongful requires that one knows the difference between right and wrong. In this case, ignorance of some vital information or knowledge that can assist in making this distinction usually excuses one from blame for a wrongful act. If one did not know about certain moral standards in a foreign country, let us say, and acted in a wrongful manner, one could be accused of misconduct, but not be held morally responsible. A similar lack of knowledge might arise because one is unfamiliar with certain situational factors. Ignorance resulting from circumstances such as described in these cases would excuse wrongful behavior.

On the other hand, deliberately keeping oneself ignorant, by not reading a crucial report or memo that might provide some important information, provides no excuse for moral culpability. This sometimes occurs in large corporations to "protect" executives and shelter them from moral responsibility. In circumstances where one can control one's ignorance, one can still be accused of intentional wrongdoing. *Intentional wrongdoing* then characterizes the deliberate and willful (planning, knowing in advance) aspects of carrying out of actions that might also be known to be wrong.

Clear cases of cheating, stealing, lying, bribery, conflicts of interest, denying the rights of others, and so forth would fall under this category of misconduct, that is, intentional wrongdoing. As mentioned, there are conditions that can excuse one from responsibility from this type of misconduct. There are also mitigating factors that can reduce the level of responsibility for these kinds of action. Velasquez (1992) identifies four such mitigating factors.

First, many moral dilemmas are surrounded by some uncertainty. If one was not quite sure how serious a certain action might be, or was unclear about a moral standard, then although one acted in a wrongful way, one's responsibility might lessen. Second, some actions are difficult to avoid. For example, in the workplace some people feel enormous pressure either from their superiors or from the demands of their job. Under such conditions, they sometimes act in ways they sense are wrong but feel powerless to avoid, and so they are not held completely responsible for their wrongful actions. Third, if one is not actively involved in the commission or omission of a wrongful act, this lack of involvement is generally accepted as a mitigating factor. The less one actively contributes to the outcome of an event, the less responsibility is attributed to that person for some occurrence. Finally, one also considers the seriousness of the injury that resulted from the wrongful action. If the misconduct is extremely serious, likely few or no mitigating factors will reduce responsibility for such action. On the other hand, less serious misconduct might itself act as a reason to lessen responsibility for such behavior. Despite the presence of conditions that can excuse or mitigate intentional wrongdoing, this form of misconduct may be summarized as the deliberate performance of actions known to be wrong.

The third sense of misconduct concerns a more particular set of actions described as mismanagement. This type of misconduct usually involves wrongdoing in bureaucratic or political organizations. Here, corporate standards of conduct; company policies; social, environmental, and fiscal rules and regulations are violated. Mismanagement might include such issues as fraud, embezzlement, lack of truth in advertising, questionable marketing practices, job discrimination, unjust collective bargaining, and breaches of employee rights.

Several of these examples are clearly criminal, but others could be related to internal procedures of an organization that may be ethically questionable. Some criminal misconduct of this sort may result in huge fines and penalties (especially in consumer, product, and environmental cases), and occasionally prison terms for some executives. On the other hand, less serious forms of mismanagement are easily dealt with and corrected on a day-to-day basis. In most instances, mismanagement involves the power and control mechanisms in place in large firms and bureaucracies, but it can also involve small businesses, the social influence of which is relatively minimal. Misconduct in larger corporations is usually carried out by more than one individual, because the network of staff and flow of information make it almost impossible for one to act alone. The scope then of mismanagement is quite broad, and it refers to misconduct at the corporate or political level. Many of the issues taken up in the applied portion of this text will refer to misconduct as mismanagement.

KEY CONCEPTS

improper behavior	intentional wrongdoing
actions difficult to avoid	active involvement
seriousness of injury	mismanagement

Summary

This chapter covered a substantial amount of terrain, but it sought to focus on and examine some of the central ideas, difficulties, and concerns surrounding ethical discourse. It began by discussing the general area of value inquiry known as axiology, because ethics is basically interested in value issues. In that section, several important distinctions were made between moral and nonmoral values, and various kinds of values were delineated. There was also a brief excursus into purposes and types of definitions. This was included to point out the complexities and intricacies of our use of language.

The next section treated the topic of ethics proper. Ethics involves the study of criteria used to judge events, actions, and people in terms of right or wrong. Several features of ethical questions were addressed to indicate the distinctiveness of ethics. This section concluded by considering what ethics is not, and it was compared to feelings, authority, the law, and religion.

Morality, the subject of the third section, emphasized the practical aspects of rules and standards as they are situated within a social context. Four distinguishing features of morality, were examined, as well as the concepts of a moral position, the object of morality and the motives for moral behavior. This discussion conveniently led to an examination of moral reasoning and moral development. The focus of the latter was on the cognitive-developmental theories of Kohlberg, but we also considered an alternative view proposed by Gilligan. When we turned to address moral reasoning, three central elements were identified, namely, moral standards, evidence, and moral judgments. Finally, we suggested, borrowing from Simon, that impartiality, consistency, and coherence in practice were general guides toward sound moral reasoning.

In the fifth section, the nature of ethical conduct was considered. The discussion here included such issues as voluntariness, determinism, free will, responsibility, unintended consequences, acts of omission, and the involvement of others. Because the notion of ethical conduct marked off what is generally considered commendable behavior, we then briefly investigated the character of misconduct. Three senses of misconduct were examined, namely, improper behavior, intentional wrongdoing, and mismanagement.

At several points throughout this chapter reference was made to ethical principles and moral standards. Yet it was never made clear just what these axioms were, who proposed them, and what justifications might exist for them. The next chapter will explore, in considerable detail, the main theories of ethics we have inherited from some of the greatest philosophers and thinkers in Western history.

Questions for Consideration

1. Define axiology and describe the various senses of the word "good."

2. Why are definitions important? What types of definitions are there? Finally, what sorts of problems can be avoided by defining terms appropriately?

3. How do normative and nonnormative ethics differ?

4. Compare the positive features related to ethics Billington presents with the negative characteristics White introduces.

5. Describe the four distinguishing characteristics of morality proposed by Beauchamp.

6. Explain the relationships between a moral position, the object of morality, and motives for moral behavior.

7. Delineate the salient features of Kohlberg's six-stage moral development scheme. What are Gilligan's main objections to this model?

8. What are the main elements of sound moral reasoning?

9. How are the following terms and expressions related to ethical conduct: voluntariness, free will, determinism, soft-determinism, responsibility, unintended consequences, acts of omission, and involving others?

10. Describe the various senses and meanings of misconduct.

References

Beauchamp, T. L. (1991). *Philosophical ethics: An introduction to moral philosophy* (2nd ed.). New York: McGraw-Hill.

Billington, R. (1988). *Living philosophy: An introduction to moral thought.* London: Routledge.

Copi, I. M. (1982). *Introduction to logic* (6th ed.). New York: Macmillan.

Cornman, J. W., & Lehrer, K. (1974). *Philosophical problems and arguments: An introduction* (2nd ed.). New York: Macmillan.

D'Arcy, E. (1963). *Human acts: An essay in their moral evaluation.* London: Oxford University Press.

Feibleman, J. K. (1967). *Moral strategy: An introduction to the ethics of confrontation.* The Hague: Martinus Nijhoff.

Findlay, J. N. (1970). *Axiological ethics.* London: Macmillan.

Frankena, W. K. (1973). *Ethics* (2nd ed.). Englewood Cliffs, NJ: Prentice-Hall.

Freeman, J. B. (1988). *Thinking logically: Basic concepts for reasoning.* Englewood Cliffs, NJ: Prentice-Hall.

Gilligan, C. (1982). *In a different voice: Psychological theory and women's development.* Cambridge, MA: Harvard University Press.

Kohlberg, L. (1987). *Child psychology and childhood education: A cognitive developmental view.* New York: Longman.

Marias, J. (1941/1967). *History of philosophy* (S. Appelbaum & C. C. Strowbridge, Trans.). New York: Dover.

Minton, A. J., & Shipka, T. A. (1990). *Philosophy: Paradox and discovery* (3rd ed.). New York: McGraw-Hill.

Nowell-Smith, P. H. (1967). Religion and morality. In P. Edwards (Ed.), *The encyclopedia of philosophy*, (Vol. 7, pp.150-158). New York: Macmillan and The Free Press.

Pepper, S. C. (1960). *Ethics*. New York: Appleton-Century-Crofts.

Rachels, J. (1986). *The elements of moral philosophy*. Philadelphia: Temple University Press.

Salmon, M. H. (1989). *Introduction to logic and critical thinking* (2nd ed.). Englewood Cliffs, NJ: Prentice-Hall.

Shirk, E. (1965). *The ethical dimension: An approach to the philosophy of values and valuing*. New York: Appleton-Century-Crofts.

Simon, R. L. (1991). *Fair play: Sports, values, & society*. Boulder, CO: Westview Press.

Velasquez, M. G. (1992). *Business ethics: Concepts and cases* (3rd ed.). Englewood Cliffs, NJ: Prentice-Hall.

Webster's new collegiate dictionary. (1977). Springfield, MA: Merriam-Webster.

White, T. I. (1988). *Right and wrong: A brief guide to understanding ethics*. Englewood Cliffs, NJ: Prentice-Hall.

CHAPTER 3

MAJOR ETHICAL THEORIES

Chapter Objectives

- to consider ethical theories in which the consequences of behavior are directed toward some stated good, purpose, or end
- to examine ethical theories in which moral obligations and maxims guide and influence one's conduct
- to investigate ethical theories in which justice is viewed as a supreme moral standard
- to become familiar with the ethical concerns associated with sport management
- to discuss methods for choosing a particular ethical theory

---

By turning to theoretical considerations, we will, in this chapter, examine a variety of classical and modern ethical principles that can be employed when making moral decisions. This diversity is evident because there has never been a consensus among moral philosophers throughout history as to the underlying reasons for ethical judgments. Consequently, numerous questions can be raised that refer to the grounds of ethical conduct, and there are generally no single right or wrong answers to these questions.

For example, do people act primarily out of self-interest? Can they be genuinely concerned for the welfare of others? Do people behave morally out of a sense of duty or moral obligation? Are moral standards universal, or are they culturally bound and relative? Are ethical decisions simply based on individual subjectivity? What are the moral grounds for justice and fairness? What constitute individual, human, civil, moral, and legal rights?

Once again, these basic questions, and there is a wealth of others, have never been answered in a complete and satisfactory manner. Yet by posing them and trying to arrive at some reasonable answers to them, one should be able to understand and appreciate further the complexity of ethical decision making. The point then is not to become discouraged by plurality. Perhaps the best one can do is to analyze the distinctive character of different ethical principles and, from there, to recognize some of the assumptions of ethical judgments.

This chapter then will proceed by examining four main categories of ethical theories and concepts: teleological, deontological, justice and rights. In each category, several specific strands of thought will be introduced and investigated. This taxonomy is neither complete and exhaustive, nor does it follow any prescribed chronology. Its content, however, provides an adequate theoretical background for the applied purposes of this text. So the reader does not feel utter despair over the prospect of considering a number of alternative theoretical viewpoints, a final section will be devoted to the issue of choosing a theory.

Teleological Theories

Because we are now trying to assess the rationale for and foundation of moral standards, let us begin with a general description of one of the main categories of ethical principles. Teleological theories in ethics rely on some "concept of the good or the humanly desirable" (Olson, 1967, p. 88). As we noted in the previous chapter, candidates for what is good or desirable are numerous. Frankena (1973) lists pleasure, power, knowledge, self-realization, and perfection as possibilities for what counts as good. He further notes that these are nonmoral values in the sense outlined in the section on axiology in the last chapter. That is, these sorts of good need not carry a prescriptive meaning. To judge an action right, correct, or good, the identification of the nonmoral sense of good must be made or implied to avoid circularity. For example, if one were to claim that people should pursue healthy activities to reduce health-care costs, the idea that being healthy is good in itself might be established in a nonmoral sense.

A teleologist then would claim that one has a moral obligation to promote whatever nonmoral good is deemed worthwhile or that on balance one should seek the greatest measure of this good over its opposite. So, if one's nonmoral good is pleasure and one is faced with a moral problem, the moral decision or action taken must reflect pleasure to the greatest extent when compared to pain. In this sense, teleological ethics emphasizes the real and possible consequences of ethical conduct, rather than, let us say, the character or intentions of a moral agent. White (1988) calls this a "results-oriented approach."

Many moral decisions are made using a teleological method. Whenever one weighs the benefits and costs of some action (or inaction) when confronted with a moral problem, one focuses on the consequences of one's behavior. Donating money for charity rather than spending money on some luxury might be based on a teleological calculus. The sports expression "no harm, no foul" is results oriented (White, 1988). The point is that if the end (a particular action, some slight contact in basketball, for instance) produces less or no harm, then perhaps the greater or greatest good (continued play in the game toward the pursuit of excellence) can be sought. Of course, this sort of view is contentious. What should count as harm? Can one foresee all possible forms of harm that might result from one's actions? These are just two general criticisms of teleological ethics, and more will arise as we examine specific brands of this principle.

Egoism

As mentioned above, teleologists make ethical decisions and act from some accepted nonmoral good. Disputes about what this good should be are legion. For some, the only good thing worth pursuing is that which fulfills one's personal interests, needs, and desires. The name given to ethical views that subscribe to the idea of self-interest is *egoism*.

This teleological stance has some appeal, for in many instances, it would be highly unusual to act against one's own interests. But some forms of egoism go further and maintain that all our moral actions are guided by self-interest. Telling the truth, keeping one's promises, not cheating, and the like are adhered to because there are personal advantages or benefits to be gained from doing so (Harman, 1977). Even acts of benevolence, such as charity, volunteerism, and heroism are, or at least can be shown to be, prompted by self-interest. For example, one might save a drowning child because one wants to be recognized as a hero or one enjoys the challenges of high-risk situations. Therefore egoism insists that ethical conduct is invariably motivated by the dictum "what's in it for me." But is the doctrine of egoism feasible? Do people always act from self-interest?

What is immediately clear is that egoism rules out unselfish or altruistic behavior. Altruism claims there are situations in which one does act in the interest of others, sometimes to the extent of sacrificing one's own interests. Most traditional and religious moral philosophies hold some type of altruistic position (e.g., the Golden Rule, "love thy neighbor"), and other-regarding acts are often considered the hallmark of morality (Palmer, 1991). Basic moral considerations, such as respect for persons, justice, fairness, and the like, tend to acknowledge the interests of others, yet egoism rejects this sort of concern for other people. If egoism is right, or is at least plausible, then it seriously challenges many commonly held views about morality, and it needs to be examined in greater detail.

There are two main versions of egoism in ethics. The first is known as *psychological egoism*. This view states that it is part of human nature to act according to one's own interests. Human beings simply cannot behave otherwise. They are always motivated to act by placing their own interests above those of others as a matter of course. Even when it looks as though one is acting unselfishly, by helping others for example, upon closer examination, a self-centered motive can be found (Porter, 1980). One wants to feel good, one wants to alleviate the feeling of pity, one wants public recognition, or one wants to elevate one's stature in the community could each be a possible motive for assisting others. To the psychological egoist there is no escaping some self-interested motive for one's behavior. To think that one can genuinely act from a concern for others is a facade.

In the history of philosophy, Hobbes (1588-1679) was the first important figure to elucidate the tenets of psychological egoism. He exerted great effort to demonstrate that all actions are guided by self-interested motives. In many ways this followed from his declaration that "...the condition of man...is a condition of war of every one against every one..." (Hobbes, 1651/1962, p. 103). What he meant is that the natural disposition of human beings is to be self-seeking and in conflict with others. If there are actions that seem like personal sacrifices on behalf of others, they can occasionally be performed because such sacrifices can also be interpreted to be in one's own interest. Perhaps by making some sacrifices now, greater personal advantages will accrue later. But as one might suspect, under this scheme, every action can be understood from a self-interested perspective.

This kind of interpretive reasoning about the motives of behavior demonstrates one of the weaknesses of psychological egoism. Merely because the motives of actions can be interpreted or reinterpreted as self-seeking does not necessarily prove the soundness of psychological egoism. This view only demonstrates that it is *possible* to ascribe self-interested motives to actions, but this possibility does not provide substantive proof for the theory (Rachels, 1986).

Another criticism of psychological egoism as an ethical theory concerns its insistence that *by nature* people act from self-interest. If it is part of human nature to be self-seeking, then the theory has nothing to recommend to people. They cannot help acting other than in a self-interested way. If this is so, then it excludes the possibility of praising or blaming people for their ethical conduct. They had no choice in the matter to begin with (Porter, 1980). Although there are more persuasive arguments in favor of psychological egoism, and each of them contains flaws, there is one other related major criticism against this ethical standpoint.

What are we to make of a theory that can explain, without exception, the true motives of all human conduct? In the sciences, no such all-inclusive theory is possible. A scientific hypothesis by definition must leave open the possibility of being refuted by counterevidence or a superior competing hypothesis. In fact, it must clearly indicate countervailing conditions in order to demonstrate its strength as a hypothesis (certainly so if the hypothesis is to have predictive value). For example, to show the cogency of the theory of gravity, one would have to know the conditions that prove the theory wrong, namely, seeing things heavier than air float (Palmer, 1991). The same empirical demands can be made of psychological egoism.

If the genuine motive of every action can be identified (in this case, a self-interested one) and no action can be picked out as evidence against psychological egoism (i.e., all expressions of altruism are emphatically denied), then the content of the theory is vacuous. An irrefutable theory is logically impossible. There would be nothing to hold up contrary to the theory to support its validity. As Rachels (1986) eloquently states, "Paradoxically, if we do not allow some way in which we might be mistaken, we lose all chance of being right" (p. 64).

Although the proponents of psychological egoism (especially Hobbes) explain away altruistic motives, they also claim that human experiences of concern for others are sincerely wrong and discount them. People, of course, know better. This refusal to accept and take seriously a set of real human experiences also weakens the case for psychological egoism. Thus, the rejection of altruistic experiences as counterevidence, the restricted sense of the nature of human beings, plus the reinterpretation of motives, are serious criticisms against psychological egoism. Perhaps another version of egoism is more palatable.

Rather than say people are naturally motivated to act out of self interest— that is, people in fact do act out of self-interest—*ethical egoism* asserts that people *should* act from a self-seeking posture. The first view, psychological egoism, is, therefore, an explanation of human nature and the motivation of conduct, whereas the second theory is a justification for how people ought to act, regardless of how they do behave (Beauchamp, 1991). Ethical egoism then tries to supply a basic reason for human actions, and that reason is self-promotion.

So when one is confronted with an ethical dilemma, one's only duty as a moral agent ought to be to advance one's own interests. According to Rachels (1986), three types of arguments are usually offered to support this theory. The first generally claims that by looking after one's own interests, everyone is better off. No one would be meddling in other people's affairs because each individual would be seeking what is best for him- or herself. Conservative economic and political policies often subscribe to this view. But from a philosophical perspective, this argument is fallacious, and in fact, it supports an unegoistic position. To assert that "everyone is better off" demonstrates a concern for the interests of others and this notion, by definition, is foreign to an ethical egoist.

A second argument for ethical egoism states that altruism is a pernicious doctrine because it encourages people to become dependent and reliant on others, and it diminishes the value of the individual. In this view, altruism is criticized for it asks one to make sacrifices on behalf of others, and denies the interests of the individual. Personal ambitions are stifled by altruism, and so the only moral principle devoted to individual achievement and personal worth is ethical egoism.

The difficulty here concerns the extreme presentation of altruism, which practically no one accepts. A more charitable and realistic account of altruism would at least say that both the interests of the individual and the interests of others ought to be considered when making moral decisions. Moreover, describing altruism as an extreme position, rejecting it, and then serving up ethical egoism (another extreme) as an alternative is hardly convincing, and one view certainly does not follow from the rejection of the other.

This brings us to the third argument in favor of ethical egoism. This position is less radical and accepts some common moral rules, such as telling the truth, keeping one's promises, not cheating, and the like. This is surprising because these rules typically convey a concern for others. But rather than view these rules as separate other-regarding guides for behavior, this account tries to demonstrate that common-sense morality can be unified and explained by a single principle, namely, ethical egoism. So in the long run, one ought to tell the truth, to keep promises and to not cheat because these actions provide personal advantages. If one consistently violated these moral rules, one would likely be considered untrustworthy, unreliable, and subversive. Having this sort of reputation would not help toward advancing one's own interests. Ethical egoism, therefore, can explain everyday moral standards and preserve the idea of promoting self-interest.

Rachels (1986) levels two criticisms against ethical egoism. The theory states there are personal advantages to be gained in the long run from following common moral rules, say telling the truth. But it does not say that this is always the case. So, in some particular instance, substantial gains could be achieved from not telling the truth. This argument then does not stress seriously enough that moral rules ought to be upheld even in the face of some personal gain. Second, although one might reason that it is in one's best interest not to cheat on exams, for example, there still could be a more basic reason for not cheating on tests. The complete range of challenges of an exam would be lost by cheating, and one could prefer to be tested to the fullest extent. Thus, for some activities, there could be fundamental reasons for complying with moral rules. The reason of self-interest might be secondary, and it is definitely not the only reason. Therefore, this enlightened form of ethical egoism is unsatisfactory.

Each of the three arguments for ethical egoism falls short of the mark. But there is a more serious charge against ethical egoism. As discussed in the previous chapter, among the distinguishing features of morality are universalizability and a related notion that one should be able to recommend one's moral standards to others. It is reasonable then to ask how these criteria of sound ethical principles relate to ethical egoism. If each person were a committed ethical egoist, there would likely be constant struggle and conflict to fulfill his or her own interests (much as Hobbes described). The ethical egoist could say that some individual interests and advantages would overlap. But this admits to a world that could potentially contain *shared* rather than *self* interests and defeats the egoist doctrine (Frankena, 1973). The universalizability of ethical egoism is logically implausible.

A related point is that it would be to the ethical egoist's advantage that not everyone adopt this posture. That is, the greatest gains could be made if some people were not ethical egoists, for there would be less conflict with others. This alternative would seem to follow if universalizability is unobtainable. But this creates a scenario in which people are divided between "them" and "us," egoists and nonegoists, and the interests of the first group outweigh those of the second group. This, however, raises the question of what justification egoists offer to prefer their interests over those of nonegoists. Unless there are relevant differences in the characteristics of each group, no difference in value and treatment between them is warranted. In fact, ethical egoism *arbitrarily* grants itself this privileged status, just as most racist and sexist theories do. Any ethical principle that arbitrarily places itself on a higher moral plane in relation to others can be confidently rejected (Rachels, 1986).

KEY CONCEPTS

teleological   egoism   psychological egoism
altruism   ethical

Utilitarianism

Egoism proved unsatisfactory as a teleological ethical theory because striving for self-interested nonmoral goods fails to meet some of the central demands of sound moral reasoning. Although none of these goods were specifically examined, like pleasure, knowledge, power, perfection, and so on, the point was that none of these could be pursued from an exclusive self-seeking perspective. There is, however, a popular modern ethical principle that does account for the social well-being of others while seeking to attain certain nonmoral goods.

Utilitarianism posits that the only good worth pursuing is pleasure or happiness. For this reason, it is sometimes labeled a form of *hedonism*, from the Greek word *hedone*, meaning pleasure (Raphael, 1981). The only moral duty one has is to promote the greatest amount of happiness. Happiness is usually considered the totality of different pleasures. Pain is the opposite of pleasure and is bad, and by its reduction or removal, one enhances pleasure. So in general, utilitarians wish to create conditions to maximize pleasure and minimize pain. But the obligation toward achieving this sense of happiness is extended to include and account for the pleasures of everyone.

The social imperative here is critical. Utilitarianism insists that one person's happiness is just as important as the next person's. As Mothershead (1955) explains, "Human happiness is the good. This being true, the standpoint of utilitarianism is inevitably democratic.... Happiness is primary; whose happiness it is, is secondary" (p. 223). Utilitarianism, therefore, is not grounded foremost in self-interested motives (though some utilitarians do make egoistic claims). Because altruism is not entirely ruled out, the general formula of utilitarianism can be stated as "the goodness of an act depends on its giving the greatest happiness to the greatest number" (Pepper, 1960, p. 112). The determination of whether an action is right or wrong then depends on this principle.

As one can easily see, it is the consequences or possible consequences of behavior that serve as a gauge for conduct to be judged good or bad. This view is known as consequentialism. Actions that produce the greatest benefits are correct, whereas those that create harmful effects are to be avoided. So an athletic director who has sufficient funds in his budget to renovate both men's and women's locker rooms should select this option, rather than upgrade one or the other facility. All athletes would be served and benefit from the first choice, whereas the second option accommodates fewer athletes.

From a utilitarian perspective then, conduct is seen primarily as a means toward happiness. More specifically, such behavior must be practical and useful, hence the derivative term *utility* in the name utilitarianism. Not only can particular actions in given circumstances be evaluated from a utilitarian standpoint, but many bureaucratic and governmental policies also are decided by employing this approach. Tax, health, and licensing policies, for example, are often determined according to the utilitarian formula, that is, by or as providing the greatest benefits to the greatest number of people. In many ways, utilitarianism is a convenient and efficient way to make judgments of a practical and ethical nature. What makes a particular behavior or policy right then is that its consequences lead toward pleasurable ends (happiness); the behavior or policy has utility because usefulness generally creates greater benefits for more people, and the pleasure(s) of each person affected by such action is (are) equally valued. The difficulty, of course, is deciding what and how to measure the results of conduct or a policy to determine whether a particular course of action or policy should be followed.

Bentham (1748-1832), perhaps the first individual to formally articulate the tenets of traditional utilitarianism (though he did not coin the term), tried to quantify pleasures and pains under the following seven categories: intensity, duration, certainty, propinquity (how soon experiences are felt), fecundity (the likelihood of future pleasurable experiences), purity (how free from pain the experiences are), and extent (the number of others who are affected) (White, 1988). Bentham believed one could calculate the goodness of an action by listing the pleasures associated with the action, applying a numerical value (say +1 to +10) for each of these in terms of the above categories, then finding the total. After one does the same for any pains (say -1 to -10) associated with the action, then the resultant sum, either in favor of pleasures or of pains, would tell an individual what course of action to follow. A positive total would be good, and the behavior ought to be carried out. A negative total would be bad, and the action ought to be avoided (Wheelwright, 1959).

Bentham's hedonistic calculus is a strictly objective procedure for determining the value of an action. But how effective is this method? What does one do if the resultant sum is zero? Can all pleasures and pains be quantified? What should count as a pleasure and a pain? Can the latter be objectively determined? These are all important questions. However, for Bentham, morality was only concerned with quantity and the final tally, what we presently refer to as "the bottom line." In fact, to avoid some of the above questions, Bentham held that any and all pleasures were equivalent. So whether one enjoys digging ditches, washing cars, playing tiddlywinks, watching sports, performing classical ballet, doing math, or just about anything else, each is given the same status as a pleasure (White, 1988). There are no intrinsically better or worse pleasures according to Bentham, although some activities may provide greater pleasure than others for different people. From a sociopolitical perspective, Bentham also insisted that his form of utilitarianism is strictly democratic ("one person, one vote"). No one can tell you what to enjoy and what is enjoyable, and if hopscotch provides you with more pleasure than poetry provides, then it is a more valuable activity (Palmer, 1991). But is there anything wrong with saying all pleasures are equal? One person who thought so was Bentham's disciple and godson, John Stuart Mill (1806-1873).

Mill, who did introduce the term utilitarianism, was dissatisfied with the claims that only the quantity and the equal status of pleasures were the most relevant considerations when estimating the consequences of behavior. If this were the case, many mundane and ignoble pleasures could be legitimately pursued. Mill believed that certain pleasures were superior to others and these provided greater utility (Billington, 1988). In his view, pursuing knowledge and appreciating cultivated activities like art, music, drama, dance, literature, and science are superior to activities than doing the dishes, sunbathing, attending professional wrestling matches, watching soap operas on television, and the like. Mill feared that if the latter pleasures were equally justified pursuits when compared to the former, and they were also widely accepted, then culture would be reduced to a lowest common denominator. He, therefore, set out to refine Bentham's ideas.

Mill argued that Bentham's exclusive quantitative approach only worked when dealing with "lower," more basic pleasures. When considering "higher desires," the quality of pleasures, not merely the quantity, was needed to better assess the value of certain actions. If some behavior produces pleasure that is qualitatively superior, but its duration is shorter, then its cumulative value might be greater than an alternative action that provides longer enjoyment but is relatively mundane.

In some ways, Mill's concern here is intuitively correct. If society decided that to achieve "the greatest good for the greatest number" it had to do away with arts and sciences, many creative, original, and ennobling activities would never be realized. Human dignity and imagination might erode to base levels, and general happiness might not be attained. To emphasize this point, Mill (1861/1969) went so far as to say, "It is better to be a human being dissatisfied than a pig satisfied; better to be Socrates dissatisfied than a fool satisfied" (p. 237). Therefore, to preserve intellectual and creative integrity the quality of pleasures has to be acknowledged. But Mill's improved version of utilitarianism has several shortcomings.

First, by delineating "higher and lower" pleasures, who is to say which provides the greatest happiness? For many people, the simple pleasures of life (like bowling once a week) do offer them enormous happiness, whereas some intellects and artists have led and continue to lead unhappy, agonizing, and sometimes destructive personal lives (think of the number of "cultivated" individuals in history who had nervous breakdowns, went insane, or committed suicide). So the mere separation of different levels of pleasures does not guarantee any more or less happiness (Porter, 1980). Moreover, who is in a position to judge the quality of a pleasure?

Mill, in fact, believed one has to be competent or cultivated before passing judgment on this issue. That is, if one is unrefined in cultural matters, one is unqualified to decide what pleasures are superior. Along similar lines, Mill also thought plural voting in "democratic" elections should occur, with the vote of the educated to count for more than that of the uneducated (Schneewind, 1967).

What these views strongly suggest is a form of elitism. In order to preserve a "high" cultural and sociopolitical standard, Mill designated some people and their judgments to be more valuable than others (Palmer, 1991). So by attacking one aspect of utilitarianism, its "lowest-common-denominator" flaw, Mill abandoned the deeply rooted democratic feature of utilitarianism.

Mill's revision of utilitarianism is also weakened because by asserting the duality of pleasures and the legitimacy of elitism, he ceased to support the hedonistic aspects of the doctrine. The pursuit of pleasure is no longer the supreme nonmoral good in his account. By introducing the notion of quality of pleasures, only certain pleasures, acquired and appreciated by a select segment of the population, afford and promote happiness. Other pleasures, the "lower" ones, are deemed less worthy, and some likely unworthy altogether, even though they may be enjoyed by some people. If pleasures and people can be divided as such, and Mill does say it would be better to maintain human dignity and be dissatisfied, then this is a serious departure from hedonism. He seems to be describing a particular way of life as being more valuable than a pleasurable one (Porter, 1980). Although the pursuit of all pleasures need not be at the core of utilitarianism, Mill attempted to refine this idea but came up short when he departed from this central utilitarian theme.

However, perhaps the most serious charge against Mill's version of utilitarianism, and traditional utilitarianism in general, are some of the intuitively wrong conclusions one can arrive at when following this principle. Consider the following example. In the most important game of the year, the coach of a Division I football team had a decision to make about whether or not to return a player to the game after he suffered an injury. On an earlier play, the athlete had been knocked unconscious but regained his composure after a short while. Both the trainer and the team doctor strongly advised against the player's returning to the game. But on a crucial series of downs, the coach ignored their advice and ordered the player onto the field. On the very next play, the player was involved in a vicious tackle, which led to a game-winning score, and he was rendered unconscious again. This time, however, he lapsed into a coma, and several hours later he died.

When questioned afterwards, the coach reasoned that the athlete looked fine, he often returned players to the game after similar injuries and injury reports, the athlete was recently orphaned and had no known relatives (and, therefore, was not going to be dearly missed), he was a sophomore and not well known on the team, he was needed in the game to secure a win for his team, and his contribution to the team, the college, and the community achieved a greater level of general happiness.

As far-fetched as this example may appear, the coach's reasoning is sound based on utilitarian grounds. The beneficial consequences of playing the athlete perhaps outweighed any suspected harmful effects. Most people, however, intuitively sense the coach was unjustified and wrong in his action, especially based on the strong advice he was given. The example points out that, in some circumstances, utilitarianism can lead to conclusions many people would find hard to accept. The athlete certainly did not deserve to be sent out to play, and to reason that the promotion of happiness ("the greater good") was attained by the sacrifice of this one life is hardly the kind of justice many people would agree with (Ewing, 1953). Therefore, to focus principally on the consequences of behavior can sometimes lead to a breach of some deeply rooted moral standards, like justice and granting people their due.

Similarly on utilitarian grounds, one could conceivably lie, cheat, or steal, if these actions lead to greater happiness. It is for this reason that later utilitarians introduced the distinction between *act-utilitarianism* and *rule-utilitarianism*. The former follows closely with traditional utilitarianism by considering the actual or possible consequences of actions in given situations that produce the greatest utility. There are, however, problems with act utilitarianism. In addition to the difficulty of knowing the full range and extent of all the consequences of an action, two different actions in a specific instance might produce identical outcomes. If the first involved lying or cheating and the second did not, then either action could be followed according to act utilitarianism, because they produce the same results (Frankena, 1973). Human intuition would say that one should carry out the second action, but this cannot be recommended from an act-utilitarian perspective.

When faced with this sort of dilemma, rule utilitarians argue that one should formulate a general rule that when followed would more consistently lead to a greater amount of happiness. So the second course of action, referring once again to the preceding example, should be exercised because one should adhere to the rule that lying and cheating are generally more harmful and do not lead to greater happiness. Rule utilitarianism has an advantage here by taking into account instances in which rules of justice, fairness, equality, and the like are part of ethical problem solving. However, a difficulty with this approach might be that one could make certain exceptions to rules (Palmer, 1991). So one might establish the rule that cheating in sport is acceptable as long as one does not get caught by the officials. But adding exceptions to rules would likely lead to undermining rule utilitarianism altogether. The more exceptions created, the less clear and consistent the application of rules become (much like what is implied in expressions like "a bureaucratic nightmare" and "a catch-22").

The emphasis on the consequences of actions challenges some basic ideas about behavior many people deem just plain wrong, like lying, stealing, cheating, breaking promises, abandoning a friend, and failing to repay one's debts. It has been shown that utilitarianism can, in many instances, provide a method to resolve ethical dilemmas by pointing to the outcomes of behavior. But in some circumstances, moral intuitions tend to prevail, and one feels compelled to be guided by them. One question then, which we will address more fully in the next section, is, are there actions that must be followed out of a sense of duty, no matter what their consequences? Before we proceed to examine this question, this section will conclude by briefly addressing another teleological ethical theory that tries to combine elements of duty and a concern for consequences.

KEY CONCEPTS

utilitarianism	hedonism	Bentham's calculus
Mill's critique of Bentham		consequentialism
higher and lower desires		critique of Mill's version of utilitarianism
act utilitarianism		rule utilitarianism

Situation Ethics

As the name implies, this type of ethical approach is similar to act utilitarianism in that it takes into account particular actions and circumstances when one is faced with a moral problem. That is, ethical decisions and actions will arise exclusive to a set of given social conditions. No two contexts can be treated as similar, but each must be viewed as a separate, distinct episode. As such and in one sense, only the consequences of ethical judgments and behavior directly linked to discrete situations are the most significant. This feature of situation ethics provides a connection to utilitarianism. But where is the character of duty located?

Because each situation is unique, some advocates of situation ethics assert that no predetermined general rules can be applied when one is faced with a moral dilemma (Frankena, 1973). Each case must be viewed from its own perspective. For this reason, Billington (1988) calls situation ethics a type of ethical relativism. Distinct circumstances generate and govern different sets of rules, and what is right is a product of a given situation.

But rules cannot always inform what one should do because in some contexts there are no rules to appeal to, or the rules do not readily apply to a certain situation. This development might demand the creation of particular rules by which to act, but they would be relevant only to a specific situation. Thus, in a given context, telling a lie or turning one's back on a friend might be justified, and this enjoins people to be extremely sensitive to the uniqueness of moral situations. One is, therefore, duty bound under this ethical principle always to search for distinct rules or maxims by which to follow and reject the application of general moral standards in a hard and fast manner (Hudson, 1970).

So far, the description of situation ethics has not revealed its teleological dimension. Fletcher (1967), an important proponent of situation ethics from a Christian perspective, did supply one supreme value that should guide all ethical considerations. He maintained that "only one thing is intrinsically good, namely, love: nothing else" (p. 15). From a religious perspective, this has become known as "the ethics of love" or *agapism*. This brand of theological situation ethics contains utilitarian elements as well as a duty-bound feature. In this case, one is obliged to derive all decisions and actions from the value of love. Whether this takes the form of considering only one's actions in a given situation or developing and relying on rules, both must be based on the principle of love. There could, of course, be nonreligious supreme values that could serve as various foundations for situation ethics, like justice, self-realization, and perfection. The point is to demonstrate that situation ethics can be guided by specific nonmoral goods in a teleological sense.

Despite such noble overriding values, situation ethics has its drawbacks. In practice, one does have general rules, maxims, or principles that one follows, and one implicates these in different situations. How can one simply erase the influence of previously learned ethical guidelines and look at each moral episode in an entirely new and fresh way? Certain moral standards are bound to be part of one's ethical deliberations, and the uniqueness of any situation would not likely convince one to completely give up these principles, if only temporarily. Many people already know that torture, slavery, rape, incest, and a host of other abhorrent activities are morally wrong, no matter what. One hardly, if ever, approaches these issues with a blank slate, and so their moral status is quite plain regardless of the situation. Yet the relativistic strain in situation ethics leaves open the question of the wrongfulness of such acts.

Moreover, at least one important weakness emerges if we consider Fletcher's situation ethics specifically. Because love is the one unconditional principle here, it becomes difficult to discern and specify how other important principles might apply in a given situation, if they do at all. For example, how does love tell people what to do in the case of distributing justice? Fletcher (1967) makes a point to say that love and justice are equivalent and justice is love distributed; but he also imports, to some degree, a utilitarian calculus when making ethical decisions. Borrowing the utilitarian approach at least indicates or suggests that love on its own may not be sufficient to handle the demands of some ethical dilemmas, and other nonagapeic principles are also significant. Frankena (1973), for one, argues against a pure morality of love and says it needs to be supplemented by a principle of justice.

Although situation ethics possesses some certain flaws, it offers an interesting combination of ethical principles. It may be viewed from a teleological perspective by reflecting a supreme value; it may contain a utilitarian strain by considering the consequences of behavior in particular situations; and it may possess the quality of insisting one be duty bound to certain rules and maxims once they are established in a given context. In the next section, we will turn to an examination of ethical theories that state that actions and rules are right or correct regardless of the consequences that may follow from them or of whether they promote some nonmoral good.

KEY CONCEPTS

context and duty   specific rule development
agapism   critique of situation ethics
combining elements of ethical principles

Deontological Theories

Many people feel an obligation to act in a certain way because they just know it is the correct thing to do. Keeping promises, telling the truth, respecting others, honoring one's parents are viewed as right in themselves. These maxims, and the behavior generated from them, are rarely questioned, and many would claim they apply in all circumstances. Yet if there are some action-guiding principles or rules one accepts as intrinsically valuable, what sort of rules are they, and in what ways is one obligated to them? These are at least two central questions we will investigate in this section.

The term generally used to describe theories where moral obligation does not involve a consideration of the outcomes of action is known as *deontological*. As Garner and Rosen (1967) explain, "Deontological theories of obligation hold that things other than (but, perhaps, in addition to) consequences determine which actions are morally right" (p. 25). The word deontology is derived from the Greek, *deon*, meaning "duty" or "obligation" (Beauchamp, 1991). Some have even called this ethical approach, *the ethics of duty*. What this theory emphasizes is the moral nature of specific standards and one's behavior irrespective of the results they produce. Once justification is given for the soundness of these guidelines and actions, then one's moral duty can be firmly established in any context.

Deontological theories easily can be contrasted with utilitarianism, because the latter is distinguished as a results-oriented approach. Whereas some reasoning along utilitarian lines can lead to injustice or treating people undeservingly (as demonstrated in the previous section), deontologists usually are not confronted with these sorts of problems. In fact, it will turn out that respect for persons, personal autonomy, motives, commitment, and other similar ideas impose moral obligations that can outweigh whatever benefits might result from our actions. In fact, to strict deontologists it does not matter whether the consequences of behavior are good or bad. One's only duty is to adhere to accepted and well-established moral standards.

Deontological theories can also be contrasted with certain elements of situation ethics. Whereas the latter can be guided by a commitment to a supreme value (e.g., love) whereby one accepts a principal duty, in most versions of situation ethics, the consequences of actions in a given context are usually assessed, and no previously established rules are brought into consideration. In the main, deontological theories reject these utilitarian and rigid context-bound features. But the question remains, where do intrinsic principles originate?

Some deontologists appeal to God's or a Supreme Being's divine commands; others claim the moral superiority of certain rules and actions is known through intuition; some hold that reason can tell us what is right; and still others claim there are principles and actions that are correct by their very nature (Beauchamp, 1991). Usually in each case, some rationale is given to establish moral standards to which one owes one's allegiance. Once the soundness of these maxims is in place, one must carry out one's obligation to live up to such standards.

As in the earlier section of this chapter, we will again examine three kinds of approaches. No one of these deontological theories is presented completely, but the variations among them will disclose how the notion of duty is alternately expressed. We will begin with a relatively simple type of deontological viewpoint and move toward more complex versions of this ethical principle.

The Golden Rule

Perhaps the most well-known moral maxim in Western history is the Golden Rule. It is mostly associated with the Hebrew and Christian bibles and has been suggested as *the* foundation for morality both in ancient and modern times (Raphael, 1981). Because the Golden Rule was, and is still, a highly revered moral standard, it deserves our attention from a deontological perspective.

Many people believe the Golden Rule was first enunciated by Jesus in the expressions "love thy neighbor as thyself," and "do unto others as you would have them do unto you." In fact, however, the Golden Rule has an older tradition that predates the time of Jesus and the emergence of Christianity.

In the Hebrew bible, the final portion of Leviticus, XIX, 18 reads, "...thou shalt love thy neighbour as thyself...," and in verse 34 in the same chapter it is written, "The stranger that sojourneth with you shall be unto you as the homeborn among you, and thou shalt love him as thyself..." (Hertz, 1980, pp. 502 and 504). Generations of Jewish prophets and scholars quoted or paraphrased this verse as a supreme teaching to guide human conduct. If one now only considers these religious versions of the Golden Rule, without worrying too much about any differences in their formulation, how should one come to understand this basic principle?

In the first instance, the Golden Rule clearly places an emphasis on altruism. One's primary motive for ethical behavior should be to act unselfishly with regard to others. This seems to be the hallmark of religion in Western history. The ideas of charity, helping those less fortunate, and comforting the sick and weak have a central place in Western traditional religions. Trying to put oneself in the place of others is also an attempt to express a deep concern for the condition and welfare of other people. We have already seen how extreme forms of egoism reject altruism as a motive for ethics. The Golden Rule, however, stresses that one should be kind and thoughtful toward others and should assist those in need. The question is, to what extent can one act selflessly?

For one thing, total self-sacrifice would lead to social absurdity. Imagine if everyone worked completely for the good of other people. That is, one would tend exclusively to the needs of others, whereas others would tend to one's own needs. This sort of arrangement would be highly unlikely because differences in individual wants and desires would be so varied that no reasonable level of satisfaction would ever be gained (Mackie, 1977). There could also arise the situation whereby if one only worked for the good of others in the most unselfish manner, no one would accept the benefits of such work, and overall general happiness would decline (Ewing, 1953). So in the extreme, living entirely for others is an untenable form of altruism. But the Golden Rule does not advocate this. It does not say that one should love another "more than" oneself, but "as thyself." One of its assumptions then is the notion of self-love.

Both Judaism and Christianity espouse the idea that regard for the self is a fundamental feature of human existence, hence the expression "as thyself." Taking into account one's own interests along with those of others is a legitimate enterprise in ethical deliberations. In fact, the self-interested dimension is sometimes understood to be a more basic quality of human beings, whereas our concern for others must be learned (Shirk, 1965). Christianity, more so than Judaism, has often seen self-love as a debilitating, sometimes evil and sinful, human trait. It has proposed doctrines of self-denial or *asceticism*, the renunciation of material, bodily, and personal pleasures, as a way to curb the desires of the self.

As before, such extreme positions are generally implausible interpretations of the Gold Rule. On the one hand, it is unlikely that if one led a life of self-denial, all others would want to be treated in this same way. As Billington (1988) writes, "I am unlikely to make much of a contribution to my neighbour's wellbeing if I am indifferent to my own" (p. 25). In the opposite extreme, some people exude so much love, concern, and care for others, it is sometimes embarrassing to the recipients, or such sentiments are viewed as disingenuous and can put people off. So the idea of "doing unto others" has its limits in both these negative and positive senses. By bringing together a regard for others as well as consideration for oneself, the Golden Rule tries to temper radicalism in either direction. It also serves as a universal maxim.

Anyone who adopts the Golden Rule is committed to placing everyone on an equal moral plane. The emphasis on impartiality is guaranteed here because one is willing to accept the same actions for oneself as that being recommended to others. No one is, therefore, considered arbitrarily superior in terms of moral worth. But even though this moral equality exists between individuals, as we saw above, the treatment of individuals as one would like to be treated cannot be taken literally (Ewing, 1953). Again, one might accept living as a hermit, but most other people would not want to be considered according to this lifestyle. Moreover, the way one would prefer to be treated may not be the right way a person ought to be treated. So, one would prefer to not receive a parking ticket, but if one clearly breaks the law, getting a parking ticket is rightly what one deserves. Despite not making a moral exception in individual cases, and, therefore, holding to the idea of universalizability, the Golden Rule can still lead to unappealing and unwarranted practices.

The religious formulations of the Golden Rule have much to recommend. They teach one to be benevolent toward others, to place some importance on self-interested pursuits, and to regard everyone as moral equals. The desire to adhere to the Golden Rule as one's duty is perhaps a good general guide to behavior. But one drawback alluded to in the problems addressed above is the difficulty of applying this principle in specific cases (Brandt, 1959). Consider the example of capital punishment.

Those who advocate this sort of punishment could invoke the Golden Rule by

·claiming that some death row inmates agree they should be killed for their crimes. Occasionally convicted murderers come to realize they do not deserve to live for what they have done, and so are willing to accept capital punishment as a form of justice. In this case, there is no breach of the Golden Rule for those who face execution for their crimes. Moreover, even though the bible teaches the Golden Rule, capital punishment is a justifiable form of retribution, and examples are replete in scripture. By contrast, those who oppose this supreme penalty also point to the Golden Rule and argue that loving one's neighbor means expressing reverence for human life and that other, less severe forms of punishment are more just. Consequently, there are no clear answers in some particular cases if one were to rely exclusively on the Golden Rule.

As we noticed above and in the latter specific case, interpretations of the Golden Rule can vary. If this is so, then how it is understood and applied in different situations can also be diverse. The Golden Rule, therefore, does not prescribe precisely what one ought to do in many specific instances. This is one of the major weaknesses of this maxim. In what follows, a nonreligious deontological theory will be examined that, in one of its pronouncements, has an affinity with the Golden Rule.

KEY CONCEPTS

deontological	ethics of duty	golden rules
selflessness	self-love	asceticism
benevolence	moral equality	

Kantian Ethics

One of the greatest philosophers in Western history was Kant (1724-1804), a quiet academician, who lived as a bachelor and never ventured very far from his birthplace, Koenigsberg in northeastern Germany (then known as Prussia). Perhaps his greatest contribution to philosophy was in the area of ethics, and his works continue to have tremendous influence on those who agree and disagree with his thought.

Kant reacted against any hint that moral behavior should and could lead to good or beneficial consequences, like happiness, perfection, self-realization, and the like. According to Kant, ethics has nothing to do with satisfying some identifiable end. For this reason, he is definitely not a teleologist. In fact, if one could demonstrate that an act was carried out to arrive at some desirable outcome, this would disqualify the act as an instance of ethical behavior (Palmer, 1991). But this raises the question of how moral behavior can be recognized as having no association with some consequence.

In the early portion of *Foundations of the Metaphysics of Morals*, in a famous quote, Kant (1785/1959) wrote, "Nothing in the world...can possibly be conceived which could be called good without qualification except a *good will*" (p. 9). Based on this statement, Kant developed the view that ethical conduct can emanate only from someone who possesses a good character. Someone with such a character behaves morally from a pure sense of duty, rather than from a consideration of the results of actions (Brandt, 1959). From a Kantian perspective, if keeping one's promises, not lying, respecting one's parents, paying one's debts, not turning one's back on one's friends, and the like are performed because these actions provide some kind of advantage or gratification, they are no longer ethical actions. This is so because there would always be alternative motives attached to these actions. For Kant, the only motive for ethical conduct is what human beings will in a strict, unadulterated sense of duty. He, therefore, was one of the first ethicists to examine seriously the notion of duty for duty's sake (Ewing, 1953). He also tried to demonstrate the soundness of this basic tenet by relying on one's ability to reason clearly, and he began by making an important distinction in the way people use the term ought.

On the one hand, one could tell someone, "If you want to improve your health, then you ought to start exercising" or "If you desire to be a better racquetball player, then you ought to practice more." These everyday typical examples make use of the term ought in a practical way. Although a course of action is being recommended ("start exercising" or "practice more"), it is suggested only as a means to fulfill some wish ("improve one's health" or "be a better racquetball player"). Kant (1785/1959) called such "if-then" statements where *ought* is found, *hypothetical imperatives*. That is, the *ought* refers to a practical plan or requirement one should follow if one want to satisfy some particular desire. But this sort of imperative (or obligation) is relatively weak, because if one were to renounce the desire, then one would no longer be bound by the recommended action (Rachels, 1986). The binding force of hypothetical imperatives then depends on what one wants, and there is no moral relevance related to one's desires.

A genuine moral ought, however, is unconditional according to Kant. It does not rely on any desire or on any further qualification. So to say "you ought to treat your sister in a fair manner, if you love her or if you want her to be fair in return" is not an example of a moral statement because various conditions are attached to the ought clause. Kant would say "You ought to treat your sister in a fair manner" and stop right there. The imperative (or obligation) here is absolute, and no qualification can be linked to it for it to be a moral claim. For just think, if one did not want one's sister to be fair in return or did not love her (and these are possibilities), then the binding force of the imperative is not very strong; it really involves a practical matter, and hence it no longer falls within the domain of morality. (As mentioned earlier, Kant relied on human ability to reason carefully about ethical issues because he firmly believed the foundation of human existence is based on the fact that humans are rational beings. His ethics is grounded not in intuition, divine authority, desires, consequences, and the like, but firmly in reason. Therefore, his moral arguments, if sound, must be accepted by any rational individual; not doing so would be tantamount to renouncing one's very nature.)

It is clear from the above discussion there are different degrees of duty.

Hypothetical imperatives involve a weak level of duty only insofar as one wishes to fulfill some desire, whereas genuine moral imperatives demand an ultimate sense of duty based on reason. But the question remains: What gives the latter their absolute quality when it comes to duty, for this is the only motive acceptable for moral behavior? Kant provided three formulations to what he called the principle of the *categorical* (absolute) *imperative*. All moral obligations will necessarily conform to this principle.

The first version of the categorical imperative is as follows: "Act only according to the maxim by which you can at the same time will that it should become a universal law" (Kant, 1785/1959, p. 39). One can easily see that Kant appealed to the idea of universalizability as the supreme test to decide if a particular rule or action is right and, therefore, to be followed or carried out with a pure sense of duty. But before one can employ the categorical imperative as a test, two preliminary steps must occur.

First, an individual must have in mind some rule of action, known as a maxim (Garner & Rosen, 1967). This will be the personal guide by which individuals conduct themselves, and so numerous maxims can exist. For example, the beliefs that it is good to marry and have children, to do volunteer work, to give part of one's income to charity, and to help one's neighbor are all maxims of various sorts. There need not be any agreement between people about any particular maxim. So not everyone is required to give to charity, to marry and have children, to be a volunteer or to help one's neighbor. But Kant did insist that each person must arrive at or will these maxims autonomously. His idea of autonomy is a difficult one and is often misunderstood.

In brief, what Kant was saying is that each person's action-guiding maxims must be willed from a rational posture, independent of any desire or influence (Beauchamp, 1991). Thus, it is fairly clear when a child is told by her father to help her grandmother up the steps, thereby following a rule like "always help the elderly," the child is not acting autonomously. The child is likely acting from obedience and is being influenced by her father, whom she wishes to please. When the child matures and perhaps later accepts the maxim and autonomously wills it as a rational agent, only then would a resulting action contain moral worth. At this stage, too, the maxim possesses authority because it is derived from a rational stance.

Autonomy of will does not simply involve an individual's capacity to make personal decisions and to create and be responsible for a certain kind of lifestyle. Merely establishing rules by which to govern one's own life is not what Kant meant by autonomy. As Beauchamp (1991) explains, "Kant's theory of autonomy is to be explicated in terms of moral *self-legislation*: If a person freely determines the principles under whose direction he or she will act, the person is a law-giver unto himself or herself, and thus is autonomous" (p. 181). There is a difference then between rule creator and rule legislator. The former produces action-guiding rules primarily as an expression of his or her liberty, whereas the latter individual autonomously wills maxims that emerge from one's nature as a being who possesses reason, and whose maxims, therefore, are valid for all rational beings. The idea of autonomy is a central feature of Kantian ethics to which we will return later.

The second preliminary step required before using the categorical imperative test concerns the relationship between some moral act and a maxim. In this case, the moral agent must choose to have his or her behavior conform to a maxim, so that one is indeed acting from the maxim (Garner & Rosner, 1967). If an individual did not choose to have a particular action described under a maxim, the person would only be acting according to some rule, rather than *from* the rule.

Once these conditions are met, the categorical imperative then asks a person to consider whether a given maxim can be followed consistently by everyone at all times. This procedure will determine whether an action-guiding rule can be made an objective and absolute (universal) standard, whose binding force at this point is contained within a law. The maxim as a universal law should possess no contradictions or inconsistencies. As Shirk (1965) explains, "we should act in such a way that everyone else could so act, with consistent and harmonious consequences for all" (p. 187). If the maxim passes the test of the categorical imperative, it then can be accepted by any rational individual. Because people possess reason, they cannot deny their obligation to moral laws (Wheelwright, 1959). For Kant, ultimate respect for moral laws is a derivative of the human ability to reason, and this compels people to apply the strictest sense of duty toward such laws. But what are some of these universal laws?

Kant provided several examples. He considered whether suicide could be accepted as a universal law. If a person contemplated self-destruction based on the maxim "end your life when a longer life would lead to more pain than pleasure," then this rule would be self-contradictory when held up against the test of the categorical imperative. In this instance, the maxim assumes a certain love for oneself, the very notion that drives one toward sustaining life, and so the maxim contradicts a principle on which it is founded. Suicide, therefore, cannot be universally willed.

Can the neglect of natural talents be universally accepted? Suppose one was gifted in some area, but instead of developing this gift, one decided to live an idle, indulgent, and pleasurable life on the beaches of the Caribbean. Kant believed that choosing idleness and pleasure as a universal law over the improvement of natural abilities contradict the nature of humans as rational beings. He reasoned that even a person devoted to seeking pleasure is still acting as a rational person who wills that his or her talents be developed. In this case, the individual's abilities have provided him or her with a life of pleasure seeking. It would be contradictory, therefore, to will that natural talents be neglected because one cannot foresee how one's gifts might be utilized.

Next consider the person who would decide that she or he no longer wishes to assist others when they are in need. Can the maxim "do not help others in distress," be willed in a universal manner? No, said Kant, because one would eliminate any future possibility for help for oneself, and again, this would be self-contradictory.

Kant's main example to demonstrate the existence of universal laws and how they are derived from reason concerns the case of making false promises. Suppose one needed to borrow money from someone else and promised to pay back the money, but knew that one would not repay the debt. Promises of this sort could not be universally willed for that would lead to a contradiction. Ultimately no one would believe such promises, and so the very thing promises do would be nullified, thereby making promises logically impossible. Some have applied the self-contradictory nature of false promises to other examples.

Lying presupposes the general condition of truth -telling, whereas cheating in sports assumes the overall condition that most players adhere to the rules of the game. In other words, if everyone lied or cheated, these activities would be self-defeating. People generally have to be telling the truth in order for lying to work, for this is what the person lying counts on in order for the lie to bear fruit. Similarly, the cheater in sports does not want everyone to violate the rules; otherwise, cheating would offer no rewards. So Kant would declare that maxims involved with lying and cheating could not become universal laws and these actions are immoral in all social contexts.

The first version of the categorical imperative reveals whether one's action-guiding principles are consistent or contradictory. For Kant, this moral test not only appeals to one's sense of reason, but it also ensures that no individual can be considered an exception when acting from a maxim. That is, "when we make an exception for ourselves, declaring that the action is wrong in general but we can do it nonetheless, that is a certain indication that our action is immoral" (Porter, 1980, p. 183). The idea of impartiality then is an essential feature of Kantian ethics, and in this respect it is similar to the Golden Rule. It also is clear that the categorical imperative is a procedure that takes into account the rational nature of others. This other-regarding dimension is so central to Kant's ethics it is the basis of the second formulation of the categorical imperative.

In this version, Kant (1785/1959) asserted, "Act so that you treat humanity, whether in your own person or in that of another, always as an end and never as a means only" (p. 47). Here Kant was stressing the intrinsic worth of human beings as rational selves. The primacy of selfhood, autonomy, and self-determination for all rational beings simply because they are rational ensures that no amount of exploitation of people can be morally justified. Moreover, this formulation of the categorical imperative, whose substance is apparently identical with the first version, cannot place conditions upon people in order that they be treated as ends (Korner, 1955). So one cannot force others to adopt a certain way of life and then treat them with human dignity. Once again, people are ends in themselves by virtue of their existence as rational selves. Slavery, torture, political oppression, sexual harassment, and all forms of exploitation are immoral and cannot be justified and condoned.

Kant was not suggesting that one exclusively, in all one's affairs with others, view them as ends. Part of one's relationship with others is on an instrumental level, as it is with employers, clerks, co-workers, and even one's parents. The point is that one should not treat others "as a means *only*" (emphasis added). On a fundamental level and as much as possible, others ought to be accorded genuine respect and be treated with dignity even when they are considered as a means to some end (Beauchamp, 1991). So athletes should not treat a trainer or equipment manager *just* as a specialized servant who performs specific auxiliary tasks on demand, but as an autonomous, independent human being, with her own interests, desires, and needs, who performs essential supportive services. One, therefore, needs to be sensitive to the kinds of relationships one has with other people and recognize an ultimate concern of respecting the intrinsic worth of human beings.

The idea of treating others "always as an end" carries other implications like not harming others, respecting their rights, enhancing their well-being, and trying to further their ends (Rachels, 1986). It also means holding in high esteem rationality itself. Respect for persons means that one regards others as having the capacity to make choices, and to deny others the ability to choose is to treat them as a means.

In the above false-promise example, if the borrower told the lender he did not know if he could repay the loan, then the lender would be given the opportunity to decide whether or not to extend the loan on some other basis. Consider how a person might feel if he discovered someone had lied to him. Aside from any practical consequences of the lie, the individual would likely feel insulted, as though the lie were an affront to his integrity as a person. Some moral experiences, therefore, can tell people whether they treat others primarily as ends or as means. Such experiences can also be utilized as a kind of test to determine whether one's maxims are morally sound or inconsistent. So for Kant, a fundamental aspect of human dignity is to respect others as autonomous, rational beings. When one does treat others as ends as such, this provides a further indication that one's maxims can become universal laws.

By combining elements of the first and second versions of the categorical imperative, Kant provided a third formulation. He basically stated that one should act as, "a legislative member in the realm of ends" (Kant, 1785/1959, p. 53). Now the term realm extends the idea of willing self-imposed laws to all members of a community (Raphael, 1980). If a society, in principle, could account for and unify each person's capacity to will universal laws and always to treat others as ends, then at one and the same time, one would be both a legislator of laws and a subject of them.

What Kant was saying is that, in theory, if every person in society utilized reason to create self-imposed laws, this would lead all persons to will the same universal laws. One's duty toward the law would then be absolute from a social perspective. No longer would coercion or force be needed to uphold the law because in the realm of ends all individuals are legislators and subjects. Because in such ideal circumstances, members of society would be collectively willing identical self-imposed laws, not to comply with such laws would be contradictory.

In essence, what Kant was describing is a pure form of democracy. Each member of society would be given the freedom to make independent decisions (liberty), all choices would carry the same value (equality), and each person would make decisions as a member of a community (fraternity) (Raphael, 1980).

In the three versions of the categorical imperative several salient features of Kantian ethics emerge, and it would be helpful to review these at this juncture. In the first instance, the notion of an absolute duty as the only motive for moral action (resulting from a good will) required a coherent foundation based on reason alone. Kant introduced the distinction between hypothetical and categorical imperatives to demonstrate how the term ought is employed. In the former case, which is based on desire, "ought" claims could not be considered morally relevant, nor could the sense of duty here be deemed very strong. A genuine moral ought creates an absolute (categorical) obligation that must be accepted by all rational beings. To establish this duty as ultimately binding, two conditions need to be met.

First, an individual must autonomously will a maxim, or an action-guiding rule. The notion of autonomy here is linked to people's fundamental nature as rational beings. Second, a person must choose to act *from* the maxim rather than act according to the maxim. Once these steps are taken, one can employ the principle of the categorical imperative, as a sort of test to determine whether a maxim is morally correct. Three versions of the categorical imperative were examined.

The first formulation emphasized the idea of universalizability. One asks, "Can the maxim be followed consistently by all people at all times?" In this way the maxim acquires the character of a universal law that can be accepted by all rational persons and adhered to with a strict sense of duty. Any maxim that turns out to be self-contradictory is immoral. This particular moral test ensures impartiality so that no one can be made an exception to a certain rule. The second version of the categorical imperative stressed the importance of human dignity. We are always to treat others as ends and not merely as means. Here we have an ultimate concern to respect the autonomous and rational capacity of others. We must, therefore, enhance the well-being of others, advance their ends, respect their rights, and not harm them. Finally, the third variation consisted of an ideal political situation in which the collective will of all members of a community creates self-imposed laws and in which opposition to such laws would be contradictory.

Although many features of Kantian ethics conform to moral experiences and they do seem to be rationally grounded, how cogent are these views? One difficulty surrounds the idea that maxims can be universalized. Frankena (1973) points out that conflicts can arise between two duties. Suppose one upholds the universal laws never to tell a lie and, always to help someone in trouble. Then one day one is confronted by a known killer (a hit person) who asks the whereabouts of someone one knows. If one tells the truth one would likely endanger the potential victim's life; if one lies, however, one would be assisting the person one knows. In either case, one could not simultaneously uphold both laws. Where then should one's absolute duty reside? Kant had no satisfactory way to resolve this dilemma, but consider the following.

If one were to modify the maxim by saying "never tell a lie unless by doing so you preserve someone's life," the maxim would no longer apply in a universal way, but it would be connected to specific instances. Perhaps if there are two conflicting laws, one could be selected as having greater value over another (Porter, 1980). So in the above example, saving a person's life takes precedence over never telling a lie. In this way, a hierarchy of laws could be established. But again, this would not agree with the principle of universalizability, and the application of laws would be context specific. There would also be the problems of deciding what one law would dominate all others, and whether or not the application of this law would be guaranteed in every moral situation. In any event, Kant believed that universal laws did apply in all circumstances without exception, so such modifications to the principle of universalizability are unhelpful.

Difficulties raised in the preceding discussion indicate that, in some instances, certain practices people generally think are wrong could be morally justified. So stealing food to feed one's children during wartime or a famine could be approved by most of us. Doctors sometimes make decisions to withhold medical treatment in extremely severe cases (especially if death is imminent), thereby not acting to preserve life and curtail human suffering, and this behavior may be morally justified. So the idea that a universal law is applicable in all situations without exception, may be unrealistic in practical terms. In fact, for some critics, there can be no such laws because no maxims can be identified that apply strictly in all situations (Porter, 1980).

Conflict also arises with regard to the second formulation of the categorical imperative. Suppose one is in a position to help only one of two individuals who equally need one's assistance. How does one decide which person should be helped? If both individuals are to be treated as ends so that one is to further their interests, advance their well-being, and the like, it becomes virtually impossible to resolve this dilemma. Kant's principle identifies which maxims are moral because they demonstrate respect for human dignity, but in reference to the preceding example "it does not give me a criterion for deciding which of them I should help" (Raphael, 1981, p. 60). If there is no standard to decide which person's ends one should respect, then Kant's principle is of limited value in some contexts.

Also at issue are certain practices we sometimes commend, but either they cannot be carried out universally or it would be too much to require strict obligation to them. For example, on one hand, self-sacrificing conduct can occasionally be recommended and be seen to be virtuous in some instances (we certainly would not want to say it is not virtuous) (Porter, 1980). On the other hand, such conduct could not be performed by everyone; otherwise, no one would be the recipient of such behavior. Consider another example: heroic conduct. Although acts of heroism are often viewed as morally correct, people cannot be required to act in heroic ways if the opportunity might call for it. No one can morally demand that someone enter a burning apartment building to save some of its tenants. This does not mean that heroic behavior has no moral worth, but that one's moral obligations cannot extend to include certain practices.

It is here that Kant's general notion of duty is sometimes unclear. Many maxims can be universalized and, therefore, be candidates for undivided duty, but this does not necessarily mean the maxims are moral. So, always put on one's left shoe first or comb one's hair before brushing one's teeth could each be a universal law (i.e., followed by all people at all times), but what sort of absolute moral obligation do people have to such laws?

Frankena (1973) indicates that Kant did not adequately provide a way to tell whether or not one is dealing with a moral issue and where one's duty lies. Palmer (1991), however, defends Kant on this point and claims, "What gives an act *moral* worth is not simply the fact it *can* be universalized, but the fact it was chosen as a moral act" (p. 328). This reminds us once again that it is the motive for one's actions that ultimately decides the moral content of behavior (what issues from a good will). That is, when one acts from a posture of duty for duty's sake the action is said to be a moral one. The difficulty here, of course, is knowing what people's motives are. These motives may not be evident from their actions, and it may not be helpful to ask people what their motives are (they might not know, or they might be confused about the matter). For these reasons, the idea of absolute duty remains questionable, and some critics contend no such pure stance is possible. Although one's intentions or motives are surely part of moral reasoning and conduct, they are likely not the *only* factors underlying the notion of duty, and they provide limited help when one tries determine what counts as a moral act.

Despite the shortcomings discussed above, and there are several others we will not address, the appeal of Kantian ethics rests on a number of important points. For one thing, it stresses that people must remain strictly impartial. All rational beings are equally considered from a moral point of view. Moreover, although it may be impossible to will universal laws with no exceptions or to act from a pure sense of duty, these can still be useful rules of thumb by which to guide human behavior in some contexts. That is, as ideals these notions cannot be totally discounted. Perhaps the most significant claims within Kantian ethics concern the stature of the moral agent. Kant elevated the individual as a moral authority based on the ideas of autonomy and rationality. This insight removed morality from the realm of external authorities including religion. Kant altered the focus of ethics by turning toward each person as the ultimate source of morality, and this was a major shift in the history of ethics, felt even today.

KEY CONCEPTS

good will or character	duty for duty's sake
hypothetical imperative	rationality
3 formulations of the categorical imperative	maxim
autonomy of will	self-legislation act according to a rule
act from a rule	consistency and contradiction

impartiality   persons as ends
conflicting duties   strict application
acts of self-sacrifice   acts of heroism

Ross's Prima Facie Duties

Before we leave the area of deontological theories, one other relatively recent viewpoint that follows in the Kantian tradition will be briefly examined. As mentioned in the previous section, Kant's system could not resolve a conflict between one's duty toward two universal laws without breaking one of them. There was just no way to decide which law was to take precedence unless one was willing to make certain exceptions (e.g., never lie except when it helps someone in danger), and Kant would have none of that. For this reason, some deontologists have introduced the notion of plurality whereby several principles operate to account for certain overriding concerns. The most noted philosopher to develop this line of thought was W. D. Ross (1877-1970), and it is to his work that we now turn.

Like Kant, Ross was committed to a nonconsequentialist approach toward ethics (e.g., he strongly opposed utilitarianism), and he too placed considerable importance on the notion of duty. Unlike Kant, he did not view duty as an absolute obligation. As we noted above, there was no way to resolve the dilemma when two universal laws came into conflict in a given situation, thereby making it impossible to decide where one's duty resided. Ross, therefore, proposed an alternative to the absoluteness of Kant's sense of duty.

To set out this new position, Ross presented a distinction between actual or "proper" duty and conditional or "prima facie" duty (Ross, 1930). What one actually ought to do or what is actually right can be derived from rules that permit certain exceptions. So, if one made an appointment to meet a friend for a racquetball match, but learned one's mother had to be rushed to the hospital (she had a known heart condition), breaking the date to play tennis (even leaving the friend unknowingly stranded) would be morally justified in order to be at the side of one's mother (especially if one promised to do so in such a situation). Here, the rule "never break a promise except in personal emergencies" would be followed so that one's actual duty took into account an exception.

A prima facie (which means at first glance, apparently so, or self-evident) or conditional duty follows from exceptionless rules. However, such a duty is not yet an actual duty because it can be superseded by other overriding obligations. In this instance, there will always be more reason to adhere to a prima facie duty unless it is outweighed by another duty. For example, one has a prima facie duty always, as much as possible, to keep one's promises. If one is a doctor who makes a date to play tennis with a friend and no emergency arises, one has a moral obligation to show up for the game. But if one faced a conflict in which another prima facie duty was pressing, for instance, saving a person's life, then this second duty would likely outweigh the first. It would be at this point that one could then declare one's actual duty that would follow from a rule containing an exception, although keeping promises and saving lives are separate prima facie duties (Frankena, 1973).

Note that Ross is committed not to the idea of absolute duty, but to the consideration of different competing duties. Prima facie duties follow from rules that can be said to be internally without exception. By considering other prima facie duties one is not introducing exceptions to certain rules, but one is instead weighing one "exceptionless" rule against another and trying to formulate what one's actual duty is that can contain an exception clause. This point is often missed by some readers.

Now one might ask, "What are some of these prima facie duties?" Ross provided a list that he claimed is not exhaustive, and the correctness of these duties he accepted as self-evident (hence prima facie). Many have been critical of him on these two counts (cf., Garner & Rosen, 1967), but it is still useful to know his list of prima facie duties which are (a) to keep one's promises, (b) to make restitution when one wrongfully harms others, (c) to return any services when one has benefited from the services of others, (d) to distribute rewards and punishment based on merit, (e) to do good on behalf of others, (f) to improve oneself in terms of virtue and intelligence, and (g) not to injure others (Brandt, 1959; Ewing, 1953; Ross, 1930).

On the surface, this pluralistic approach toward duty appears sound, and something like prima facie duties are more reasonable than Kant's unconditional duty. But here also Ross is not totally in the clear when it comes to conflicting duties. Ewing (1953), Brandt (1959), Garner and Rosen (1967), and Frankena (1973) all point out that Ross has not provided sufficient criteria to decide which prima facie duties ought to take precedence over others in conflict situations. Ross (1930) conceded as much when he stated, "For the estimation of the comparative stringency of these prima facie obligations no general rules can, so far as I can see, be laid down" (p. 41). Other criticisms include counterexamples that demonstrate how some of Ross's prima facie duties are occasionally inconsistent and sometimes can be applied in morally questionable circumstances. It also has been shown by critics that some of his duties approach utilitarian themes and calculations that he strongly opposed.

Notwithstanding these criticisms, Ross's ethical theory can at least be said in some instances to do no worse than other ethical theories (Ewing, 1953). Even utilitarians must often admit to having no criteria for deciding between competing pleasures and pains. Although Ross rejected utilitarian grounds to establish moral obligation, and he preferred a self-evident view for the moral value of prima facie duties, his approach is generally in accord with ethical concerns on a common-sense level. That is, many everyday moral evaluations and decisions are based on the notion of duty and are often consistent with moral intuitions. So on Ross's account, an emphasis on duty might not lead so readily to situations in which better overall consequences might result from some personal injustice (as could happen when following a utilitarian approach). Yet on the other hand, the pursuit of virtuous ends cannot be entirely neglected to make way for moral obligations, for the latter often presuppose such ends (Ewing, 1953). Ross's prima facie duties, therefore, provide an important ethical concept, yet one that must be accepted with some reservations.

This ends our discussion of deontological theories, and it was made clear that morality here was based on a number of central themes, such as ultimate moral principles, character, duty, and motives. In the next section, we will focus on another major ethical theory, a category that considers the topic of justice as a basic tenet of morality.

KEY CONCEPTS	
nonconsequentialist	actual or "proper" duty
conditional or prima facie duty	weighing prima facie duties
critique of Ross's ethical theory	

Theories of Justice

The notion of justice usually falls under the domain of social philosophy. Here, moral problems are framed by such concepts as fairness, desert (what one deserves), entitlement (what one is entitled to), and the distribution of goods and services that people claim as citizens of particular societies (Beauchamp, 1991; Palmer, 1991). Issues of justice more generally involve matters where what is due or owed is considered. For example, company policies, rules, and regulations might be in place to ensure fairness in hiring, nondiscriminatory practices in promotions, fair grievance and negotiation procedures, just benefits packages, and the like. Specific rules are usually governed by more general principles, such as equality between people, fair treatment by others, protection from harm, ownership rights and obligations, and distributive and retributive justice (Beauchamp, 1991; Frankena, 1973). In most instances, social justice is conceived in both these general and specific senses.

Because this section is really not concerned with criminal activities and the fairness of penalties attached to such behavior (retributive justice), the focus here will be on distributive justice. The latter refers to the distribution of benefits and burdens assumed by members of a society. Paying taxes, for example, is a distributed burden, whereas food stamps, welfare, unemployment, and workers' compensation checks are distributed benefits. Distributive justice is usually based on the premise that certain qualities people possess should be linked with the way societal benefits and burdens are correctly distributed. For instance, company promotions ought to be given to those who are in line for a promotion, those who possess excellent skills, those who have improved their performance significantly, and those who have achieved recognized standards of accomplishment.

Many examples of distributive justice involve at least two general features. First, there is usually a comparative component. If two similar individuals in similar situations are treated differently for better or worse, there may be grounds to say an injustice has been committed (Frankena, 1973). So what one person or group deserves is often compared to the desert of another person or group. Not all justice issues are comparative, but many of the distributive variety are. Second, distributive justice involves some element of scarcity over which there are conflicting or competing claims. This usually applies to benefits (Bowie & Simon, 1977). If a promotion is seen as a benefit, the available positions to which people can be promoted are typically limited. A just selection process, therefore, must be established when several people apply for promotion.

The comparative and scarce dimensions of distributive justice are still insufficient bases by which to make decisions of fairness, desert, entitlement, and the like. What is also needed are specific criteria by which to establish just rules, procedures, and regulations. Frankena (1973) lists three major categories that can serve as criteria in these instances. First, justice may be founded on what people *deserve* or *what* they merit. This criterion is known as *meritarian*, which refers to the distribution of some good (e.g., happiness) based on the expression of some virtue (e.g., honesty). Second, justice may involve treating others as *equals* so that the distribution of benefits and burdens is equal as well. An *equalitarian* criterion is typical of democratic societies. Finally, justice may be based on people's *needs* or their *abilities* or both. This criterion is the foundation of a Marxist view of justice.

In the following subsections, a further explication and critique of these criteria and their relationship to various theories of justice will be presented. The theories to be covered include egalitarian, libertarian, utilitarian, and Marxist perspectives. This cursory examination should provide a sound overview of a difficult topic.

Egalitarian

In most ethical theories, the meaning of equality plays a major role. Whether one speaks about the equal status of individuals or the equal value given to people's preferences or the treatment of others as equal, some basic sense of equality is needed. A reasonable understanding of equality is also required to determine relevant differences and inequality in given situations. But unlike other ethical positions, the meaning of equality and inequality is a central tenet of an egalitarian theory of justice (Beauchamp, 1991).

One form of egalitarianism holds strictly to the dictum that justice means treating equals as equals and unequals as unequals. Based on this formula, one is able to render consistent justice decisions (Bowie & Simon, 1977). This extreme egalitarian view considers people to be sufficiently alike so that all people are to be treated equally. That is, all benefits and burdens ought to be equally distributed because, morally speaking, all people are equal. A major flaw here is that people are not identical or equal to one another, and so the premise of the argument is false (Wheelwright, 1959). People do not have the same backgrounds, skills, opportunities, needs, interests, physical appearance, and the like. Consequently, there can be no possible way to distribute benefits and burdens so that identical results are achieved.

Some have suggested that equal treatment rather than equal outcomes is the proper way to understand the egalitarian position. So those who have special needs, like the poor, the sick, and those with disabilities, should be provided with greater benefits so inequalities can be corrected (Raphael, 1981). This revision of egalitarianism tries to create advantages proportional to the needs of others in special cases. What this view does *not* suggest is that those who have superior talents and skills be given additional incentives and rewards so that the advantages they already possess are enhanced further. If this enhancement were carried out, disparity between the distribution of benefits and burdens would continue to exist, and an egalitarian society would not be established. But this modified version is still not free of problems.

Is there a fair financial distribution if parents outfit one child in an ice hockey program and a second child in a soccer program? If the first child is only interested in expensive sports, should the second child be "penalized" as a result? In this case, it may be contentious whether or not a just distribution of benefits and burdens should be based solely on special interests or needs (Bowie & Simon, 1977). Because of such criticisms a further revision to egalitarianism maintains that an equality of opportunity to fulfill fundamental needs is required. Affirmative action is one concrete way to implement this last form of egalitarianism, but here too, there are strong objections to affirmative action programs (Beauchamp, 1991). Rather than continue to explore and critique different versions of egalitarianism, let us turn to discuss one of the most compelling contemporary statements related to this theory of justice.

Over two decades ago, Rawls (1971) produced an egalitarian view of justice in his important book, A *Theory of Justice*. According to Rachels (1989), this work is revolutionary because it returned moral philosophy in this century from a mostly theoretical area of study to one where working principles could be implemented to create a just society. Second, Rawls's book revived aspects of contract theory in social philosophy and joined it with deontological elements, thus creating the first significant alternative and challenge to utilitarianism, which had dominated social and political philosophy for about a century. Unfortunately, and given the relevance of this work, only an outline of Rawls's egalitarian theory can be offered here.

We have already discussed how utilitarianism can lead to situations in which injustices are committed, especially in breach of individual rights or what people deserve, to attain the greatest good for society. The potential to arrive at such a circumstance has no place in a system of social justice. Rawls, therefore, set out to construct a theory to avoid violations of justice, even those that exist only in principle.

The procedure or method he followed to locate and establish sound social principles is rooted in the expression "justice as fairness" (Rawls, 1971). Any social structure or institution that fails to ensure that individuals are treated justly needs to be abandoned or reformed. But who determines what counts as "justice as fairness"? Rather than present some utopian vision that people work toward, Rawls proposed a hypothetical situation in which free, equal, and rational people will have to make their own basic decisions about creating the just society. In this way, their decisions are produced by and turned back on themselves. But because of the individual and collective nature of this process, people will be constrained by the judgments of others. People will realize that not everyone can receive the largest share of any particular good. There will be a recognition that both cooperative and competitive elements will operate to guide people's decisions. Yet despite potential rivalries, free, equal, and rational people will likely choose to create a society that promotes advantages for all (Falikowski, 1990). This will entail that some form of mutual understanding will exist between people where justice and equality are fundamental considerations. Rawls then understood society as consisting of some type of social contract in which tacit agreements are made between members of a society. But how exactly does a Rawlsian society emerge?

Rawls (1971) suggested that, theoretically speaking, people create principles of social justice from an original position where impartiality is maintained. From this standpoint, people are placed behind a "veil of ignorance." That is, individuals have no knowledge of their race, class, physical appearance, mental capabilities, social status, natural talents, monetary worth, society's socio economic and political structure, and the like. The "veil-of-ignorance" construct ensures individuals cannot devise principles of justice that favor only themselves. Members of society must take into account the interests and decisions of others because there is no guarantee that a particular judgment will result in personal advantages. Again, one does not know in advance how one will fare in the end. As Raphael (1981) explains,

> The hypothesis of making the calculation under a veil of ignorance about one's personal situation is a method of adding impartiality. If I have to provide for my own interests in any and every possible contingency, I am providing for the interests of anyone and everyone, not just for my own. (p. 72)

By making free, equal, and rational choices under this thought experiment, Rawls contended people can devise mutually agreeable principles of justice that are fair. Two main principles arise from his proposed scheme. First, people would maximize the amount of liberty (political, religious, speech) they can exercise, and second, once this liberty is in place, primary social goods like wealth, power, self-respect, and opportunities would be distributed to the advantage of all (Beauchamp, 1991). The latter principle implies that inequalities can exist in a just society, as long as the whole of society benefits from such inequalities and everyone has a fair opportunity to acquire unequally distributed goods. Because these principles are generated from behind the veil, they produce the effect of moving toward greater equality for disadvantaged members of society. The conditions created by Rawls's method, therefore, are consistent with his "justice as fairness" credo. It is also clear from this discussion that Rawls objected to desert and merit as founding principles of a just society, as well as traditional forms of utilitarianism. His preferred society stresses the maximization of equal liberty, greater equality for the disadvantaged, and the fair distribution of social goods where inequalities can exist for the benefit of all.

Now that an outline of Rawls's egalitarian theory of justice has briefly been presented, a sport-related application of his procedure and a short critique are in order. Simon (1991) analyzes the problem of unequal distribution of scarce benefits in elite sports by employing the Rawlsian method of social justice. This problem centers on the issue of whether or not a handful of athletes *deserve* or *merit* the enormous fame and fortune they receive because of their natural talents. In light of the conclusions above, personal desert in itself cannot serve as the ground for justifying inequalities. The only room for desert or merit lies in a just set of rules or regulations created impartially behind the veil of ignorance. So, Olympic athletes deserve the medals they receive if they and others abide by rules created independently of desert considerations. If such rules are created in accord with Rawls's procedure, then not only can a mild form of desert exist but inequalities can also exist. Athletes may receive a disproportionate amount of scarce benefits in a free-market economy because such inequalities in the long run benefit society and the disadvantaged.

Simon (1991) is uncomfortable with this reasoning because it minimizes the idea of desert and could lead to conditions in which respect for persons is undermined. In particular, in a Rawlsian view, athletic talent might be considered community property to be developed and expressed independently of the interests and choices of the individual athlete. This of course would be disrespectful of people as autonomous agents. Should all seven-footers be compelled to play basketball? Should people not acknowledge the efforts to excel and the improved performance of one athlete over another when they both possess similar natural abilities?

Inequality of results is often a consequence of personal abilities and assets some people wish to develop and others recognize, without the added necessity of creating benefits for all and improving the lot of the disadvantaged. Simon (1991) suggests that perhaps in a Rawlsian society there is some room for individual merit in order to retain respect for persons. Based on this amendment, elite athletes are justified and deserve to be disproportionately rewarded for their natural abilities. But they should also recognize that their personal assets are fortuitous and that if they are being rewarded by society, they have an obligation to those worse off, a conclusion that results from being behind the veil of ignorance.

In addition to Simon's misgivings about aspects of Rawls's theory, other criticisms have been raised as well. Rawls of course advocated a liberal society where a premium on fairness and equality exists. This also happens to be the kind of society Rawls lives in, and so he seems to be speaking from an ethnocentric and biased position (Palmer, 1991). This criticism can be extended because some claim his original position is not neutral but assumes a liberal, individualistic view of society. Rawls provided no sound arguments to reject other social arrangements (e.g., a theocracy) that some might choose even behind the veil of ignorance

(Bowie & Simon, 1977).

Another criticism is the special kind of self-interest Rawls assumed people would adopt, which tends toward playing it safe in case one ends up unlucky. If the stakes were high enough to become extremely wealthy, let us say, some might decide to take their chances and risk being paupers in the original position (Raphael, 1981). An additional criticism goes as follows: If complete ignorance of one's own interests and identity is required, then signers to Rawls's social contract are not legally bound. No contract can ask of its signatories to forgo all knowledge of themselves, and so the contract must be deemed invalid (Palmer, 1991). Finally, Rawls has been criticized for not protecting individual rights where the redistribution of benefits and burdens will require undue state interference. Rawls's theory only works because it is assumed that social goods are heaven sent, when they are really produced historically through the resourceful efforts of individuals. In other words, social goods belong to people, and treating these goods as if they did not is a violation of people's rights (Beauchamp, 1991).

This ends our discussion of an egalitarian theory of justice, which has much to recommend despite its weaknesses. In the next subsection we will focus on a libertarian perspective that relies heavily on the protection of people's rights and directly challenges some egalitarian ideas.

KEY CONCEPTS

desert	entitlement	retributive justice
distributive justice	comparative	scarcity
meritarian	equalitarianism	needs and abilities
egalitarian	equal outcomes	equal treatment
equality of opportunity	justice as fairness	social contract
original position	veil of ignorance	liberty
primary goods	Simon's critique	ethnocentrism
prudent self-interest	violation of rights to social goods	

Libertarian

Unlike the egalitarian perspective in which justice as fairness involves equal opportunity so that those disadvantaged can gain greater equality, libertarians in the main do not hold to such a premise. A libertarian asks only that fair procedures, rules, and regulations be in place in society to ensure that people have the freedom to make social and economic choices as they please. Any attempt to restrict people's liberty in this regard is deemed unjust. The distribution of benefits and burdens is carried out by creating conditions whereby people can freely control their lives to pursue their own interests. Those who are more industrious and contribute more to their own success and to that of society rightly deserve to be rewarded more than do others who contribute less. The rights of liberty, happiness, property, and such are taken seriously by libertarians who would prefer minimal government intervention in the lives of citizens.

There are of course objections to the libertarian account of social justice, and these will be raised later in this subsection. Once again, however, there is a well-known contemporary spokesperson for this position, and we will turn to his thought to explain further the libertarian view.

As a challenge and alternative to Rawls, Nozick's (1974) compelling work called *Anarchy, State, and Utopia* follows traditional and more recent views of libertarianism. Nozick begins with a critique of the anarchist's position that "no state has legitimate authority over its citizens" (Minton & Shipka, 1990, p. 462). Essentially, the state interferes in the lives of people through the principle of the right to command. For example, that state can tax people and compel them to go to war. For anarchists, the state violates individual rights (suppose one does not want to pay taxes or go to war) on the basis that it provides protection for its citizens. Nozick reasons that the anarchist view is incorrect, because anarchy would still result in some grand protective agency's emerging and operating as a state-like entity. Nozick concludes that anarchy would logically create a "minimal state" that can be defended as just (Palmer, 1991).

No state, whether socialist or capitalist in nature, should try to reach a just society by redistributing benefits and burdens. A state's only mandate is to ensure that people have an absolute right to liberty so they can make social and economic decisions in the most free and unencumbered way possible. Some theories of justice (e.g., utilitarianism) employ end-state goals whereby the distribution of benefits and burdens is determined in a nonhistorical way. Society might be better off if the rich were forced to share their wealth with others, but for historical reasons (e.g., if such wealth was acquired legally and legitimately), people cannot morally make these demands (Bowie & Simon, 1977). Similarly, if a state were to follow some patterned formula for redistributing benefits and burdens, it would always lead to some infringement of a person's liberty.

Because Nozick is critical of nonhistorical end-state principles and patterned formulae employed by some theories of justice, he proposes an entitlement theory of justice (Beauchamp, 1991). This theory refers to some basic rights contained in three main principles related to the acquisition, transfer, and rectification of goods or "holdings." Nozick (1974) borrows ideas of ownership from John Locke (1632-1704), a 17th-century moral and political philosopher, and claims that " Locke views property rights in an unowned object as originating through someone's mixing his labor with it" (p. 174). So, in the 17th century, explorers in North America could cross the Mississippi, set up a camp, and claim all the territory before them for France, England, or Spain. This kind of original acquisition, however, can worsen the situation for others, like native peoples. Because resources like land are scarce, Nozick (1974) agrees with Locke's proviso that acquisitions can occur as long as they do not worsen circumstances for others and some sort of baseline situation is maintained.

In addition to acquiring holdings, a person has a right to transfer personal goods if this transfer is done in a legal and legitimate way in accordance with the above disclaimer. So transactions, such as selling, purchasing, gift giving, and inheriting, are certainly appropriate in a minimal state. Finally, one has the right to defend one's holdings in the event they come under harm and to exact punishments against those who are guilty of such harmful practices. In order to seek rectification in such instances, the libertarian demands that the state intervene, and this is the only area where it can do so (Palmer, 1991).

It is clear that the above three principles and their related rights work optimally in a free-market, capitalist society. When pure procedural guidelines are followed in the latter areas and basic rights are upheld, then social justice can prevail. There is also a recognition that ownership and monetary inequalities will exist in the minimal state. Despite the proviso Nozick introduces, he defends such inequalities by saying they are unfortunate, but not unjust (Palmer, 1991). Intuitively, one might find Nozick's libertarian view harsh and unsympathetic to the plight of those less fortunate. Some critics object to his ideas on these grounds. In the remainder of this subsection, a number of criticisms will be raised against the libertarian position, and a sport-related example will be discussed.

One of the main criticisms against Nozick's brand of libertarianism is the premium he places on economic rights. By doing so, he restricts the notion of individual rights, which can include the right to decent education, health care, environment, living standard, and the like (Bowie & Simon, 1977). Further, Nozick does not provide an argument to claim economic rights supersede noneconomic rights. He merely presupposes the former are absolute, and this is an arbitrary move on his part. Moreover, in most of Nozick's transactions he presumes that those involved are on an equal footing. In the real world, however, acquisitions and transfers often occur between parties who have different levels of power and wealth. Justified outcomes may still be unfair even though power and wealth are acquired legitimately (Beauchamp, 1991).

Another criticism against the libertarian view relates to the meaning of "original" acquisition. How can one possibly determine when and where such an acquisition took place? Wars fought over territory do not resolve this problem, and merely looking back through history leads to an unclear and unhelpful regress (Palmer, 1991). Another area that is vague is Nozick's proviso that ownership not worsen the situation of others below a baseline level. First, to suggest such a baseline logically means that some rights must be given up to support this "safety net." This then would undermine Nozick's absolute and firm stance on noninterference when it comes to individual liberty. Second, Nozick sometimes suggests that the only situation in which people might be worse off is one that leads to their death (Bowie & Simon, 1977). Other than that, ownership can extend to impoverish the lives of others, and again, this might be unfortunate, but not unjust. Many people would not tolerate such a lack of concern for others and would find it difficult to claim this is just.

The above criticisms are sufficient to reveal that libertarianism contains some serious flaws and shortcomings. Nevertheless, the wide attention given to Nozick's work by way of criticism also suggests the importance of his ideas. By way of closing this subsection and in light of the above discussion, a sport-related example will be taken up.

Once again we will turn to Simon (1991), who discusses the distribution of basic benefits of sport. Unlike scarce benefits, such as fame and fortune, basic benefits refer to goods available to all sport participants. These would include having fun, improving one's health, improving one's skills, learning to cooperate with teammates, being challenged by opponents, and the like. Whereas scarce benefits are exclusionary (not everyone can acquire fame and fortune), basic benefits are nonexclusionary (everyone has access to and can acquire these goods). Given this distinction, Simon asks whether or not all persons have the same right to the basic benefits of sport. The latter issue centers on the idea of positive rights and liberty.

Positive rights establish that people are obligated to provide the basic benefits of sport to those who wish to pursue and enjoy these goods. This obligation must be manifested in concrete actions, and it usually means some cost is involved, either money or time or personal effort. So a positive right to participate in sport with opponents who supply challenges means that some people would be obligated to become opponents. Suppose the state were to guarantee the latter, then this would surely violate the liberty of those individuals designated as opponents. Libertarians at this point would argue that such interference is unjustified and the redistribution of the basic benefits of sport, therefore, undermines individual liberty.

Simon (1991) objects to the libertarian critique on two fronts. First, even though one cannot claim a positive right to ensure opponents, there may be other positive rights claims that are justified. So, to maintain a decent standard of living, people may have the right to basic education, including physical education where the benefits of sports are enjoyed. Thus, the rejection of one basic benefit of sport as a positive right does not mean that all such benefits need be rejected. Second, the libertarian insistence on noninterference when it comes to individual liberty is suspect. Because the libertarian does permit a protection agency to ensure personal liberty itself is maintained (the minimal state), then he or she acknowledges that some social support system is valuable. The latter is a positive rights claim that obligates citizens to support the protection agency. If this is the case, then perhaps other positive rights claims (like basic education), which create social obligations, also ensure individual liberty. Despite these criticisms, Simon (1991) admits that the libertarian critique of positive rights warns us about the intrusive nature of these claims and that entitlement to the basic benefits of sport is not a clear-cut issue.

The libertarian view of social justice presented above places a premium on individual freedom and autonomy. People are able to best serve their own interests and act on their abilities when left alone with no interference from others or the state. In the next subsection, justice from a utilitarian perspective will be examined. Because utilitarianism as an ethical theory was introduced earlier in this chapter, the following short discussion will focus on the justice themes of this view.

Utilitarian

It was earlier shown how acts of injustice could result from a utilitarian calculation in which the consequences of behavior are a foremost concern and decisions are made in order to achieve the greatest good for the greatest number. Criticisms of traditional, act- and rule-utilitarianism were raised because, in each version, situations could arise in which basic principles of justice were violated. For example, there could be instances where one should lie, cheat, steal, or kill if one or more of these acts produce a greater level of general happiness. Moreover, if two courses of action lead to identical utilitarian consequences and one happens to involve cheating, there are no criteria to recommend one of these forms of behavior over the other. Finally, establishing rules that prohibit objectionable conduct, like lying, stealing, and cheating (because in general they lead to more harm), often requires the attachment of exceptions to such rules and, eventually, the creation of a quagmire of complicated rules.

These general criticisms may not directly reveal injustices related to the social distribution of benefits and burdens, the main topic of this section. Therefore, the remainder of this subsection will consider only utilitarianism and issues related to just distribution.

Some sense of equality is contained in the idea of distributive justice, yet for most utilitarians there is a greater emphasis on the interests of the community rather than on those of individuals. That is, society is overvalued whereas individuals are undervalued (Beauchamp, 1991). As a result, the distribution of benefits and burdens may result in unjust practices. Frankena (1973) writes.

> It still may be, however, that they [utilitarians] distribute the balance of good over evil produced in rather different ways; one action, practice, or rule may, for example, give all the good to a relatively small group of people without any merit on their part..., while the other may spread the good more equally over a larger segment of the population. In this case, it seems to me that we should and would say that the former is unjust and wrong and the latter morally preferable. (p. 41)

If cases of unjust distribution can arise on a utilitarian calculation, then conflicts can arise between utility and justice (Raphael, 1981). It may also mean that utility alone is insufficient to determine the best way to distribute benefits and burdens, and so nonutilitarian principles of justice would have be attached to a utilitarian approach. Mill recognized this conflict between utility and justice and addressed the problem in no uncertain terms. Essentially, he claimed that justice itself is part of the principle of utility and everyone has a right to be treated justly (Beauchamp, 1991). When one considers making decisions about what to do by weighing the potential consequences of one's actions, one is in fact establishing the most just alternatives. Because the desires and wants of each person are treated equally in a utilitarian analysis, justice becomes a moral right of every person. Therefore, a society's ideas about justice are served by and are a part of a utilitarian account (Bowie & Simon, 1977).

Critics of this argument, which declares justice is dependent on utility, point out that it only holds in hypothetical situations in which equality between persons and a just distribution can be worked out. In the real world, however, a cost-benefit analysis could recommend actions or programs that in fact result in unbalanced distributions, such as a health care system that denies access to disadvantaged members of society (Beauchamp, 1991). Earlier and later rule-utilitarians at least can respond by saying that short-term or one-time cost-benefit analyses may pose the preceding difficulties. If this is the case, then alternatives or modifications to rules that govern fair distribution of and access to programs and actions are needed. This means that in some versions of utilitarianism egalitarian principles can be introduced as rules to ensure the widest and fairest possible distribution of some benefit (Frankena, 1973). The critic might say now that the value of equal distribution is right or just in itself and is not just a utility-maximizing factor, even if the former happens to result in the latter. In this way the utilitarian can always claim justice relies on utility. But the connection between equal distribution and utility-maximization is contingent, and so the utilitarian endorses this relationship on a relatively weak foundation.

To illustrate the latter point, suppose funds are available to improve the athletic locker room facilities at a university. The funds may be used to greatly improve either the women's or men's locker rooms, or moderately improve both. Suppose also that the men's facilities are larger than the women's and that they are used more extensively, thereby requiring more funds for improvement and upkeep. On a utilitarian calculus, there might be a strong case to channel the funds to renovate only the men's locker room and forgo improving the women's facilities. But suppose a more equal distribution does indeed maximize utility so that the funds should be used to moderately improve both locker rooms. If the latter was decided, the main reason would not be because it is more just or fair or deserving for women to have comparable decent facilities; it just so happens that this pattern of distribution results in greater utility. For some, this kind of reasoning might not seem right because justice can and should be considered independently from utility. That is, some things are right or just in themselves.

As stated previously, utilitarianism is a powerful ethical theory and is typically employed in the establishment of corporate and public policies. It is a rational approach for determining right and wrong, and it seeks to remove feelings, intuitions, and hunches from moral considerations (Rachels, 1986). On the other hand, utilitarianism does face a serious challenge from principles of justice that are accepted as strong foundations for creating a just society. For this reason, many contemporary moral philosophers accept some of the basic tenets of utilitarianism but attach other nonutilitarian principles to it.

There is another prominent view of justice that differs radically from those considered above by suggesting that a form of socialism, or even communism, is the best type of social arrangement. Contained in this political idea is a theory of justice attributed to Marx (1818-1885), whose thought dramatically influenced the course of world events in this century.

KEY CONCEPTS

community versus individual interests   utility and justice
equal distribution and utility-maximization

Marxist

To understand a Marxist theory of justice, even in brief, requires a minimal comprehension of Marx's world-view. Therefore, this subsection will initially outline some general themes before treating specifically the topic of justice.

Like his predecessor Hegel (1770-1831), Marx believed that human history progressed toward the realization of some greater good and overall improvement. Unlike Hegel, who viewed this progression as idealistic, Marx was a committed materialist concerned with actual, empirical facts. He held that change and advancement must occur in the real world and there were social scientific principles that governed the evolution of human societies (Perry, Chase, Jacob, Jacob, & Von Laue, 1989). The main laws that guided human affairs were connected to economic and technological means that structured and ordered people's lives. Therefore, in every age, material conditions created particular social and political arrangements. So, machine-powered factories spawned the Industrial Revolution, which dramatically altered the social lives of those who lived in growing cities. The limited modes of production in the Middle Ages resulted in the feudal system, in which peasants worked for the nobility under generally harsh and oppressive conditions. The efforts of all individuals were thus interconnected historically as products of their social environment (Palmer, 1991). Marx's scientific understanding of human societies then is based on what is known as *historical materialism*.

But, according to Marx, human history also unfolds as a struggle. In most of this history, there has always been a small group, usually the wealthy and upper class, who controlled the means of production. Relationships like those of the master and slave, the lord and serf, the capitalist and laborer attest to the historical reality that economic power generally remained in the hands of the few. Those in power primarily served their own interests, and they established the dominant ideas of the day, thus creating a certain reality for all members of society (Marx & Engels, 1848/1948). Usually, this reality became altered when economic conditions changed or social stability was weakened, or both. For example, slavery in the United States was abolished, in part, because technological innovations and methods became more efficient than human labor, and political thought was divided. Because the interests and power of the ruling class differed from the majority working class, there has always been conflict between these groups. Marx hoped to see societies progress so that the majority's interests would be served in a classless social structure.

As Marx interpreted the social conditions of 19th-century Europe, he noted another important development. His critique of capitalism tried to demonstrate that the worker was no longer organically connected to that which he produced as he had been in previous eras. Most factories and industries operated more efficiently when labor was divided, and so the worker was compelled to engage in menial, piecemeal tasks. Ultimately, the laborer became *estranged* or *alienated* from the fruits of his labor and from himself (Marx & Engels, 1848/1948; Matson, 1987). The worker was dehumanized, exploited, and by necessity had to sell his labor to the capitalist for subsistence wages under the poorest working conditions.

Marx saw a tremendous injustice under these conditions. He believed that human beings sought freedom to express their natural, creative, and productive selves and that capitalism stifled and perverted these pursuits (Melchert, 1991). He also predicted capitalism was doomed to failure as a matter of course as were earlier socio-economic structures. His ideas about how and what to replace capitalism with have left an indelible mark on the history of the 20th century. What is the just society that he envisioned?

The inevitable destruction of capitalism would be precipitated by two main events. There would be a wide polarization between a much smaller wealthy, ruling class and the vast majority of laborers. The majority would then become poorer, embittered, restless, and inevitably desperate to improve their condition. Once this occurred, the masses would instigate a revolution to overthrow the existing government and the capitalists, abolish private property, control the means of production for themselves, and create a new social order (Marx & Engels, 1848/1948). There would no longer be any classes, the state would no longer protect the wealthy, and there would be a fair distribution of goods and services. A Marxist theory of justice would then be introduced to establish a just society.

At least three main principles are part of this theory. First, the needs of people would be divided between genuine or true needs and false needs (Palmer, 1991). Genuine needs are based on the real nature of human beings as biological and social creatures. Food, shelter, clothing, education, health care, love, and creative needs are examples of true needs. False needs are artificial desires for luxury items, or wants that set some people apart as privileged, or desires created whose main purpose is to earn profit. Clearly, a just state would ensure that true needs are fulfilled, whereas false needs are exposed and done away with. Second, all resources, methods of distribution, and forms of production would be publicly owned and democratically controlled. Finally, each worker would choose his or her profession or vocation based upon his or her desire and ability. Marx envisaged no specific social roles in the classless society. Each person could act upon her or his talents and creative aspirations because there would be no strict divisions of labor. Individual potential and needs would be identical to social, community needs. As Marx and Engels (1848/1948) put it, "In place of the old bourgeois society, with its classes and class antagonisms, we shall have an association, in which the free development of each is the condition for the free development of all" (p. 31).

Justice in a Marxist society amounts to a total restructuring of people's economic and social lives. The implications of a classless society would ensure a fair distribution of goods and services, and benefits and burdens. But there are a number of drawbacks to Marx's theory of justice. First, he paints a rather optimistic picture of human nature such that people are genuinely cooperative, not selfish and competitive (Palmer, 1991). The Marxist response to those who hold the latter view is that they only conceive human beings through alienated lenses because they live in alienated cultures. In many instances, however, human history and experience have shown people to be both cooperative and competitive, and there is no strong evidence to say basic human nature is captured by one or the other expression.

Second, one could question the distinction between true and false needs. When do genuine needs become exaggerated so as to declare them as false? Who is to make this decision? Here, individual freedom and interests would be curtailed at the expense of community interests. For example, if one wanted to produce a more efficient, spacious automobile as a matter of need, the classless society might deem such a car a luxury. It would seem then that Marx's insistence that collective and personal interests become identical really undermines individual autonomy. Personal preferences would be obliterated because they would actually be social preferences. This raises a related criticism: Why should the meaning of the good life, the just society, be predicated on working-class ideals? Do laborers know the real meaning of life any more than other groups of people? Is there such a meaning? These questions point to some specific difficulties with Marx's theory of justice (Palmer, 1991).

Finally, if Marx's economic and social principles are indeed scientific and contain predictive value, then few of his speculations have materialized. There have been numerous Marxist revolutions around the globe since the 19th century, and many occurred in unlikely countries resulting in oppressive regimes (Perry et al., 1989). In recent years, the collapse of most socialist and communist countries appears to be a triumph for Western capitalist, democracies. Many theorists and historians have tried to explain the so-called failed attempt of the Marxist social experiment. It would take us too far afield to discuss these explanations, but suffice it to say, human history has not ended, and there are certainly weaknesses in Western socio-political structures. Perhaps at another moment in history, under different conditions, and with certain modifications, some manifestation of Marx's theory of justice will occur.

This ends our exposition of various theories of justice. Each theory disclosed a number of distinct principles and assumptions about creating a fair means to distribute social benefits and burdens. Some theories were more radical than others, some have had a profound influence on world affairs, and others have yet to be realized in practice. In a number of the above discussions reference was made to individual rights. This will be the topic of the final section of this chapter, and it will be a relatively short section.

KEY CONCEPTS

historical materialism	modes of production	means of production
class conflict	estrangement or alienation	destruction of capitalism
genuine and false needs	public ownership	classless society
critique of Marxist justice		

The Concept of Rights

The issue of rights is often central to ethical theories because rights place demands on others as obligations or as noninterference with people who declare rights. Human rights, natural rights, liberty rights, inalienable rights are part of the language of rights. Generally, rights guarantee certain freedoms or a particular way one is to be treated by others, an institution, or the state (Beauchamp, 1991). Rights also have a strong, but not necessary, connection to power and interests. If one claims a right to something, it can mean that one possesses a certain amount of power or one is securing a particular interest (e.g., the right to vote). But some rights have no power or interest component attached to them. Native peoples may have rights and an interest to recover parcels of land, but because of past treaties, they have no power to do so.

For some, rights are viewed as entitlements. That is, the latter are rights to something and are held as claims against others (Beauchamp, 1991). For example, when one exercises one's right to privacy, one also claims that others not infringe on that right. Two types of entitlements are described by Bowie and Simon (1977) when they assert, "Legal rights are entitlements that are supportable on legal grounds, while moral rights are entitlements that are supportable on moral grounds" (p. 58). The important point is that whereas rights entitle people to something, they place restrictions or limitations on what others can or cannot do.

Many people reasonably understand the idea of rights as described above because it is part of human language and everyday reality. However, the subject of rights is a relatively new area in moral and political philosophy. Before the 17th century, people were obligated to the king, the lord, the Church, and the like, and rights were not a consideration in political thought. With the Enlightenment, and specifically, the American and French revolutions, rights became and have continued to be a significant topic in moral and social philosophy. The philosophical debate surrounding rights is lengthy, difficult, and implicated in many particular issues. In the remainder of this section, we will only discuss the idea of obligations and then identify several kinds of rights to gain a basic, general understanding of rights.

Rights and Obligations

We have already indicated in the subsection on deontological theories the important role duty plays in ethical considerations. Similarly, the notion of obligations has a special relationship to rights. As Wheelright (1959) indicates, "the idea of a right is logically correlative with idea of specific duty, or obligation" (p. 223). For example, if one has a right to speak, then others have an obligation to allow that person to speak. If one has a right to privacy, then the police have an obligation not to barge into one's home without justification. Because there is usually a logical connection between rights and obligations, propositions involving rights can be translated into obligation statements, and vice versa (Beauchamp, 1991). The previous examples then can be reversed to read the obligation clause first and then the rights clause. According to Urban (1930), there are at least three senses in which rights and obligations are related.

The first sense refers to legitimate claims one makes to a right that establishes a corresponding obligation on others. If one legally acquires a piece of land, then others are obligated to acknowledge this ownership and not challenge this possession. Here, there may be legal grounds that create both rights and obligations.

Another sense of rights and obligations focuses more so on the individual. Owning a tract of land does not necessarily mean that one can do anything at all on one's property. A right to ownership also means that one has an obligation to develop the property appropriately within the law and in consideration of others. If one wishes to build an addition to one's home, city ordinances and bylaws must be followed, and often neighbors must be notified and agree with the type of improvement. Rights, therefore, sometimes carry personal obligations in acknowledgement of the law and others.

Finally, although rights tend to imply obligations, some theorists argue the reverse is not always the case. This means that there may be types of obligations that cannot be translated into rights claims. Even though, morally speaking, one may be obligated to give charity, one cannot claim charity from others as a matter of right. Charity seems to be the kind of gesture based on a personal standard, and so the obligation established here is of a special type beyond strict moral guidelines. This has led some to distinguish between perfect and imperfect obligations (Beauchamp, 1991). Legal rights, for example, imply perfect obligations, whereas some moral rights imply imperfect obligations. One drawback with this distinction is the difficulty by which to determine each type of obligation. Still, the idea that some obligations cannot be characterized as rights claims is an important feature to keep in mind as we next examine several types of rights.

freedom and treatment by others   power and interests

entitlement   rights and duties   legitimate claims

individual emphasis   obligations not as rights

Kinds of Rights

Because a number of different rights have been mentioned already, it would be useful to briefly identify and describe them. The classification of rights developed by Beauchamp (1991) will be the basis of this discussion because he provides the most extensive list of different rights. The first kind of right and the most easily recognizable is a moral right. These are rights claimed by individuals by virtue of their nature as moral beings (Urban, 1930). *Moral rights* are determined by a system of moral principles and theories. "Punishing" someone who violates a moral right may not involve legal sanctions but perhaps shame and public censure. The right to an abortion versus the right to life debate is one glaring example of a rights issue with deep moral sentiments and "punishments."

Legal rights are determined by a system of laws. Although there is usually a close link between legal and moral rights, there need not be. Some laws guarantee or deny rights that are immoral in themselves (e.g., the system of laws under apartheid). Legal rights tend to be more definitive than moral rights because the former are established in writing, have been tested in the courts, and are historically related through precedent cases (Wheelwright, 1959). Legal rights are also embodied in the workings of the state to uphold, protect, and enforce these rights. Appeals to the state by individuals and groups can determine whether legal rights and their corresponding duties have been protected or violated. Under a system of law, punishments for breaking legal rights are generally more severe than those for violating moral rights. Because these two types of rights are often indistinguishable or the former are viewed as an extension of the latter, both legal and moral penalties for rights violations can be similar. The main point is that legal rights are established by laws, the courts, and the state, and they are linked, but not necessarily so, to moral rights.

Another kind of right emerges from documents like the U.S. Constitution or the Declaration of Independence, which declare certain rights as absolute. So the rights to life, liberty, and property are sometimes seen as *inalienable or absolute* rights that no countervailing conditions can supersede. But can the preceding rights or any others be deemed absolute? If the right to life were an absolute, then no wars would be justified, one could not kill in self-defense, and capital punishment would be inconceivable. But many special circumstances can be raised where so-called absolute rights are overruled on moral and legal grounds (Wheelwright, 1959). For this reason, *prima facie* rights perhaps better describe what is meant by rights like life, liberty, and property. That is, if there are competing demands or conditions when considering these rights, then the claim one actually makes is a prima facie right (Brandt, 1959). Only in the absence of any conflict is one able to claim an absolute right (but again, the latter is extremely difficult to establish). For this reason, the state may interpret or amend basic rights to accommodate special conditions. Prima facie rights, therefore, are tentative because they are claimed until overridden by other competing claims.

The provisional nature of exercising rights sometimes leads to conceiving of rights as *fundamental* and *derivative* (Beauchamp, 1991). This distinction was suggested above when legal rights were described as extensions of moral rights. Urban (1930) accepts this approach because he sees both civil and political rights as extensions of moral rights. Civil rights would provide citizens protection to exercise two species of moral rights, physical rights (life, liberty, property) as well as mental activity (freedom of thought, of religion). Political rights would provide the means for citizens to create favorable social conditions to exercise the preceding moral rights. Beauchamp (1991) adds to this discussion by indicating that some rights are originally created and others flow from them (e.g., the right to an adequate standard of living is original), whereas other rights refer to bodies that possess certain powers to create laws and policies (e.g., a state legislature). Many fundamental and derivative rights are determined by basic social needs. For example, health care, food, shelter, clothing, and other necessary items required for a decent standard of living are often criteria for determining which rights are fundamental and which are derivative. In many instances, the distinction between these rights helps to establish public policies and corrective methods when dealing with social programs.

Rights involved in the development of social policies and programs usually are the final two categories of rights, known as *positive* and *negative* rights. Positive rights refer to claims so that receiving certain goods and services improves one's welfare, whereas negative rights refer to one's liberty such that others are not to interfere with one's liberty (Beauchamp, 1991). Because of the correlation between rights and obligations, a negative right simply means others are obligated to leave the rights bearer alone. Negative rights as noninterference rights are generally contained in various documents that set out to protect certain freedoms and liberties that people wish to exercise.

A positive right, however, means others are obligated to provide the rights bearer with some particular good or service. We have already presented some implications of positive rights for sport in the libertarian subsection in this chapter. The main question there was, if basic benefits of sport could be claimed as a positive right, is it reasonable for society to assume this burden? It was clear in that discussion that positive rights are generally more difficult to deal with. Both positive and negative rights then must be identified to know what sort of obligations these claims have against others.

This concludes not only our discussion of rights but also the lengthy exposition of major ethical theories. Each section has tried to convey to the reader different and complicated ideas and themes within moral philosophy. Although the account provided here is by no means exhaustive, the reader has been exposed to some of the most prevalent ethical theories. Two final subsections will close this chapter.

KEY CONCEPTS

moral rights   legal rights   inalienable or absolute rights
prima facie rights   fundamental and derivative rights
positive and negative rights

Selecting a Theory

Once individuals understand and appreciate the variety, limitations, and advantages of ethical theories, they must still confront the issue of choosing a theory or make ethical decisions that have different theoretical assumptions. But this choice is not an easy one. Each of the theories and concepts presented in this chapter has particular flaws and weaknesses. How then is one to act according to any given theory?

The question of selecting an ethical theory is itself problematic. Does it mean that one is entirely committed to a specific theory or that a single theory must be implicated in every moral situation? To answer yes to these questions leads to a rigid, inflexible approach, and such a posture is likely unreasonable and impractical. In many instances, ethical conflicts do not permit the application of a solitary theory. These dilemmas often have numerous conditions attached to them, special exceptions, unclear motives, unpredictable outcomes, and a host of other extenuating circumstances. To suggest that a single theory can account for and deal with all contingencies surrounding a particular moral problem is likely asking for and expecting too much.

There is also a hidden and unfounded bias in trying to adhere to one ethical theory. Someone who lives by just one set of ethical precepts is sometimes described as on solid ground, unswerving, and deeply committed. But in some cases such devotion can lead to untenable and sometimes immoral acts (e.g., the strict deontologist who never lies and tells a known killer the whereabouts of a potential victim). The notion that no alternative points of view have merit and that one's own position is exclusive and ideal also seems to be unreasonable. For these reasons at least, some contemporary moral philosophers have advocated a kind of pluralism when it comes to choosing "a theory."

Moral pluralism asks that one develop and accept elements of several ethical theories. Commenting on this multidimensional approach, Beauchamp (1991) writes,

> The virtue of a philosophical pluralism is that it cheerfully acknowledges a wide variety of moral conflicts, recognizes the extraordinary range of disagreement in contemporary moral philosophy, and tolerates different traditions without attempting to force them into an artificial unity. (p. 296)

Being committed to diversity and eclecticism may seem to some a sign of weakness and uncertainty. To others, like the authors here, adhering to pluralism demonstrates strength, insight, and sensitivity. By considering aspects of several ethical principles, one appropriates the advantages each principle has to offer, places issues in better perspective, and encourages more critical and challenging thought. Moral pluralism, therefore, offers the broadest conceptual framework by which to judge ethical problems. The remainder of this section will outline two such pluralistic approaches.

Rachels (1986) presents a multifaceted moral theory by asking the question "what would a satisfactory moral theory be like?" He begins his answer by suggesting that such a moral theory should be without hubris, a kind of inflated or false pride. For too long human beings have exercised their power and will over their environment, other creatures, and fellow beings in a morally superior manner. Even though we are rational creatures, who can articulate reasons for our actions and be consistent in our conduct, we have not yet overcome serious disagreements, conflicts, injustices, and other difficulties. Rachels (1986) identifies three basic ideas to overcome hubris: (a) impartiality, (b) fair rules that serve everyone's interests, and (c) modest caring for others. He adds to these components the concept of responsible agency, which maintains that human beings are free to make choices and that treatment toward others be returned in kind. Combining these elements, the fundamental principle of morality without hubris is that "we ought to act so as to promote impartially the interests of everyone alike, except when individuals deserve particular responses as a result of their own past behavior" (Rachels, 1986, p. 143).

This formulation incorporates utilitarian and Kantian ideas. There are consequentialist considerations here, as well as the requirements to remain impartial and treat others as ends. To test his moral theory, Rachels turns to the area of justice and fairness. We have noted that utilitarianism can lead to injustice when it comes to punishment, and it can lead to treating people as means. Rachels' theory, therefore, addresses these flaws by insisting on its Kantian dimensions of impartiality and respect for persons. Utilitarianism also finds it difficult to deal with the issue of desert. By focusing on the outcomes of certain actions and their overall social good, what people deserve is rarely an issue. On Rachels' account, however, personal agency, effort, and past actions can lead to justifiable unequal treatment. So, people should be promoted because they have worked hard, not because the promotion provides overall benefits for the company or because of natural endowments and abilities, like intelligence and physical appearance, should be rewarded (in the Rawlsian sense). In the area of fairness and justice then, morality without hubris is able to provide more plausible answers to concerns that single theories find problematic.

Rachels himself is the first to admit that his moral theory is a modest attempt to account for the nature and interests of human beings and the ways they confront and view moral issues. Still, this example of moral pluralism provides a satisfactory and sound approach when dealing with ethical problems. Zeigler (1984) is a leading sport and physical educator who also recommends a pluralistic ethical approach that sport managers and others ought seriously to consider.

In brief, in Zeigler's view, three major philosophical positions are brought together to create a step-by-step procedure for making ethical decisions. From Kant, Zeigler borrows the idea of universalizability to demonstrate that one's ethical judgments need to be consistent. To ensure that the consequences and outcomes of one's moral actions are considered, Zeigler turns to Mill and the two versions of utilitarianism (act- and rule-utilitarianism) addressed previously. Finally, ideas on intention, virtue, and voluntariness are appropriated to understand the nature of motivation and blameworthiness within moral behavior. It is Zeigler's contention then that all three positions must be applied when making ethical judgments, and he calls this procedure a "triple-play approach." Although Zeigler then superimposes the above steps on various legal arguments, for our purposes, it is sufficient to note that he adopts a variety of sources toward the formulation of moral decisions. Choosing ethical theories then is not an insurmountable task as long as one recognizes the strengths and weaknesses of one's selections, and one can apply them to concrete situations intelligently.

KEY CONCEPTS

moral pluralism   eclecticism   morality without hubris
the "triple-play approach"

Summary

This chapter set out to introduce and explain some major ethical theories and concepts. It grouped these around the categories of teleological, deontological, and justice theories and the concept of rights. In the first section, egoism and its several versions were built on the idea of self-interest. Utilitarianism developed the principle of the greatest good for the greatest number of people, and situation ethics adhered to the idea that every circumstance must be treated independently and on its own terms while fulfilling some supreme value.

Deontological theories, by contrast, emphasized the notion of duty and motive. The first of these duty-oriented theories was the Golden Rule, generally described as "do unto others as you would have them do unto you" or "love thy neighbor as thyself." Kantian ethics were featured next by stressing the categorical imperative, impartiality, universality, and utmost respect for persons. Finally, Ross's prima facie duties tempered some Kantian principles by dealing with the issue of competing and conflicting duties.

In the third section, four theories of justice, specifically distributive justice, were examined. The egalitarian view was concerned with the issue of equality. One important version of this theory introduced by Rawls was explained at length. His method of taking an original position and operating behind a veil of ignorance tried to ensure that people were treated equally and given equal opportunities and that the disadvantaged were helped. The libertarian perspective insisted that justice requires little or no state interference in people's affairs. People are entitled to exercise their liberty unencumbered, and if inequalities emerge, this is unfortunate, but not unjust. A utilitarian approach is often employed in justifying social programs by calculating both the costs and benefits and the overall good such programs provide. Finally, a Marxist view of justice explained that people have historically been engaged in a class and economic struggle. Consequently, from this struggle, laborers have been alienated from their work and themselves, and the only way they can overcome their plight is to engage in a social and political revolution and create a classless society where their creative selves can flourish.

The final theoretical section discussed the idea of rights. After rights were defined, the special relationship between rights and obligations was considered. The section closed by briefly describing several different types of rights. It was shown how the notion of rights operates on a number of levels and in a variety of circumstances.

The chapter ended with a short comment on selecting a theory. After a brief critique of the selection process, moral pluralism was offered as a coherent and more complete approach toward choosing "a theory." Throughout the chapter, and to varying degrees, both sport management and non-management examples were raised to help the reader understand better the above content. Because many of the theories and ideas will be referred to in Part III of this text, the reader will have more opportunities to learn how the above principles relate to concrete situations.

Questions for Consideration

1. What are the main differences between teleological and deontological ethical theories?
2. Identify the main types of egoistic theories and critique each of them.
3. How do Bentham's and Mill's versions of utilitarianism differ?
4. Describe examples that demonstrate weaknesses with utilitarianism.
5. What are some supreme values people might adhere to when following a situation ethics approach? How are these values implicated in this approach?
6. Why is the Golden Rule considered a deontological theory?
7. How do Kant's hypothetical and categorical imperatives differ?
8. Identify the three versions of the categorical imperative and critique each of them.
9. How are Ross's prima facie duties an advance over Kantian ethics?
10. Describe Rawls's "original position" and "veil of ignorance" expressions, and explain how his theory is an egalitarian one.
11. How does Nozick's minimal state compare with Marx's classless state?
12. Why might utilitarian reasons not convey a sense of justice when distributing benefits?
13. For each type of right described in the section on rights, show how obligations are related in each case.

References

Beauchamp, T. L. (1991). *Philosophical ethics: An introduction to moral philosophy* (2nd ed.). New York: McGraw-Hill.

Billington, R. (1988). *Living philosophy: An introduction to moral thought.* London: Routledge.

Bowie, N. E., & Simon, R. L. (1977). *The individual and the political order: An introduction to social and political philosophy.* Englewood Cliffs, NJ: Prentice-Hall.

Brandt, R. B. (1959). *Ethical theory: The problems of normative and critical ethics.* Englewood Cliffs, NJ: Prentice-Hall.

Ewing, A. C. (1953). *Ethics.* London: The English Universities Press.

Falikowski, A. F. (1990). *Moral philosophy: Theories, skills, and applications.* Englewood Cliffs, NJ: Prentice-Hall.

Fletcher, J. (1967). *Moral responsibility: Situation ethics at work.* London: Westminster Press.

Frankena, W. K. (1973). *Ethics* (2nd ed.). Englewood Cliffs, NJ: Prentice-Hall.

Garner, R. T., & Rosen, B. (1967). *Moral philosophy: A systematic introduction to normative ethics and meta-ethics.* New York: Macmillan.

Harman, G. (1977). *The nature of morality: An introduction to ethics.* New York: Oxford University Press.

Hertz, J. H. (Ed.). (1980). *The pentateuch and haftorahs* (2nd ed.). London: Soncino Press.

Hobbes, T. (1962). *Leviathan: Or the matter, forme and power of a commonwealth ecclesiastical and civil* (M. Oakeshott, Ed. & R. S. Peters, Intro.). New York: Collier Books. (Original work published 1651).

Hudson, W. D. (1970). *Modern moral philosophy.* London: Macmillan.

Kant, I. (1959). *Foundations of the metaphysics of morals* (L. W. Beck, Ed. and Trans.). Indianapolis, IN: Bobbs-Merrill. (Original work published 1785).

Korner, S. (1955). *Kant.* London: Penguin Books.

Mackie, J. L. (1977). *Ethics: Inventing right and wrong.* London: Penguin Books.

Marx, K., & Engels, F. (1948). (F. Engels, Ed. and Trans.). *The communist manifesto.* New York: International. (Original work published 1848).

Matson, W. I. (1987). *A new history of philosophy: Modern* (Vol. 2). New York: Harcourt Brace Jovanovich.

Melchert, N. (1991). *The great conversation: A historical introduction to philosophy.* Mountain View, CA: Mayfield.

Mill, J. S. (1969). *Utilitarianism.* In E. M. Albert, T. C. Denise, & S. P. Peterfreund (Eds.), *Great traditions in ethics: An introduction* (2nd ed., pp. 227-252). New York: D. Van Nostrand. (Original work published 1861).

Minton, A. J., & Shipka, T. A. (1990). *Philosophy: Paradox and discovery* (3rd ed.). New York: McGraw-Hill.

Mothershead, J. L., Jr. (1955). *Ethics: Modern conceptions of the principles of right.* New York: Holt, Rinehart and Winston.

Nozick, R. (1974). *Anarchy, state, and utopia.* New York: Basic Books.

Olson, R. G. (1967). Teleological ethics. In P. Edwards (Ed.), *The encyclopedia of philosophy* (Vol. 8, p. 88). New York: Macmillan and The Free Press.

Palmer, D. (1991). *Does the center hold?: An introduction to Western philosophy.* Mountain View, CA: Mayfield.

Pepper, S. C. (1960). *Ethics.* New York: Appleton-Century-Crofts.

Perry, M., Chase, M., Jacob, J. R., Jacob, M. C., & Von Laue, T. H. (1989). *Western civilization: Ideas, politics & society* (3rd ed.). Boston: Houghton Mifflin.

Porter, B. F. (1980). *The good life: Alternatives in ethics.* New York: Macmillan.

Rachels, J. (1986). *The elements of moral philosophy.* Philadelphia: Temple University Press.

Rachels, J. (Ed.). (1989). *The right thing to do: Basic readings in moral philosophy.* New York: Random House.

Raphael, D. D. (1981). *Moral philosophy.* Oxford: Oxford University Press.

Rawls, J. (1971). *A theory of justice.* Cambridge, MA: Harvard University Press.

Ross, W. D. (1930). *The right and the good.* Oxford: Clarendon Press.

Schneewind, J. B. (1967). John Stuart Mill. In P. Edwards (Ed.), *The encyclopedia of philosophy* (Vol. 5, pp. 314-323). New York: Macmillan and The Free Press.

Shirk, E. (1965). *The ethical dimension: An approach to the philosophy of values and valuing.* New York: Appleton-Century-Crofts.

Simon, R. L. (1991). *Fair play: Sports, values, & society.* Boulder, CO: Westview Press.

Urban, W. M. (1930). *Fundamentals of ethics: An introduction to moral philosophy.* New York: Henry Holt.

Wheelwright, P. (1959). *A critical introduction to ethics* (3rd ed.). New York: The Odyssey Press.

White, T. I. (1988). *Right and wrong: A brief guide to understanding ethics.* Englewood Cliffs, NJ: Prentice-Hall.

Zeigler, E. F. (1984). *Ethics and morality in sport and physical education: An experiential approach.* Champaign, IL: Stipes.

PART II

PERSONAL AND
PROFESSIONAL ETHICS

Wade Austin, (1985). Reprinted with permission.

CHAPTER 4

PERSONAL ETHICS— RIGHTS AND RESPONSIBILITIES

Chapter Objectives

* to explain the specific moral duties of those within the sport management realm, namely the sport manager, athletic director, athlete, coach and media personnel

Who is responsible for ethical and unethical behavior in sport? **Everyone is responsible**. Ethics is not optional, a condition that thus places the responsibility on all those associated with the sport industry, including fans. Sometimes it is difficult to separate the responsibilities of the player, media, coach, sport manager, sport director, sport business, and so forth. Although each individual or organization contributes something different to the sport setting, the moral expectations of each situation should be the same in terms of ethical behavior. The examples presented here and subsequent ethical expectations for each are not restricted to only a specific role. The reader should pay particular attention to the sharing of responsibilities for ethical behavior in the sport setting.

The Sport Manager

Being responsible for one's intentional personal and professional actions and behaviors as a manager within the context of sport requires personal reflection and exploration from the ethical perspectives presented. Ross (1989) points out that responsibility refers to a general project or task for which an individual is accountable or answerable. According to Becker (1973), the concept of responsibility "is the notion expressed to explain the concept of agency which is invoked for the attribution of praise or blame, the assignment of obligations and duties, and the actual sanctioning associated with the practice of holding people responsible" (p. 128). The social institution of sport and the individuals who serve as managers of such programs are certainly not exempt from being responsible, as has been indicated in this text.

As questions of moral behavior are raised in the business setting, it is important that corporations and especially sport businesses be thought of as social enterprises the existence and decisions of which are justified insofar as they serve public or social purposes (Dahl, 1975). Dahl explains further that the corporation cannot be considered only as a profit-making enterprise. "We the citizens give them special rights, powers, and privileges, protection, and benefits on the understanding that their activities will fulfill purposes" (pp. 18-19). This indicates that there is a contractual relationship between business and society and that the nature of the contract is explicit. Bowie and Duska (1990) explain that "the corporation must not only benefit those who create it; it must benefit those who permit it (namely, society as a whole)" (p. 113).

Applying ethical principles regarding the responsibility and behavior of all those involved in sport including players, coaches, and spectators, Eitzen (1988) introduces ethical principles which represent the ideals of sport and our professional obligation to the institution of sport and those who participate. These principles include:

1. Athletes must be considered ends and not means.
2. Competition must be fair.
3. Participation, leadership, resources, and rewards must be based on achievements rather than on ascribed characteristics.
4. The activity must provide for the relative safety of the participants. (pp. 17-30)

Acknowledging and protecting the rights of others are key factors within ethical behavior. It is the right of the athlete to be treated fairly and with respect and dignity by all those involved with the sport program. In the spirit of sportsmanship, opponents should not resort to willful injury or other means of intimidation. The rules of the game, coaching, and equipment should provide for the welfare of those participating. There exists the perception that the concept of coercion and social control of athletes reigns high in many American college Division I athletic programs due to the emphasis on winning. Sport administrators must be certain that the philosophy of their programs is consistent with ensuring the rights of those involved.

Fair competition in sport incorporates the involvement of physical prowess, which necessitates that the contestants not take part in cheating or artificially enhancing their performance in order to give a team or an individual an unfair advantage. Actions that violate the spirit of the sport are considered unethical.

Equal opportunity and equal access to sport must be ensured. The participants of sport should be determined by ability and motivation rather than by the discriminating factors of gender, race, ethnicity, or social class.

sport managers' professional obligations
fair competition

The Athletic Director

The athletic administrator carries the responsibility for ensuring that the athletic programs are sound and ethically managed. This responsibility includes personnel, resources, facilities, development, and all athletic programs. Question areas regarding the ethical behavior of sport administrators include

1. Promoting gender equity regarding equal facilities, equipment and budget for girls'/womens' athletics
2. Scheduling teams that create a mismatch
3. Hiring and firing coaches solely on the win-loss record
4. Regarding "win at all costs" as the ultimate test of the participation and competition
5. Allowing team physicians to administer pain-killing drugs to players so that they may continue to play when injured
6. Allowing the trainer to dispense performance-enhancing drugs.

Protection of the players is an utmost consideration by athletic coaches, trainers, and administrators. Not only must the health and safety of athletes be a consideration, but it must also be ensured that athletes neither act nor be coached in ways that lead to the intent to harm an opponent or teammate. Still another question open for much ethical debate concerns those sports in which the intent is to injure the opponent or sports that encourage such conduct.

Because the rules of sport provide an equal base for all who participate, these rules are considered to be binding on all. But ethical standards or practices are advanced indicating how individuals ought to behave rather than how they actually do behave. Unethical practices do occur and are considered to be widespread. Therefore, if everyone or every team takes part in unethical practices, are such actions justified? Although illegal recruiting practices, transcript tampering , and anabolic steroid use, for example, do occur, these resulting instances still deviate from the intended contest and thus violate the spirit of the rules. The gaining of a competitive edge in the ways noted are violations of the rules, not strategies of the game. Players are no longer on an equal footing in these instances and are no longer striving together in contest, but rather are considered to be engaging in unethical behavior. Such conduct also undermines the integrity of the sport in question.

areas of ethical responsibility of the athletic director
player protection   rule violation issues

The Athlete

Once again, the responsibility for all ethical decisions and practices is shared among those who are associated with sport and physical activity. Sportsmanship is the most widely known term associated with ethical behavior in sport. It is concerned with both the written as well as unwritten rules of sport. The definition of this term, however, is not only associated with the athlete. It may be expanded to include spectators, opponents, coaches, athletic directors, and everyone else associated with sport. Sportsmanship ensures that the play will be fair, safe, and within the rules. People are all too familiar with the numerous violations of unsportsmanlike conduct in the form of unnecessary roughness, placing the opponent at an unfair disadvantage not within the rules, and general unruly behavior.

Although aggression is to be controlled by the rules of the game, its encouragement by coaches, administrators, and trainers alike must be restrained to avoid violent outbreaks. The violence that may occur in sport either as a result of coaching techniques, encouragement by fans, or reactions within the game offers still another area for ethical debate. The fine line which exists between what is condoned within the contest and what is literally illegal in North American society is difficult to discern. The violence and brutality of boxing and ice hockey are legitimized within the boundaries of the ring and the ice. Certain actions outside these realms are condoned by neither the society nor the legal system.

Eitzen (1981) identifies two forms of cheating in sport, namely, normative and deviant. Normative cheating is those illegal acts that are accepted as part of the game. These actions either are ignored or receive minimal penalties. Deviant cheating, on the other hand, is an illegal act that is not accepted. Drugging a racehorse, tampering with equipment, and accepting bribes are examples of deviant cheating. The resulting punishment is greater for these actions. Although these are grave offenses, Eitzen (1981) expresses a concern for normative cheating and how it violates ethical principles, but is still accepted. He and others offer the following examples of normative cheating:

1. Intentional fouls in all sports.
2. Intentional pass interference by football players.
3. Basketball players who pretend to be fouled.
4. Basketball players coached to bump the lower half of a shooter's body because referees are more likely to be watching the ball and upper half of the shooter's body.
5. Offensive linemen in football coached to use special but illegal techniques to hold or trip the opponent without detection.
6. Use of loopholes in the rules to take unfair advantage of opponents.
7. Wetting the nets in basketball to prevent the fast break.
8. "Doctoring" the home field in baseball. (For example, a fast team can be slowed down by digging up or watering the basepaths or by putting sand in the takeoff areas.)

9. Application of a substance to the baseball by pitchers.
10. "Corking" the bat in baseball. (The bat is hollowed out and the wood replaced with various substances to make it more powerful.) (Bowyer, 1982, pp. 308-309)
11. Curving the blades of ice hockey sticks beyond legal limits to make them more effective. (Axthelm, 1983; Bowyer, 1982; Ostrow, 1985)

The normative form of cheating exists within sports as well. In football, ice hockey, and basketball (which is supposed to be a noncontact sport), violent play occurs but usually no penalty is assessed. It seems that in these sports, such actions are socially rewarded, and the intimidating, hitting, and gang tackling are part of the strategy. Crowd-pleasing violence in the form of fights is also a tactic condoned by those coaching, playing, and marketing sports.

KEY CONCEPTS

sportsmanship   violence   cheating

The Coach

The ethical behavior of coaches also may be called into question. In their quest for successful teams and the rewards of winning, violations of recruitment, eligibility of athletes, and violent motivational techniques have been utilized. The ethical or unethical behavior of coaches deals with some of the following areas:

1. Physically or verbally assaulting athletes
2. Treating athletes in a dehumanizing manner
3. Encouraging the use of drugs to enhance performance
4. Encouraging cheating in any form
5. Ignoring educational goals of athletic programs
6. Not reporting violations by coaching peers

Coakley recommended to the United States Olympic Committee Coaching Symposium that a coaches' code of conduct be developed (cited in Nielsen, 1994). He indicated that the highest priority for a coach is establishing relationships with athletes that can assist the athlete in positive ways. Initially, coaches must establish expectations for what they consider to be appropriate conduct for the athletes and personnel in their charge. In establishing such expectations, coaches will have to balance the external expectations or those outside influences, which are so great, with their own in order to be able to develop a code of ethics.

Coakley also identified those barriers or contradictions that hinder the development of a code of ethics for the coach. First of all, the issues associated with ethics are sensitive ones and are difficult to approach. Then, too, there are many contradictory aspects to this area. Sport is often seen through various sets of moral lenses different from those used for other situations in society. Much more is permitted to occur in sport than is allowable elsewhere in society. For example, some coaches are able to get away with physically and psychologically abusing players. However, if the same type of maltreatment occurs in the classroom, such action is unacceptable and leads to different consequences (Nielsen, 1994).

KEY CONCEPT

areas of unethical behavior of coaches

The Media

The ethical role of the media in the promotion and reinforcement of negative stereotypes regarding racial minorities and women is also questioned. Misrepresentation or the lack of representation of women in sport magazines is abundant. The focus on female athletes usually gives attention to their physical appearance rather than their athletic skills and abilities. It is not uncommon to find sexist language in the media when references are made to girls and women in sport.

Gambling in sport is another area rich with unethical motives and practices, yet it has a long history and association with sports. The media have been accused of legitimizing gambling in sports because the media report point spreads, information, and advertising, all of which make gambling more accessible. In those states in which gambling is illegal, the media would be supporting this activity through providing such information. Therefore, the corruption of sport is thought to occur somewhat, but not entirely, because of the practice of gambling and its relation to the media.

Many place blame on the media for unethical behavior in sport. The glorification of violence in sport is often used to promote events. Some children choose as role models the individuals at the heart of the action. Slow motion and continuous viewing of plays that are particularly violent are considered to create a more violent response from fans (Eitzen, 1988).

Determining what is "news" and what is "sport news" is another dilemma facing the media. What should be private information regarding sport figures and what should be public? Determining what is newsworthy and in what respect pose ethical problems for those writing about and broadcasting sports. Because of the position athletes and professional players hold in society the media transform them to heroes. Individuals whose professional and amateur work is exposed to and dependent on the media and spectatorship are constantly in the public eye and additionally scrutinized.

KEY CONCEPTS

stereotyping	misrepresentation	sexism
gambling	promoting violence	news versus sport news

Summary

Specific responsibility for ethical sport programs is a part of everyone's personal responsibility. The individual in charge of the situation, the administrator, cannot function alone in attempting to carry out ethical procedures. These responsibilities filter down to everyone involved in the organization. In this chapter, ethical responsibilities of the sport manager, the athletic director, the athlete, coach, and the media have been examined. Each area raises an abundance of questions regarding legal issues and ethics.

Questions for Consideration

1. How would you go about developing your own personal ethical standards?
2. How would you incorporate your personal ethical standards into the organization of which you are in charge?
3. Who else in the organization is responsible for ethics?

References

Axthelm, P. (1983, August 8). Psst, somebody may be cheating. *Newsweek,*, *122*, 74.

Becker, L.C. (1973). *On justifying moral judgments.* London: Routledge & Kegan Paul.

Bowie, N. E., & Duska, R. F. (1990). *Business ethics* (2nd ed.) Englewood Cliffs, NJ: Prentice Hall.

Bowyer, J. B. (1982). *Cheating: Deception in war and magic, games in sports, sex and religion, politics and espionage, art and science* (pp. 271-323). New York: St. Martin's.

Dahl, R.A. (1975). A prelude to corporate reform. In R.L. Heilbroner & P. London (Eds.), *Corporate social policy* (pp. 18-30). Reading, MA: Addison-Wesley.

Eitzen, D.S. (1981). Sport and deviance. In G.R.F. Luschen & G. Sage (Eds.), *Handbook of social science of sport* (pp. 400-414). Champaign, IL: Stipes.

Eitzen, D.S. (1988). Sport and deviance. *Journal of sport and social issues, 12,* 17-30.

Nielsen, W.V. (1994, Winter). Ethics in coaching: It's time to do the right thing. *Olympic Coach, 4,* 2-4.

Ostrow, R. (1985, March 21). Tailoring the ballparks to fit needs. *USA Today,* p. 1C, 2C.

Ross, S. (1989). Locus of responsibility: Ethical behavior in sport. *International Journal of Physical Education, 26,* 19-22.

CHAPTER 5

PROFESSIONAL ETHICS AND SOCIAL RESPONSIBILITY

Chapter Objectives
- to learn about the value of social responsibility
- to identify the features of the ethical profile
- to indicate social responsibility and ethics within the sport setting

Discussion regarding ethics and social responsibility has increased in recent years as the call for accountability on the part of all those associated with the management of sport has been made clear. The recent certification program initiated by the NCAA (requiring athletic programs of NCAA institutions to be certified) as result of the Knight Foundation Commission report (1991) is certainly a part of such a call for accountability. As academic integrity, financial integrity, governance, and commitment to equity are explored within the athletic departments of educational institutions, it is obvious that ethics and social responsibility are at the forefront of this movement for certification. The responsibility of a professional sport franchise to a city or community is also an issue of social responsibility as are the responsibilities of the individual player, all sport programs, and the managers who administer such programs.

The Relevance of Social Responsibility

The concept of social responsibility involves a moral and legal accountability on the part of individuals for self and others. It denotes reliability and trustworthiness and reflects on one's behavior. Questions regarding the nature of the complex relationship between society, sport, and the formal organizations of sport are raised within social responsibility. There is a distinction, however, between the concepts of *corporate social responsibility* and *business ethics*. To clarify this distinction, social responsibility is directly related to the social contract that exists between the business (i.e., sport) and the setting or society in which it operates. Ethics, on the other hand, mandates that individual(s) or an organization act in accord with the rules of moral philosophy. Both seem to lead to the same end, but may at times be different in their approach.

In order to gain a better understanding of the breadth of social responsibility, it is necessary to understand this concept as a *social contract* or what is known as accepted obligations, duties, and relationships between organizations or institutions and the people which relate to the corporate impact on the welfare of society (Steiner, 1972). This makes the social responsibility of sport, as with any business, a significant part of the social contract.

Within the social contract, profit maximization and social involvement are not necessarily contradictory concepts. It is possible for both of these goals to coexist. Recently, much attention has been given by businesses in general to employee welfare, support for minorities, consumer satisfaction, community improvement, and environmental protection. It has been noted, however, that such emphases have not had a unified collective impact on public opinion. The reason for this situation is perhaps attributable to the fact that these objectives are not explicit and do not appear to fit into an overall plan within organizations.

Both concepts have been regarded as outside or external to strategic planning processes in corporate codes of ethics. Such codes seem to be directed more toward those issues that influence profit than toward social responsibility or the concerns of society. Ethics presents more specific demands than does the concept of social responsibility, thus providing a base or foundation from which to function. Both concepts, however, are subject to the problems of interpretation, by the public as well as those within the organization(s). This particular problem could perhaps be eliminated by a carefully designed mission statement that would clarify the intentions of the organization.

The concept of the business or the sport setting's being amoral, that is, neither moral nor immoral is misconceived. North American society must go beyond such thinking. The realities within capitalistic democracies suggest that all businesses and their leaders must be held accountable in a moral and ethical sense for their behavior. According to DeGeorge (1986),

> the breakdown of the Myth of Amoral Business has been signaled in three fairly obvious ways: by the reporting of scandals and the concomitant public reaction to these reports; by the formation of popular groups, such as the environmentalists and the consumerists; and by the concern of business, as expressed in conferences, magazine and newspaper articles, the burgeoning of codes of ethical conduct, and so on. (p. 4)

Because business, in this case sport organizations, is a human activity, it has been and will continue to be evaluated from a moral point of view. There is no way that business can escape its moral role by merely referring to its nonhuman nature. The business or corporation is a legal entity with individuals as its legal agents and owners. Both the sport organization and the individuals working within this setting are judged by society to be liable for the behavior of its agents.

Once again, social responsibility and ethics can be successfully integrated if such concepts become a part of the mission of the organization. It is necessary for social responsibility and ethics to be a part of the core values that should permeate the entire organization, its planning process, and the implementation of all phases (i.e., organizing, leading, evaluating, marketing, etc.) of the corporate setting.

From a business ethics perspective, Robin and Reidenbach (1987) point out that the concept of the business organization is created by society and its agents and, therefore, must meet the expectations of that society or "pay the price in consumerist and antibusiness legislation" (p. 49). If the expectations are transferred to ethical theory, it is possible to use them in the development of organizational values. Robin and Reidenbach (1987) note that social systems utilize aspects of both deontology and utilitarianism in the formulation of their laws and social policies. "In the United States, cost/benefit analysis, a principal component of utilitarianism is a tool of major importance in policy making at the national, state, and local levels. Further, the concept of capitalism has strong roots in utilitarianism" (p. 49). It should also be noted that individual rights are protected at all the levels of government, as noted in the Declaration of Independence (e.g., inalienable rights), the Bill of Rights of the U.S. Constitution, and the Charter of Rights in Canada. Thus we utilize a blend of the two philosophies. But even these are subject to evolutionary change in our society. Robin and Reidenbach (1987) expand this thought further by stating:

> One problem is to determine how to treat this blend of philosophies. ... deontology, ... derived from "duty" is fundamentally concerned with the individual and tends to dominate our thinking when the plight of individuals is deemed serious. Even when reasonably sound arguments about the "greatest good for the greatest number" can be made on one side of an issue, the deontological arguments on the other side tend to dominate if individual's "rights" are seriously impaired. (p. 50)

From the social responsibility perspective, it is suggested that the organization attempt to establish a similarity or parallel between the problems it faces and the problems faced by the average family. Figure 5-1 indicates such parallels.

Basic Family Values	Basic Organizational Values
Caring for nuclear family member (i.e., husband, wife, children if any)	Caring for organization family (i.e., employees, management, stockholders)
Caring for close relatives (e.g., grandparents, aunts, uncles)	Caring for integral publics (e.g., customers, creditors)
Being a helpful and friendly neighbor	Being a helpful and friendly corporate neighbor
Obeying the law	Obeying the law
Being a "good" citizen in the community	A portion of the organization budget is allocated for philanthropic purposes
Protecting and caring for the family's home and land	Protecting and caring for the physical environment on which the organization has an impact

Figure 5-1. **Parallels between basic social responsibility values of the family and the organization.**
From "Social Responsibility, Ethics and Marketing Strategy: Closing the Gap Between Concept an Application," by D.P. Robin and R.E. Reidenback, January, 1987. *Journal of Marketing, 51*, p. 51. Copyright 1987 by the American Marketing Association. Reprinted with permission.

What the above scheme indicates is that a nuclear family type of caring for the organization's employees, management, and stockholders is significant and likened to the caring relationship among members of the nuclear family. In the organization, the consumer or customer is in a situation similar to that of a close relative. Although caring for a close relative is important and ranks higher than caring for neighbors and friends, it is still not as important as caring for members of the nuclear family. The customer should receive considerable concern that goes beyond the concept of simply not doing anything that would harm them.

KEY CONCEPTS

corporate social responsibility	business ethics
social contract	profit maximization
social involvement	parallels between the family and organizations

The Ethical Profile

Something that would benefit all organizations is a mission statement that not only guides the planning, organizing, leading, decision making, and marketing of the organization, but also serves as a guide to the organization's desired ethical profile. Such a profile projects those with whom the organization interacts and identifies how the organization chooses to interact with others. The profile identifies general guidelines for noting and creating opportunities that are ethical (See Figure 5-2).

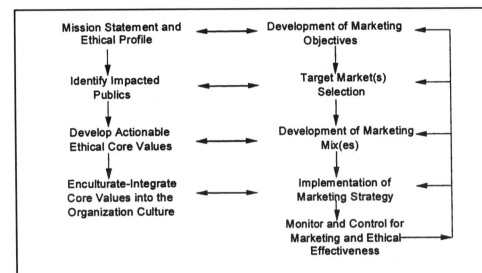

Figure 5-2. Parallel planning systems for integrating ethical and socially responsible plans into strategic marketing planning.
From "Social Responsibility, Ethics, and Marketing Strategy: Closing the Gap Between Concept and Application," by D.R. Robin & R.E. Reidenback, January, 1987, *Journal of Marketing*, 51, p. 52. Copyright 1987 by the American Marketing Association. Reprinted with permission.

In order to aid in developing a socially responsible and ethical profile, Robin and Reidenbach (1987) suggest that opportunities, threats, organizational history and mission, current corporate image, personal preference of management and owners, plus special marketing resources and competences be examined. The history of the organization, in addition to its mission and current image, gives pertinent information regarding a socially responsible and ethical profile. It is from this base that trust between the organization and the various publics develops. Once this particular aspect is tarnished, problems arise. Threats to an organization can emerge from consumers and discredit the organization. Such discrediting in turn will affect the general perception of the service(s) the organization provides or its ethical functioning. Player strikes, employee walkouts, consumer boycotts, news releases questioning the organization, and other such examples would be considered threats.

Opportunities also influence the social responsibility and ethical profile of an organization. Examining the numerous social problems that exist within North American society, coupled with the social and economic problems that affect competitors and consumers, opens the door of social awareness, and it is hoped, of social action on the part of the organization, particularly sport organizations. These organizations have the potential to provide assistance to those in need through numerous means, such as donations, making products and services available at lower costs, volunteer work, making sport facilities accessible to those with disabilities, providing public services, and promotional strategies that make consumption by different publics possible. These are just a few of the ways in which the concept of opportunity can be utilized.

Core ethical values, then, are taken directly from the ethical profile and become the guidelines for maintaining the profile itself. The deontological concern for the individual and the utilitarian concern for the "greatest good" merge or join to make up the core values. The core values are combined with those of economic and efficiency of the organization. It is anticipated that each value that is intended to guide the behavior of the organization and its members does so from a performance objective. This is exemplified in Figure 1, which utilizes the family analogy in conjunction with the ethical value system.

A problem that might exist is that individuals might not be certain of how to employ the profile dimension. It is recommended that the core value be understood and attainable. If, for example, the concept of a strong customer orientation is a goal, the profile dimension might include such statements as "treat customers with respect, concern, and honesty, the way you yourself would want to be treated or the way you would want your family to be treated" (Robin & Reidenbach, 1987, p. 55). Using the environment as an example, the core value might become to "treat the environment as though it were your own property" (Robin & Reidenbach, 1987, p. 55). For quality of products and services of the organization, making and marketing products one would feel comfortable and safe with having one's own family use would suffice as a possible attainable goal. The fundamental desire of all people is to be treated with respect and fairness. In return, individuals generally react in a positive manner. Social responsibility and moral philosophy do not have to be in opposition to business practices of organizations, but rather to assure the social values of both the business and the consumers.

Is it possible to behave ethically in a competitive world and both survive and prosper? The answer here should be a resounding yes, but there is more than just survival. Moral excellence is cited as the key outcome.

KEY CONCEPTS

mission statement   ethical core values

The Sport Setting

In conjunction with the concepts noted above concerning ethics and social responsibility, the corporate sport setting should be examined. Within the corporate setting, the players have a key role. It becomes necessary, then, to explore the role and significance of the players. Consideration must be given to players as profit-oriented laborers with acquired skills and knowledge necessary to sell their labor, which is a commodity, in an open market as an occupation and livelihood. Some would claim, however, that conceiving labor as a commodity is ethically problematic in and of itself. This Marxist view adds still another perspective from which to examine ethical issues.

The issues encountered regarding the relationships and responsibilities of players, owners, managers, and the public become worthy of examination. Further, questions concerning high school and college or university athletes and their worth as commodities should also be explored. The commitment by the educational institutions to the welfare of their athletes is paramount.

Another question brought to light within social responsibility is that of the NCAA. Although this organization may outwardly focus on the idealized functions of sport and neither necessarily nor directly reflect the intent of maximizing profit, a bottom line and perhaps a hidden agenda still exist. That is, filling stadium seats and the win-loss records in football, specifically at the Division I level, remain priority objectives. The value of the athletic programs at all levels must retain a high profile ethically, and those associated with such programs have a duty to serve it responsibly.

The sport franchise offers still another situation wherein the question of revenue generation is put forth. Does the pursuit of profit maximization take priority while labor and management forsake the public interest in favor of monetary self-interest? The sport manager must examine the revenue-generating potential of the sport franchise, the public interest of sport, and the responsibility of the franchise owner to the community, which includes guaranteeing sustained high-quality performance and an unpredictable outcome in the sport performance.

Certain obligations of the professional sport franchise do in fact exist. The product provided to the public is the competitive sport performance itself, and the public has a right to expect quality performance. The public interest of such a performance can be viewed in several ways: (a) commercial benefits related to the enhanced visibility and stimulated commerce associated with a city's big-league status; or (b) noncommercial benefits associated with the entertainment value of sport. This includes the perceived moral or educational value, such as character building or role modeling; the ideological value, such as democratic and utilitarian values of hard work, discipline, and team-work; and the capacity to generate communal identification or affiliation and the appreciation of excellence in sport performance (DeSensi, 1987).

The sport franchise owner has a direct or legal obligation in five categories: (a) to other owners in terms of abiding by the competitive restrictions in the production and marketing of the sports product; (b) to the broadcasting networks with regard to the sale of broadcasting rights and the provision of the sports product; (c) to the athlete with regard to individually negotiated salary contracts; (d) to the collective-bargaining agreements between players' associations and leagues for the provision of sport labor; and (e) to the public in terms of facility leasing, construction, or renovation agreements and safety. In addition, the direct obligation to the league promoters and public is a provision of the sports product.

The indirect obligation to the public exists in that the quality and sustained local operation of the team is of concern. Three major indirect obligations exist on the part of the team owner to the public. These include, the quality of the team performance, the unpredictability of the performance outcome, and stability of the franchise location. The sport spectator should expect the demonstration of a relatively even competition in which the outcome is uncertain and some degree of team roots whereby broad-based identification, loyalty, and support can be generated.

Sport is a significant cultural phenomenon. The potential benefits of its consumption, although social privileges, are deserving of protection under the law. Therefore, there is social significance in dealing with ethics, social responsibility, and sport law.

KEY CONCEPTS

athletes as laborers   sport-governing bodies
professional sport franchise   public interest
direct and indirect legal obligations of the sport franchise owner

Summary

This chapter discussed the concepts of social responsibility and ethics. The ethical profile and organizational values were tied together to show an attainable goal of serving the public and maintaining ethical standards within the organization. The relationships between the organization and the public were indicated as well as the ways in which the sport manager may attempt to balance profit maximization and product and service promotion, with the public interest. The social responsibility of the sport team player as well as the direct and indirect responsibilities of the team owner to the public were discussed.

Questions for Consideration

1. What is the difference between corporate responsibility and business ethics?
2. How is it possible for a sport franchise to develop a balance between maximizing profits and serving public interest?
3. Is an anticompetitive attitude necessary on the part of the sport manager to achieve social responsibility?

References

DeGeorge, R. R. (1986). *Business ethics* (2nd ed.). NY: Macmillan.

DeSensi, J. T. (1987, May). *Social responsibility and the management of sport.* Paper presented at the meeting of the North American Society for Sport Management, Windsor, Ontario, Canada.

Knight Foundation Commission on Intercollegiate Athletics. (1991, March). *Keeping faith with the student-athlete.* Charlotte, NC: Knight Foundation Commission.

Robin, D. P., & Reidenbach, R. E. (1987). Social responsibility, ethics, and marketing strategy: Closing the gap between concept and application. *Journal of marketing, 51,* 44-58.

Steiner, G.A. (1972, Winter). Social policies for business. *California Management Review, 15,* 17-24.

CHAPTER 6

MODELS AND CODES OF ETHICS

Chapter Objectives

- to identify the purposes and functions of codes of ethics
- to describe the limitations of ethical codes
- to make explicit the need for codes of ethics
- to provide sample codes of ethics

The professions of law, government, and medicine have established ethical guidelines that provide a moral framework for their practitioners. Some businesses have even followed suit, and the Ethics Resource Center of Washington, DC indicated that over three-quarters of America's major corporations have written codes of ethics. Most of these corporations also claim that they periodically update their codes of ethics (Nielsen, 1994). It has been noted also that schools of business are now providing some training in business ethics. It would seem that this information would be pertinent to those in sport and specifically sport management. It is time to establish meaningful ethical guidelines that are well developed, well publicized, and enforceable (Nielsen, 1994).

Purposes and Functions of Codes of Ethics

Regarding the concept of self-regulation and codes of ethics, Bowie and Duska (1990) suggested that ethical principles can be developed by establishing a set of rules or codes of ethics that the members of the organization are expected to follow. A set of explicit moral guidelines can facilitate a means by which individuals can monitor their own behavior. The code of ethics can be used to assist individuals and to motivate them to respond in ethical ways. The motivation to act ethically may in part result from the fact that all individuals within the organization operate within a particular moral code. Although such codes are not the ultimate mechanism to instill moral behavior, they do offer some advantages, such as

1. Motivating ethical action through peer pressure
2. Providing more stable and permanent guides to right or wrong actions than do individual personalities
3. Providing guidance in ambiguous situations
4. Controlling the autocratic power of employers
5. Specifying the social responsibilities of the organization
6. Serving the interests of the business or organization itself (Bowie & Duska, 1990).

Because businesses depend on confidence and trust, a code of ethics should help provide and maintain public trust. Incorporating such a vehicle would also assure that those involved with the particular business would behave according to the moral actions put forth in the code and that such actions would be beneficial to the business as a whole.

KEY CONCEPTS

self-regulation   motivation for ethical conduct   ensuring public trust

Limitations

Many individuals are quick to voice opposition to and negatively judge codes of ethics. Objections to organizational codes of ethics include that they are too broad and lack pattern or structure. Although ambiguities may be present in such codes, efforts toward interpretation and procedures for adopting interpretations need to be established. It is insufficient to claim ambiguity or lack of knowledge as a reason for not establishing a code of ethics. Actually, other language usages are often questioned and need to be interpreted. The enforcement of codes of ethics poses still another problem. Without enforcement, the code may not be totally effective. Bowie and Duska (1990) state that "a code of ethics without adequate enforcement is hardly a code at all. An effective code of ethics must be enforced and must have real penalties attached to it in order for it to bring about conformity" (p. 99).

Still another point is made about ethical guidelines and codes of ethics. What is considered the ethical way of doing things is not always conducive to coaches' keeping their jobs. Generally, coaches are fired if they do not win. The challenge is to maintain a successful program while subscribing to ethical standards.

Chonko and Hunt (1985) explain that codes of ethics may be ineffective if they have not been integrated into the corporate culture. Codes that are developed and placed aside are worthless. The existence of ethical codes is insufficient to effect ethical behavior unless they are enforced.

KEY CONCEPTS

objections to codes of ethics   conflicts within coaching
problems with integration

The Need for Codes of Ethics

In response to the above question still another one is posed. Why should businesses act in a moral manner? We hear statements such as "good ethics is good business," "sound business ethics means good business practices," or "it pays to be moral." The question of "why act morally" should actually never be raised. According to Bowie and Duska (1990) "the corporation should be moral because acting morally is in the interests of the corporation. Moral behavior... on the part of the corporation...is simply rationally prudent behavior" (p. 111). Further, questions such as why companies that are forced by consumers to focus on the short run should be concerned with long-term morality also need to be considered. This is evident with products that are considered fads, such as the hula hoop and other items which have held public interest for shorter lengths of time.

There are many business ventures that need not be concerned with maintaining credibility in the long term. Souvenir touting for special short-term sport events or those associated with the pop culture go into and out of business quickly as the fads and interests of society change. Often, such fly-by-night businesses are not looked upon favorably either by consumers or by more legitimate businesses. These groups consider such behavior, although profitable, not to be moral. According to Bowie and Duska (1990), what is needed is something similar to that which is in existence in general society, a combination of law and morals. Those companies that are regarded as respectable make certain that the stockholders and the consumers are aware that the products or services, or both, provided are neither shoddy nor imperfect; that the workers are treated fairly; and that the company is making an effort to assist with the problems of society. For those organizations that are not regarded as respectable, there is a conflict between the socially responsible behavior, or the demands of morality, and the demands of prudence or self-interest (p. 112).

Zeigler (1992) points out that professionals involved with sport management will "increasingly have obligations to the public, to their profession, and to their clients" (p. 9). In addition, the professional's conduct as a sport manager and his or her ethical responsibility to society must give consideration to laws, individual freedoms, equal opportunity, right to privacy, and the overall welfare of individuals for whom the professional is responsible.

Codes of ethics are probably the most visible sign of the ethical philosophy and beliefs of a company, business, or organization. In order for the code to have meaning, it must clearly state its basic principles and expectations and focus on potential ethical dilemmas that could be faced by members of the group; most important, it must be enforced. In addition, the code should be accepted by the employees before it is mandated that they abide by it. Although it is the manager's responsibility to tend to the content of the code, it is critical that the code itself be developed by as many of the employees or members of the group as possible in an open atmosphere in order to be effective (Stead, Worrell, & Stead 1990).

In order to assure successful institutionalization of a code of ethics, Stead et al. (1990) recommend that communication of the code occur at all levels within the organization, that it be distributed to new employees as a part of their orientation and possibly their selection, and that seminars on the codes be conducted so that open discussion can occur.

When the areas of sport management in which a code of ethics could be implemented are explored, coaching emerges as a primary example. Coakley (cited in Nielsen, 1994) points out the need for codes of ethics for coaching. One major purpose of such a code is basically to let all others know what to expect from the individual as the coach. Athletes are much more attuned to cases of abuse from coaching staff and have used reports of such actions in pursuing legal action and the subsequent removal of coaches from their positions.

Sexual harassment and abuse are extremely pressing issues in women's sport, particularly when males are coaching female athletes. Complaints at major universities have been brought against male coaches regarding harassment of female athletes. Whereas it is asserted that athletes may idolize coaches, romantic attraction for some seems inevitable. Acting on the attraction between an athlete and a coach is unethical, counterproductive, and professionally inappropriate. Such an act abuses the power that coaches have by virtue of their role, detracts the athlete from game-related tasks, may cause the athlete to misinterpret certain behaviors as sexually motivated, and it may cause the coach to lose objectivity in decisions relating to the athlete.

A second reason for a code of ethics is that many coaches' careers depend on the performance of the athlete(s), which may influence the coach to take advantage of athletes' time and physical well-being. Still other reasons for developing a code of ethics for coaching involve how coaches will ensure the safety of their athletes and what their beliefs are regarding the emphasis on training and winning. Nielsen (1994) indicates that

> while a code [of ethics] cannot necessarily provide answers to all
> of the issues...it can (and should) provide guidelines in ambiguous
> situations when what is ethical or proper is not clear. ... A code
> also helps to reinforce correct conduct and establish parameters
> to discourage improper behaviors. (p. 4)

Coakley (cited in Nielsen, 1994) recommended that a code for sport be a joint effort between a governing body and its coaches. His suggestion was that the United States Olympic Committee (USOC), in conjunction with its sport-governing bodies, draft codes of conduct for both coaches and other adults who control and sometimes benefit emotionally or materially from the performance of children. It would also be up to the USOC to develop, implement, and enforce such a code.

The Ethics Resource Center assists groups by reviewing, assessing, developing, and implementing codes of ethics as related to the conflicts and issues of individual organizations. This is precisely the responsibility that the USOC and other sport-governing bodies must take if such codes are to be meaningful and successful.

It is suggested that the code of ethics for coaches should (a) have as a base the social and physical development of all athletes; (b) stress the importance of a cooperative rather than command style of coaching; (c) be closely aligned with a mandatory education and credentialing program for coaches; (d) be enforced by a sport-based regulatory agency such as the USOC; (e) undergo aggressive publicity to athletes and their families and be included on bulletin boards, locker-room walls, and other places visible to athletes; (f) cover a variety of areas; and (g) serve as a list of goals and guidelines for coaches (Nielsen, 1994).

It is crucial that a code of ethics for coaches address what athletes desire from their coaches. Coakley (as cited in Nielsen, 1994) reported that competence, approachability, fairness and consistency, confidence, motivation, personal concern, and support are what athletes between the ages of 12 and 20 years of age look for most often in their coaches. Although this age group is not the only one sport managers will serve, this study offers interesting information regarding ethics, the athlete, and the coach.

In the United Kingdom and Canada, codes of ethics are developed by governmental agencies that regulate sport and coaching. The British Institute of Sports Coaches has established both a code of ethics and a code of conduct for coaches. This code of ethics is regarded as a series of guidelines rather than instructions. Nielsen (1994) pointed out that one example from this code indicates that "the good sport coach will be concerned primarily with the well-being, health, and future of the individual performer and only secondary with the optimization of performance" (p. 5).

The code of conduct also put forth by the British Institute is intended to be more specific and provides guidance in the implementation of the principles in the code of ethics. Regarding the concept of commitment, this Code of Conduct reads:

> When coaches enter into a commitment with an employer, with a team or with an individual performer, the nature of that commitment should be specifically agreed. Any such contract or terms of reference should be set out in writing and include ... the time commitment involved and an indication of the expected outcome of the coaching. (Nielsen, 1994, p. 5)

The British Institute includes the codes in its coaching certification programs with the expectation that coaches will follow them. There is also a formal complaint procedure giving individuals or organizations the opportunity to file a complaint against a coach within the context of the codes. Because the coach is encouraged to develop his or her own personal code of conduct and the athlete(s) and coach realize the expectations, there is an opportunity for the athlete(s) and coach to have a prosperous relationship.

In the United States there are very few sport organizations that have well-developed ethical codes for coaches. Because there is not an American Institute of Sport Coaches, like the ones in Britain or Canada that oversee this responsibility, an ethical code has been slow in developing or is nonexistent. The USOC, which oversees amateur sport in the United States via the Amateur Sports Act of 1978, is currently in the process of developing a code of conduct for coaches that might possibly be adopted by each national sport-governing body.

KEY CONCEPTS

short-term and long-term needs	prudent behavior	societal considerations
issues of acceptability	communication demands	
codes of ethics for coaches	British views on codes of ethics	

Sample Codes of Ethics

Concerned with the ethical actions of professionals in sport management, the North American Society for Sport Management (NASSM) appointed an ad hoc committee to study the development of a creed and code of ethics. Prior to examining these, however, one needs to understand the nature of the membership and the purpose of such an organization. This purpose is succinctly stated by Zeigler (1989):

> The North American Society for Sport Management is a professional association whose primary mission is to provide the leadership that will result in a physically active lifestyle for all North Americans. NASSM members work in positions related to healthful physical activity, and we believe that such physical activity programs should be of high quality and should encourage regular participation. Developmental activities such as exercise, sport, dance, and play should be made available for average, accelerated, and special populations of all ages. As professionals, therefore, NASSM members are deeply aware of the need to stimulate participation in the appropriate kinds of physical activity by all North Americans, regardless of age, sex, or level of competence. (p. 2)

The Ethical Creed of NASSM was accepted in June 1989 at the Annual General Meeting of this organization. It is directly related to those purposes stated above and it reads:

Members of the NORTH AMERICAN SOCIETY FOR SPORT MANAGEMENT live in free democratic societies within North American culture. As practitioners and scholars within a broad profession, we honor the preservation and protection of fundamental human rights. We are committed to a high level of professional practice and service. Our professional conduct shall be based on the application of sound management theory developed through a broadly based humanities and social scientific body of knowledge about the role of developmental physical activity in sport, exercise, and related expressive activities in the lives of all people. Such professional knowledge and service shall be made available to clients of all ages and conditions, whether such people are classified as accelerated, normal, or special insofar as their status or condition is concerned.

As NASSM members pursuing our subdisciplinary and professional service, we will make every effort to protect the welfare of those who seek our assistance. We will use our professional skills only for purposes which are consistent with the values, norms, and laws of our respective countries. Although we, as professional practitioners, demand for ourselves maximum freedom of inquiry and communication consistent with societal values, we fully understand that such freedom requires us to be responsible, competent, and objective in the application of our skills. We should always show concern for the best interest of our clients, our colleagues, and the public at large. (Zeigler, 1992, p. 35)

Another professional organization that is also defining its ethical direction and code of ethics is the North American Society for the Sociology of Sport (NASSS). In the Winter 1993 edition of the NASSS Newsletter, the importance of having a mechanism in place that allows for dialogue on moral and ethical concerns before they become divisive issues was emphasized. Although this direction serves a distinct purpose, designing and implementing such a mechanism is not a simple task.

A Bill of Rights for Young Athletes, which outlined the rights for youths in sport, was developed through the American Alliance for Health, Physical Education, Recreation and Dance (AAHPERD) . Although these points served as guidelines, a more specific Code of Ethics for Coaches developed through the Youth Sports Institute (Seefeldt, 1979). This code reads as follows:

1. I will treat each player, opposing coach, official, parent and administrator with respect and dignity.
2. I will do my best to learn the fundamental skills, teaching and evaluation

techniques, and strategies of my sport.

3. I will become thoroughly familiar with the rules of my sport.
4. I will become familiar with the objectives of the youth sports program with which I am affiliated. I will strive to achieve these objectives and communicate them to my players and their parents.
5. I will uphold the authority of officials who are assigned to the contests in which I coach, and I will assist them in every way to conduct fair and impartial competitive contests.
6. I will learn the strengths and weaknesses of my players so that I might place them into situations where they have a maximum opportunity to achieve success.
7. I will conduct my practices and games so that all players have an opportunity to improve their skill level through active participation.
8. I will communicate to my players and their parents the rights and responsibilities of individuals on our team.
9. I will cooperate with the administrator of our organization in the enforcement of rules and regulations, and I will report any irregularities that violate sound competitive practices.
10. I will protect the health and safety of my players by insisting that all of the activities under my control are conducted for their psychological and physiological welfare, rather than for the vicarious interests of adults. (Seefeldt, 1979, p 4.)

KEY CONCEPTS

features of the NASSM Ethical Creed
elements of the Bill of Rights for Young Athletes

Summary

This chapter discussed various codes of ethics that could potentially be incorporated into sport settings. The purposes, functions, and need for codes of ethics were also discussed, which would help professionals establish a basis for developing such codes for various personnel within sport organizations.

Questions for Consideration

1. How would you incorporate a code of ethics in any sport setting?
2. What procedures would you use to have the greatest input from your personnel regarding codes of ethics?
3. How would codes of ethics be enforced in sport organizations?

References

Bowie, N. E., & Duska, R.F. (1990). *Business ethics* (2nd ed.). Englewood Cliffs, NJ: Prentice Hall.

Chonko, L.B., & Hunt, S.D. (1985, August). Ethics and marketing management: An empirical examination. *Journal of Business Research, 13*, 339-359.

Nielsen, W.V. (1994, Winter). Ethics in coaching: It's time to do the right thing. *Olympic Coach, 4*, 2-5.

Seefeldt, V. (1979). Young athletes have a bill of rights: Do we need a code of ethics for coaches? *Spotlight on Youth Sports, 2*, 1-6.

Stead, W. E., Worrell, D. L., & Stead, J. G. (1990). An integrative model for understanding and managing ethical behavior in business. *Journal of Business Ethics, 9*, 233-242.

Zeigler, E. F. (1989). Proposed creed and code of professional ethics for the North American society for sport management. *Journal of Sport Management, 3*, 2-4.

Zeigler, E. F. (1992). *Professional ethics for sport managers* [Monograph]. Champaign, IL: Stipes.

PART III

SPORT MANAGEMENT
ETHICS APPLIED

Wade Austin, (1995). Reprinted with permission.

CHAPTER 7

FUNCTIONS OF SPORT MANAGERS

Chapter Objectives

- to examine the relationship between ethics and planning, organizing, leading, and evaluating as functions of sport managers
- to explore ethics within various sport settings

Chelladurai (1985) discusses the four main functions of management (i.e. planning, organizing, leading, and evaluating), indicating that they are inextricably intertwined with each other as well as with the concepts of ethics and personal, social, professional, and organizational responsibility within the management setting. Within the behavioral approach to management, the relationship between the work to be accomplished, the individuals involved in the process, and that which brings them together is the focus. Although planning is concerned with what will be achieved and how it will be achieved, organizing, leading, and evaluating are concerned with who will be carrying out the specific tasks and in what organizational configuration, what motivation will be used to encourage production, and how well the individuals carry out the task as well as the overall effectiveness of the product itself. Adherence to ethical standards and criteria is of the utmost importance in the workings of these relationships. Integrity and responsibility are to be established and maintained within the planning process and extend to the activities that are carried out and the individuals responsible for specific tasks, programs, and activities of the organization.

Planning

Within planning, the goals for the organization and its members, in addition to the activities or programs to be implemented, are set forth. Planning is the foundation and most basic of the four functions of the manager. Although planning certainly entails decision making, it is difficult to separate these two concepts from each other, but information regarding ethical decision making is covered in another section of this chapter.

Because the planning process involves defining objectives, strategies, and policies, ethical standards and principles emerge from the outset and become the basis upon which organization or project is founded. The decisions that are made regarding the planning process fit within the parameters of the model established by Filley, House, and Kerr (1976). The proposed seven-step model includes

1. setting objectives
2. identifying constraints
3. generating alternatives
4. specifying performance criteria
5. evaluating alternatives
6. selecting alternatives
7. preparing the written document.

Integrity of the organization is maintained through professional standards of behavior or professional ethics. In addition, personal ethics and social responsibility are considered in the setting of the objectives stage of the model. This is exemplified as individuals or organizations, or both, consider profitability, growth, market share, productivity and efficiency, leadership, client satisfaction, and social awareness in relation to the objectives and goals of the organization. The manner in which each of these points is undertaken relates back to the primary objective(s) and is bound by the mission and philosophy of the organization, including its ethical approach.

In the process of generating alternative courses of action within the planning process due to various constraints (e.g., biological, authoritative, physical, technological, and economic) that may hinder the progress of the plan, the manner in which each of the alternatives is evaluated should follow an established set of criteria in order to make the best choice. Although creativity and the development of new ideas should be encouraged, attempting to develop and try new approaches may lead decision makers to set aside the task of interpreting constraints and thus lead to placing greater emphasis on the task or goal at hand, rather than on the ethical concerns relating to the process and product.

Problems that may arise in the organizational goals as well as from a lack of information may limit one's rational and potentially one's ethical approach to planning. Maintaining a *rational* perspective should be *a* primary goal within the process (Chelladurai, 1985).

Organizing

The task of organizing delineates the relationships between the tasks and the individuals who are to perform them. Specifically, it is the "arrangement of people and tasks to accomplish the goals of the organization" (Fink, Jenks, & Willits, 1983, p. 46). As sport managers incorporate the principles associated with organizing (i.e., specialization, span of control, departmentalization, unity of command, and responsibility and authority) into the sport setting, they are basically setting up a decision-making process that will allow the most qualified individual to make the decision based on the best available information. Again, the close connection between ethics and decision making is brought into the functions of the sport manager within the task and responsibilities of organizing. The placement of the proper responsibilities with capable individuals takes on new meaning as one's capabilities are evaluated and categorized according to the task at hand.

What is intended, though, is that through proper organizing, the relationship between the individuals and the tasks to be completed will be efficient and free from harmful friction (Chelladurai, 1985). The function of organizing then does seem to require the combination of both human and technical skills associated with sport management.

Leading

It is within the function of leading that our personal and social responsibilities are assumed as sport managers. Leading is the task of motivating individuals to move toward the desired goal. Motivation is presented by Chelladurai (1985) as the basis of leading. With knowledge and understanding of the motivational factors that affect both the leader and follower, the process of leading can more effectively be carried out.

Personal and social responsibility must be assumed in order to understand the relationship between the behavior and needs of the follower and the task that is to be accomplished. On a human level, regard and respect for others, no matter the diversity of the group are paramount. It would be the hope that as a result of the manner in which the function of leading is carried out, mutuality and reciprocity would be evident in the personnel relationships among peers, superiors, and subordinates. A responsibility that the sport manager assumes here would be to bridge the gap (if one exists) between the goals and mission of the organization and the individuals working within the system in order to maintain the integrity of the goals sought. Once again, the skills associated with leading are relevant to the functions of organizing, planning, and evaluating as well.

KEY CONCEPTS

motivational factors   responsibilities toward others
congruence between individuals goals and organizational mission

Evaluating

Chelladurai (1985) states that "evaluating is defined as the process of assessing the degree to which the organization as a whole and various units and individuals have accomplished what they set out to do" (p. 171). The manner in which the organization, its units, and individuals are evaluated is an extremely important aspect of the sport manager's responsibilities. The evaluation of the employee should be based on the job description in order to assure that the evaluation is equitable and fair. In addition, the day-to-day tasks of the job performed should be noted (Clement, 1991). It is vital that multiple input be given from diverse perspectives within the organization, such as those of various superiors as well as those of subordinates with whom the individual works. Because organizational effectiveness and individual performance are evaluated based on prescribed criteria, obtaining the needed information to judge adequately the effectiveness of any facet of the organization or individuals within the organization, or both, is crucial. That information must also be shared with those involved in the organization in a manner that maintains the integrity of the process and the dignity of the individual(s).

Evaluation without feedback is undesirable. The manner in which the feedback is shared with employees should follow prescribed legal and ethical standards regarding evaluation. The results should be made available to the employees and discussed with them personally. A due process system should also be in place in the event the employee wishes to present an opposing position or alternative explanation to the evaluation. Employees must be afforded the opportunity to overcome any critical remarks noted in an evaluation, and proper monitoring of this situation must occur. The entire process of evaluation should be carried out in a manner that protects the rights of the employee (Clement, 1991).

KEY CONCEPTS

fairness in evaluation   multiple input   feedback

Ethical Considerations

The ethical and social responsibility of those involved with the functions discussed above include examination, evaluation, and efforts to connect the mission and goals of the organization with those working within it in order to maintain integrity. This effort in and of itself is not a simple one and requires much authentic dialogue on the part of those involved. (Concepts regarding the ethical profile of an organization and personal reflection concerning personal values, beliefs, and goals are discussed in chapter 5.) These concepts are also appropriate here.

When different sport settings are addressed in conjunction with the functions of the sport manager noted above, the following must be considered:

1. level of sport (i.e., Olympic, recreational, professional, sport for special populations, and athletics)
2. mission and goals of the individual sport programs
3. values, beliefs, and goals of the individual leaders and followers within each sport setting
4. available resources (i.e., funding, people, facilities, and equipment)
5. programs and services offered within each setting
6. individuals who will be the consumers of the programs

Once the sport manager has an in-depth understanding of the previous points (1-6), ethical responsibility for planning, organizing, leading, and evaluating can then be realized in a more complete context. At each level of sport, a consideration for all individuals who participate must be included. This includes those working as sport managers as well as those who will be the consumers of the programs and services offered. An approach that may help the sport manager focus on the sport setting and the individuals involved not only locally but also globally, is to consider the total concept of "Social Participation and Accountability, Work, Human Rights, Peace and Justice, and World Populations" (Hums, 1990). Each section of this concept will serve as a guide to sport managers as they address how to approach the functions of planning, organizing, leading, and evaluating in the individual sport settings.

KEY CONCEPTS

maintaining integrity   recognizing the totality of the setting

Moral Dilemmas in Sport Settings

The following are examples of moral and ethical issues as related to each of the preceding areas:

1. One is responsible for the planning of a building project for a new sports arena. Expenses for this project are extremely high. Considering the planning model, one is faced with the decision of choosing less than quality building supplies in order to save money. What issues are involved with this scenario, and how should one proceed with the planning project?

2. How should the organizer of an intramural program handle the following situation: Past performance in both intramural basketball and ice hockey leagues has involved numerous incidents of violent play, improper player conduct, eligibility violations, and abuse toward officials. What organizational reforms should the organizer implement to curtail and eliminate these unbecoming behaviors? Should these reforms differ in the case of men's sport as opposed to women's sport?

3. The manager of a health and racquets club notices some employees being less than courteous to the patrons and failing to fulfill their assigned duties. Some take too many breaks; others leave early and arrive at work late. However, one day the manager is called in by the club owner, who happens to relate similar deficiencies in the manager's own performance. How should the manager address and improve his or her own behavior as well as that of the employees who demonstrate unsatisfactory work? Discuss the leadership concerns and issues pertaining to this example.

4. As head football coach of Division I Eastern State University (ESU), Bob Montgomery posted a winning record in each of his 10 years at ESU. This year however, with a fairly young squad, his record fell to 4 wins and 8 losses, much to the disappointment of students, faculty, alumni, school administrators, and the community. With the prospect of the coming year looking bleak and the poor formal evaluations he was given by the athletic director and the president of ESU, Bob was concerned for his future as head football coach. Is Bob's poor evaluation a fair one? What criteria should be part of his evaluation?

Ethical Analysis

The following discussion will analyze the ethical dimensions and implications of the third example above to demonstrate how moral principles relate to a given case. Readers should try to analyze the other examples and draw their own conclusions and resolutions to any particular problems.

In general, the third case involves the role of the manager and the function of dealing with personnel. It is clear from this example that employee performance is poor, and this could have a negative impact on club members and the success of the club itself. Rectifying problems with employees is a delicate matter because the sources of the problems are not always apparent. Perhaps some employees are having difficulties at home, in their personal lives, or in the workplace. Some issues that lead to poor job performance are private matters that people just do not want to reveal and talk about.

On the other hand, the behavior of the manager in this case is relatively no different from that of the employees. The main issue here may not be what the employees are experiencing, but a lack of leadership and integrity shown by the manager. Employees may feel that if the manager is displaying a poor work ethic, then it is acceptable to live up to that standard. The owner, however, perceives the situation much differently and would want the quality of performance for all employees, including the manager, to improve significantly.

Under these circumstances, the owner might insist that the manager alter her or his behavior to set an example for the rest of the employees. Initially, the owner could identify the problems the manager is having—perhaps these are work-related or even personal—and then try to encourage the manager to make concrete changes in behavior. If specific goals and regular follow-up evaluation sessions for the manager could be established and implemented, then this might be a good first step toward significant improvement. The owner might also specify a time period to realize these changes and attach particular consequences, including the termination of the manager, in this process.

Like the owner, the manager has a mandate to supervise and assess employees under her or his charge. In this situation, the manager might proceed by showing concern for each individual in order to identify any problems shared by all employees. Having genuine interest in the well-being of others, treating others as ends and not as means, and maintaining an impartial view toward others could be some principles to follow in trying to resolve the issues in this example. These principles refer to some aspects of the deontological ethical theories discussed in chapter 3.

The application of the moral guidelines suggested above to the present case may require that the manager meet each employee privately to discuss, in a constructive way, the reasons for the poor job-related behavior. The meeting should be staged in a comfortable, nonthreatening setting to ensure that a mutual understanding of the problems is reached. Once the meeting with each employee has taken place, the manager could try to locate any common concerns that were raised in the discussions.

Let us assume that the main problem was a lack of incentive and motivation on the part of the employees because such a lack was perceived in the manager's conduct. If the manager could propose that employees help decide on strategies and standards to change their working conditions, this might create greater enthusiasm among employees to fulfill their duties. Moreover, the manager could provide assurances, through periodic evaluations, so the manager's own performance would also meet acceptable levels. Here is the possibility of a mutual, interactive process being implemented where impartiality, respect for others, and fair treatment exist at three levels of management.

Summary

This chapter discussed the functions of the sport manager in relation to the concept of ethics. When the functions and roles of the sport manager are considered, ethics is not something that should slip away or be considered in another category or as a second or third thought when one assumes work-related responsibilities. The concept and practice of ethics in regard to planning, organizing, leading, and evaluating should be ever present. It is the essence of ethics that undergirds sport managers' practices and certainly begins with the planning process and permeates each of the other functions the sport manager performs.

Questions for Consideration

1. In what areas within any of the functions of the sport manager do you envision potential violations of ethics?
2. What steps would you take to prevent infringements of ethics in planning, organizing, leading, and evaluating?
3. How would you express your philosophy regarding ethics and the functions of the sport manager to those subordinates in the sport-management setting?
4. Are specialized sport events (e.g., Gay Games, Highland Scottish Games, Maccabiah Games, Senior Games, Good Will Games, and Special Olympics) contributing to the concept of sport for all in our society?
5. The offering of midnight sports programs in cities has given many the opportunity to participate in recreational sports. What are the advantages to offering such programs? Are there objections to these programs?

References

Chelladurai, P. (1985). *Sport management macro perspectives*. London, ON: Sports Dynamics.

Clement, A. (1991). Sports law: Product liability and employment relations. In B.L. Parkhouse (Ed.), *The management of sport its foundation and application* (pp. 97-106). St Louis: Mosby Year Book.

Filley, A. C., House, R.J., & Kerr, S. (1976). *Managerial process and organizational behavior*. Glenview, IL: Scott, Foreman.

Fink, L. F., Jenks, R. S., & Willits, R. D. (1983). *Designing and managing organizations*. Homewood, IL: Richard D. Irwin.

Hums, M. A. (1990). *Model for moral development: A life issues approach for a sport management curriculum*. Unpublished manuscript.

CHAPTER 8

DECISION MAKING

Chapter Objectives
- to introduce several ethical models of decision making
- to examine decision making in sport
- to consider moral problems in sport environments

Models of Decision Making

Decision making permeates all management activities, is closely allied with the managerial function of planning, and involves making choices or the best choice from the alternatives generated. Within this process the goal to be achieved is identified, alternatives are generated and evaluated against the established criteria, and the best alternative is chosen. Rationality plays an important role in this process and affects the selection of the best means to achieve a goal and the selection of the goal itself (Chelladurai, 1985).

Decision making is rooted in philosophy, specifically in the areas of logic and reason and that of ethics and moral judgment. The philosophical treatment of these areas is normative, indicating arguments on how one **should** think and act. Descriptive models of logic in decision making are utility or probability based, and much has been done to expand such theories into examples of actual reasoning processes. This work has been integrated into business research. Normative theories of ethics are difficult to put into descriptive form, thus indicating to us that perhaps this process should move *from* the examination of the outcomes of decisions and *toward* the examination of the processes used by individuals, whereby choices are made from a number of possible outcomes (Strong & Meyer, 1992).

Using the concepts and theories discussed in the first three chapters of this text, in combination with what is proposed in Part II seems an appropriate basis upon which ethical decisions could be based. To add to this approach, work by Josepheson (1992) proposes that one examine areas of character in order to deal with decision making. These areas include

1. trustworthiness, which includes honesty, integrity, promise keeping, and loyalty
2. respect
3. responsibility, which includes accountability, pursuit of excellence, and self-restraint
4. justice and fairness
5. caring
6. civic virtue and citizenship.

Adherence to these areas will serve as a personal guide to ensure that decisions will be of an ethical quality. Although this process may sound as if it is a simple recipe to follow, much consideration must be given to the process of evaluating and choosing among alternatives. The choices involved must also be consistent with ethical principles. It is recommended that, in making either professional or personal decisions, one must be aware of and eliminate unethical options and then select the best ethical alternative. Due to the competing values and interests involved in making ethical choices, the process is rather complex. Economic, social, professional, and other pressures usually intervene in the process resulting in confusion and a question of employing the correct ethical decision.

Unethical decisions and improper conduct are often aligned with a bigger problem, which is failing to perceive the ramifications and implications of certain conduct as well as failing to express one's moral convictions in one's behavior. One's focus may be on the end, such as increasing revenue in sporting organizations or events, rather than on the promotion of an ethical ideal and how one should go about pursuing that goal in one's conduct. The employment of problem-solving skills and sound reasoning is necessary to bring to fruition a union of ethical theory and practice. An evaluation must take place in terms of the integrity of the information that is at hand and upon which the decision will be based. In addition, the ability to create alternative goals and ways to achieve them must be employed in order to eliminate unethical decisions. Foresight is also critical. The ability to envision the consequences of behavior is a skill the sport manager must develop. Evaluating the potential for risk and harm to others as a result of a decision and action is the social and moral responsibility of the sport leader (Josepheson, 1992).

One model of managerial decision making is that proposed by Trevino (1986). This model takes into consideration the concept of corporate and social responsibility that was mentioned in the introductory chapter to this text. (Keep in mind that social responsibility refers to the moral, legal, or mental accountability on the part of individuals for oneself and others.) Trevino's model indicates that there is a relationship between an individual's moral development and his or her ethical decision-making process.

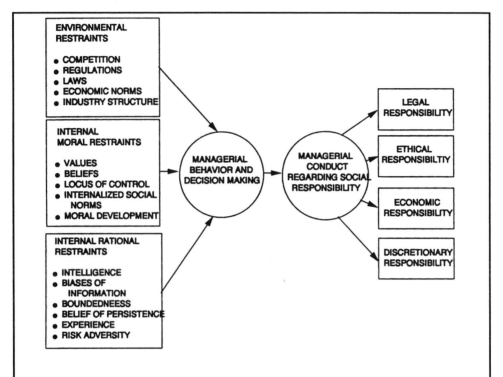

Figure 8-1. Managerial decision making model of corporate responsibility.

(Trevino, 1986) From "An Integrative Descriptive Model of Ethical Decision Making, " by K.C. Strong, and G.D. Meyer, 1992. *Journal of Business Ethics*, *11*, p. 90. Copyright 1992 by Kluwer Academic Publishers. Reprinted by permission of Kluwer Academic Publishers.

Trevino (1986) points out that environmental restraints, which include competition, laws, and social norms; moral restraints, such as values, beliefs, social norms, and moral development; and internal rational restraints, such as intelligence, experience, and boundedness, influence managerial behavior and decision making. Managerial conduct regarding social responsibility also is influenced as the setting, and its responsibilities to clients are examined in the context of legal, ethical, economic, and discretionary responsibility. Within the study of ethical decision making, theory and research by Kohlberg (1963, 1970) and Gilligan (1982) were discussed in chapter 2, but this information bears repeating. Noted are the stages of moral development, and what is indicated is that the postconventional stages of moral development can solve conflicts that lower level stages cannot because critical moral thinking is more developed in the higher stages.

The progression of Kohlberg's stages of moral development can be followed in Figure 8-2.

Stage	What is Considered to be Right
Level One - Preconventional	
Stage One - Obedience and punishment orientation	Sticking to rules to avoid physical punishment. Obedience for its own sake.
Stage Two - Instrumental purpose and exchange	Following rules only when it is in one's immediate interest. Right is an equal exchange, a fair deal.
Level Two - Conventional	
Stage Three - Interpersonal accord, conformity, mutual expectations	Stereotypical "good" behavior. Living up to what is expected by people close to you.
Stage Four - Social accord and system maintenance	Fulfilling duties and obligations to which you have agreed. Upholding laws except in extreme cases where they conflict with fixed social duties. Contributing to the society, group.
Level Three - Principled	
Stage Five - Social contract and individual rights	Being aware that people hold a variety of values; that rules are relative to the group. Upholding nonrelative values and rights regardless of majority opinion.
Stage Six - Universal ethical principles	Following self-chosen ethical principles. When law violate these principles, act in accord with principles.

Figure 8-2. **Kohlberg's Six Stages of Moral Development**
Adapted from "Moral Stages and Moralization: The Cognitive-developmental approach." By T. Lickona (Ed). 1969, *Moral Development and Behavior: Theory, Research, and Social Issues*, pp. 34-35. Copyright 1969 by Holt, Rinehart and Winston. Reprinted by permission.

What is indicated in Figure 8-2 is that at the lower end of moral development, Level I or the preconventional level (Stages 1 and 2), the individual is focusing on self and survival or obeying rules to avoid punishment or utilizing the rules only when they are instrumental to the individual. In the conventional or second level (Level II) of the model (Stages 3 and 4), the individual is subject to what is considered to be the expected good behavior and to fulfill obligations. The third level, or principled level (Level III) of moral development (Stages 5 and 6), finds the individual socially responsible, obeying rules as social contracts, and upholding rights in spite of majority opinion. This level also indicates a responsibility on the part of the individual for choosing appropriate ethical principles.

Critics of this work indicate that because Kohlberg's research used all male subjects, the work should not be generalized to both the female and male population. The findings of Kohlberg's work concluded that men developed to the higher stages of moral development and women only developed to Stage 3 of his six-stage model. The results concluded that women were viewed as inferior to men in their moral development and moral reasoning, and only when women entered into some form of activity traditionally identified as male activity could they recognize the inadequacy of this reasoning and progress to the higher stages of Kohlberg's developmental sequence. Because Kohlberg used only boys in his 1969 study, those qualities found in women, known as expressive qualities, were seen as inferior to the instrumental qualities expressed by males. The gap between women's and men's moral development, rather than being viewed as inferior, is now viewed as a different developmental process (Belenky, Clinchy, Goldberger, & Tarule, 1986; Gilligan, 1982; Kohlberg, 1969).

In her work *In a Different Voice*, Gilligan points out that the disparity between women and men is due not to the inferiority of women, but rather to a misinterpretation of the research. Gilligan's (1982 & 1988) proposal that an ethics of caring may be a valuable contribution to research in ethical development offers another approach to gender and moral development and decision making. Gilligan's (1982) proposal is inclusive of the experiences of women and projects a perspective known as women's voices. Her model includes the concepts that women's moral judgments develop from a concern for survival to a focus on goodness as seen through the eyes of others and finally to an understanding of care and responsibility for self and others. The three stages of this model offer a more complex understanding of self and others. Moral decisions for women are not based on abstract principles, but instead are grounded in the context of relationship. Decisions about conflict and morality are made with the other in mind and in relation to the situation. Moral decisions are contextual in nature.

The feminine concept of a morality of understanding is different from that of men, which is a morality of rights. Women's morality has been based on the ideal of connection rather than on the men's ideal of separation.

> Women's construction of the moral problem as a problem of care and responsibility of relationships, rather than, as one of rights and rules, tied the development of their moral thinking to changes in their understanding of responsibility and relationships

>...Thus, the logic underlying an ethic of care is a psychological logic of relationships....(Gilligan, 1982, p. 73)

Wright (1988) points out that according to Gilligan, one of the greatest conflicts for women is between responsibility and selfishness. In the moral evolutionary pattern, this conflict between selfishness and responsibility is continually reevaluated. The most reasonable context for resolving moral conflict is understanding and care.

The transitions through Gilligan's (1988) levels of moral development begin with Level I, in which survival and one's own desires and needs are primary. Transition to the next level involves the conflict between selfishness, the concern with one's own desires and needs, and responsibility to others. Here the issue is the integration of responsibility and care. In addition, connection with others is highly valued. Also on this level, the concept of women's voice is clear, one's self-worth is based on caring and responsibility for others, and self-sacrifice is seen as the highest value.

Stage	Description
Level I	survival and primary needs are foremost concerns; silence exemplified
Level II	conflict between own needs and caring for the needs of others; attempts toward integration; discovering one's voice; issues of self-worth and self-sacrifice significant gaining strength from ability to care
Level III	conflict between selfishness and self-sacrifice; responsibility toward others; concept of hurting and nonviolence; contextual considerations relevant; balancing own needs and others' needs realized as internal judgment

Figure 8-3. Gilligan's Ethic of Care.
Developed by J. DeSensi and D. Rosenberg based on Gilligan (1982). Adapted from C. Gilligan (1982). *In a different voice: Psychological theory and women's development.* Cambridge: MA: Harvard University Press

Transition from the second level of Gilligan's model to the third centers on the conflict between self-sacrifice and responsibility to oneself. This transition to visualizing oneself and one's ideas as worthwhile and valid produces a moral crisis involving the concept of selfishness. It is at this point where women begin to question the idea of self-responsibility in relation to selfishness and the question of whether responsibility should also include being responsible for oneself as well as the other. Gilligan (1982) points out that the central moral problem for women involves the conflict between the self and the other. On this level, women realize that not only do they have a responsibility to others but they also are responsible for themselves. During Gilligan's (1982) second level or the development of moral states, women envision their strength coming from their ability to care for another. This stage relates to the typical societal stereotypes for women, and women judge themselves on what others (e.g., society, males, and other groups) have to say about them.

In the transition from Level II to Level III, the concept of selfishness emerges again. The self-sacrifice question also arises. Women at this point begin to realize that their own needs are also important and that a morality of care must also include caring for themselves. A conflict point here is the emergence of the concept of hurting. The conflict of choosing whom to harm is solved by the introduction of the value of nonviolence. One is not to cause harm to another or to oneself. The principle of nonviolence governs all moral decisions, and self and the other are seen as equally valid and important. During conflicts between the self and the other, one has to decide who would be the victim. The decision in these cases is contextual and based on the best possible outcome that would benefit all involved. Again, the idea of a morality of relationship that is based on connectedness rather than separation emerges. Realizing that one's own needs have equal value with the other's, women have to choose between self and other.

> It is precisely this dilemma, the conflict between compassion and autonomy, between virtue and power, which the feminine voice struggles to resolve in an effort to reclaim the self and to solve the moral problem in such a way that no one is hurt. (Gilligan, 1982, p. 71)

At Level III women realize that they have choices and that it is possible to be responsible for others and themselves. The goodness of woman no longer comes from outside sources or external societal judgment, but is grounded internally in the idea of truth or one's own judgment of intentions and consequences of one's actions. Conflict still exists on Level III between self and other in the form of a dilemma of whom to hurt, but the issue between selfishness and responsibility has been narrowed within the concept of nonviolence.

Gilligan's (1982) three levels of transition in women's moral development lead from the initial concern towards oneself, to caring for others, to responsibility for caring for others and oneself. The issues of moral development for women involve self-worth in relation to others, acceptance of the power to choose, and acceptance of responsibility to choose oneself as well as others (Wright, 1988).

KEY CONCEPTS

Josepheson's list of character traits   factors that influence personal decisions
Trevino's model of individual moral development and decision making
environmental constraints   preconventional level
conventional level   principled level
women's voices   Gilligan's three levels of moral development

Decision Making and Sport

Sport offers many challenges that often require sport professionals to look inward and examine the consequences of their actions. The legal, ethical, and responsible actions and the choices one makes affect one and others greatly. With the theories that have been presented in this chapter regarding ethical decision making, Josepheson, Trevino, Kohlberg, and Gilligan challenge people to think through their own moral development and examine how they go about making ethical decisions.

In his discussion of ethics, Kretchmar (1994) indicates that the issues of moral sensitivity and moral callouses develop from lack of caring. Moral sensitivity involves the ability to identify moral dilemmas and in turn exhibit a concern about them. On the other hand, moral callousness involves lesser care, concern and moral sensitivity. In his discussion, Kretchmar (1994) uses the example of how during a girl's soccer game, the players themselves stopped the play when a player was injured, exhibiting a spontaneous gesture of concern for the welfare of the injured player. Much of the time, we observe sport participation that involves intimidation, violence, cheating, and lack of concern for the welfare of other players.

Kretchmar (1994) indicates that the common symptoms of moral callouses include the following:

- frequent appeals to the fact that "everyone is doing it" (therefore, how could it be wrong?)
- an inability to distinguish between what is a part of the game and what is not (if there are no penalties in the rulebook for behavior x, behavior x must be part of the game)
- difficulty in telling morally sound strategy from win-at-all-costs trickery (some blatant rule breaking is now referred to by TV commentators, for example, as shrewd strategy)
- a sense that if one is not caught, nothing wrong happened (whatever works is right). (p. 239)

Kretchmar's example of moral sensitivity and moral callouses offers a practical viewpoint of possibilities within our behavior in the sport setting. Additional characteristics that compare and contrast good and bad ethics include concepts such as self-control and rationality versus recklessness and emotionalism, a sense of fair play versus a win-at-all-costs attitude, patience versus opportunism, courage to stand by one's values in the face of difficulty versus an unwillingness to let extraneous values stand in the way of success, and altruism versus survivalism (1994). Such comparisons make clear the points to be considered as one explores one's own intentions within sport.

KEY CONCEPTS

moral sensitivity   moral callouses
characteristics of good and bad ethics

Moral Dilemmas in Sport Settings

Further situational examples of moral and ethical issues are noted in the following scenarios. What is the right thing to do?

*1. An Athletic Director at a small high school in the Midwest knows that the funds allocated to his program are insufficient to maintain the quality he desires. Uniforms are old, equipment is unsafe, facilities are crumbling. The AD gathers a group of interested people, one of whom is a wealthy beer distributor who offers to help raise money. His proposal is that the AD conduct a sanctioned softball tournament for the surrounding area. At this tournament, the AD will sell beer to the participants and the spectators. He will be given 75% of the beer sales for the athletic program if the distributor is the exclusive vendor and he is permitted to place signs in the park to promote his products. There is the potential to raise $15,000 in the venture, half from beer sales and half from tournament fees teams will pay. What ethical issues are involved in this case? What moral decision(s) would the AD make?

*2. An individual is the assistant manager of an exclusive privately owned fitness center. It became known that one of the members, who is a known homosexual, has been diagnosed with AIDS. The manager tells the assistant manager to forbid this member from using the locker room, pool, and fitness areas. There is no established policy in such a case, but the manager and the owner both disapprove of the homosexual lifestyle. Does this case involve a moral or a legal concern? What should the assistant manager do?

*3. The sports information director at a university that has a national champion team in a well-known sport has learned from a radio news report that two years prior to winning this title, a serious infraction was committed, and the NCAA has just issued a reprimand. Soon afterwards the local newspaper contacts the SID for further information. Before issuing any statements, the SID approaches the athletic director, who makes clear that the matter should not be publicly addressed. However, through a news release by the NCAA, the item is printed in papers all across the country. In the SID's position, how would you now handle this crisis? Are there any ethical problems to consider here?

*4. The Director in charge of youth sport leagues in a community learns that one of the coaches has been unusually hard on her team by demanding that the players strive only to excel, that they strictly follow rules, and that winning is the only important objective. The director also becomes aware that this same coach has embarrassed several players by yelling at them in public when they have made mistakes on the field. Further, as a consequence of low skill level, a number of players are purposely benched even though they pay the same entry fee as every other player in the league. Is this coach violating any moral principles? What should the director say to this coach to improve her behavior?

5. Reports have been forwarded to the director of women's athletics by members of a women's collegiate team that is coached by a male. The reports indicate that the coach was becoming too intimate with certain team members. He was making explicit sexual advances toward some athletes, and he was also threatening the team status of some individuals if they did not comply with his requests. How would the director verify the allegations of the report? Is the case primarily a moral or a legal matter? How should the director approach the coach to discuss these concerns?

6. Your college has just hired a black male coach for a major sport. As part of the perks and benefits package, the school has a tradition to give coaches of major sports a membership to a private local country club. In this case, however, the membership was not offered to the recently hired coach. When news of this becomes public knowledge, how should the athletic director deal with this incident? Consider both the AD's public response and private explanations to the coach.

7. The Tonya Harding and Nancy Kerrigan case in 1994 poses a dilemma associated with the Olympic sport of figure skating. The assault on Nancy Kerrigan raised issues related to athlete protection, the importance of winning, and certain rulings handed down by various sport-governing bodies. As it turned out, Tonya Harding was permitted to participate throughout the inquiry process. Was the latter decision the morally correct one? Explain your answer or consider what alternative judgment you would suggest that might be more ethically sound.

(Cases marked with an asterisk were discussed in a sport management class at Bowling Green State University, Bowling Green, Ohio)

Ethical Analysis

The following discussion will analyze the ethical dimensions and implications of the fourth example above to demonstrate how moral principles relate to a given case. Readers should try to analyze the other examples and draw their own conclusions and resolutions to any particular problems.

Ethical concerns in the area of adult-organized youth sport are particularly pervasive and serious for a number of reasons. First, there is a distinct power imbalance among the parties involved at this level of sport, namely, that between adults and children. Adults have a greater capacity to assert their authority in the case of youth, as well as to impose their values upon children. Second, children do not always have the same ability to reason and understand issues at the same level as adults, yet children may not be treated with this in mind. Third, children usually have fewer opportunities to speak and be heard around adults to effect the change deemed appropriate. Finally, adults often neglect to consider the genuine interests of children and may be too wrapped up in satisfying their own goals and ambitions. These are but a few important considerations one should try to keep in mind as the discussion turns to the youth sport example above.

Youth coaches can be a difficulty for league directors if the process for selecting coaches does not contain certain safeguards. For example, league rules could insist that an individual who wishes to coach be required to have an approved coaching certificate. This requirement might ensure that coaches have had some specific training in dealing with youth issues and that they have gained some awareness and sensitivity in handling particular youth problems. The director in this case may have made a bad original judgment in accepting the services of this coach. Perhaps the coach was not sufficiently qualified, or the coach possessed poor communication skills, or the coach couldn't relate to youth very well. If a sound selection process had been established and implemented, then some of the problems with the coach could have been avoided altogether.

On the other hand, as the example indicates, the coach was already part of the league and the director must deal with this individual. For the director, as part of the decision-making effort, the likely place to begin is to make sure one has adequate relevant information related to the coach's actions and team policies, and the experiences of players under this coach. Some type of investigation is, therefore, required. The coach should be informed about what the director has heard, and she should know that an inquiry is being conducted. The gathering of information should be carried out discretely by speaking to team members, other coaches, parents, officials, and the coach in question. We would advise that an open meeting to gather information is inappropriate because of the likely undue hardship such a forum might cause with children present. Once a sufficient amount of information has been collected, some basic moral principles can be employed to assess the case and draw relevant conclusions.

From an ethical standpoint, a utilitarian approach might be useful because this view makes explicit reference to the idea of paternalism, that is, acting or deciding on behalf of others in their best interest. In this case, children are not usually mature and rational enough to fully understand their own physical, emotional, and cognitive needs and abilities, and so adults generally make decisions on their behalf, especially in areas where safety and protection are involved.

The league director's foremost concern has to be the welfare of the participants. If the information gathered clearly indicates that children are being harmed physically or emotionally by the coach in question, then this must be brought to her attention immediately. Moreover, an explanation must be presented to the coach so she understands that she has breached some serious and basic moral guidelines. Surely no child should be publicly embarrassed in front of others, or even in private, and a youth sports league should not be an environment to condone or permit such behavior. The point should be emphasized that every child in the league is to be treated with dignity and respect, no matter what purpose the coach has in mind.

If the league is primarily for recreational purposes, then principles of fairness and equity may also be a concern. Perhaps the coach is explicitly violating league rules and objectives that ensure equal playing time for all participants, allow one practice session per week, and place a premium on participation rather than on winning. If the coach is circumventing these regulations, then perhaps her dismissal is warranted. On the other hand, perhaps the coach can pledge to change her behavior in the future.

The director might suggest to her that she enroll in a youth-coaching certification program. Perhaps team practices and contests should be monitored by a group of league representatives and parents to ensure that no further problems arise and that concrete changes are being developed. Perhaps a second coach with equal authority should be part of the team structure to temper any excessive tendencies. Finally, the director might mention that the coach listen to the needs of players about team goals, ways of practicing, and methods of rotating players in and out of games so that players are treated as decision makers as well.

Summary

Theories and concepts according to Josepheson (1992), Trevino (1986), Kohlberg (1963, 1969, 1970), and Gilligan (1982) were discussed in this chapter. Each has particular relevance for ethical decision making in sport settings. The moral development of the individual is critical in understanding how people base their decisions, establish them, and carry them out. The differences in gender regarding decision making are significant in Gilligan's and Kohlberg's work and require consideration.

Questions for Consideration

1. Based on the theories presented in this chapter, can you identify and critically examine your own decision-making process?
2. What parts of the theories presented can you incorporate into your own decision-making style?
3. What scenarios regarding the sport setting can you develop that would incorporate the models of decision making discussed in this chapter?
4. What incidents of moral sensitivity and moral callouses have you noted in the sports or sport management settings in which you have participated?
5. What examples can you give within sport of the comparisons of the characteristics of good and bad ethics?

References

Belenky, M. F., Clinchy, B. M., Goldberger, N. R., & Tarule, J.M. (1986). *Women's ways of knowing: The development of self, voice, and mind.* NY: Basic Books.

Chelladurai, P. (1985). *Sport management: Macro perspectives.* London, ON, Canada: Sports Dynamics.

Gilligan, C. (1982). *In a different voice: Psychological theory and women's development.* Cambridge, MA: Harvard University Press.

Gilligan, C. (1988). *A contribution of women's thinking to psychological theory and education.* Cambridge, MA: Harvard University Press.

Josepheson, M. (1992). *Making ethical decisions.* Marina del Rey, CA: The Josepheson Institute of Ethics.

Kohlberg, L. (1963). The development of children's orientations toward a moral order. I. Sequence in the development of human thought. *Vita Humana, 6,* 11-33.

Kohlberg, L. (1969). Stage and sequence: The cognitive-developmental approach to socialization. In D.A. Goslin (Ed.), *Handbook of socialization theory and research* (pp. 347-480). Chicago: Rand McNally.

Kohlberg, L. (1970). Stages of moral development as a basis for moral education. In C. Beck & E. Sullivan (Eds.), *Moral education* (pp. 23-92). Toronto: University of Toronto Press.

Kretchmar, R. S. (1994). *Practical philosophy of sport.* Champaign, IL: Human Kinetics.

Lickona, T. (Ed.) (1969). *Moral development and behavior: Theory, research, and social issues.* New York: Holt, Rinehart, & Winston.

Strong, K. C., & Meyer, G. D. (1992). An integrative descriptive model of ethical decision making. *Journal of Business Ethics, 11,* 89-94.

Trevino, L .K. (1986). Ethical decision making in organizations: A person-situation interactionist Model. *Academy of Management Review, 11,* 601-617.

Wright, D. L. (1988). *The relationship between women athletes' ways of knowing and moral reasoning about authority/power in daily life and sport.* Unpublished doctoral dissertation, The University of Tennessee, Knoxville.

CHAPTER 9

SPORT MARKETING

Chapter Objectives
- to discuss the obligations of sport managers to consumers
- to consider ethical issues as related to advertising

Overview of Ethics in Sport Marketing

Western society is founded on capitalist economic principles. It is not basically a negative concept to make money in modern society, but the manner in which it is done, the type of power utilized; and whom the action has coerced, disadvantaged, or in some way negatively influenced are often in question. Success in capitalistic society is driven by terms such as *the bottom-line* and *the almighty dollar*. Keeping a balance between making profit and acting in a socially responsible, legal, and ethical manner is a critical consideration for the sport manager. Financial survival and success are primary objectives. Concerns along this line are associated with (a) rivalries with competitors, (b) the power of the present suppliers, (c) the power of the consumers, (d) the power of substitutes, and (e) barriers to entry (Brooks, 1994).

Recently there has been increased attention regarding the concept of ethics in marketing due to the increase in public scrutiny over the last few decades. Dubinsky and Loken (1989) point out that marketing is the function within businesses that is most often charged with ethical abuse. Abuses within the business world and in sport have been brought to the attention of the public. As a result, the response has created increased attention and a watchful eye on the part of the consumer. Deceptive advertising, fictitious pricing, incongruence of product quality with personal philosophy, and exploitation of consumers are inextricably intertwined with the social issues of misrepresentation of minority groups in advertising, overpricing, and other such activities. Because these activities of the marketing process, even outside the sport setting, are the most visible to the general public, the abuses and misrepresentation will obviously be noticed. Attention is now directed more toward identifying such unethical business practices and their causes.

Fritzsche (1991) offers a summary of studies by Baumhart, 1961; Brenner and Molander, 1977; Chonko and Hunt 1985; and Hunt, Chonko, and Wilcox, 1984, which point out the nature of ethical issues that are encountered by those in business, specifically by marketing managers and marketing researchers. Dubinsky and Loken (1989) point out that potential ethical misconduct in marketing occurs within the following topics and positions: (a) ethical issues confronted by marketing managers, marketing researchers, advertising personnel, purchasing personnel, field and retail salespersons, and retail store managers; (b) consumers' perceptions of various marketing practices; and (c) nonbusiness professors' and marketing practitioners' beliefs about the appropriateness of applying marketing principles to social issues and ideas.

Several models have been developed for studying ethical decision making in marketing. Ferrell and Gresham (1985) prescribed a multistage contingency model of the variables that influence ethical decisions in an organizational environment. This model comprises three antecedents of ethical decision making, specifically, individual factors, such as the employee, significant others within the organization or setting; and opportunity for action.

In a similar effort, Hunt and Vitell (1986) developed a model for situations in which the individual views a particular behavior or action as having ethical content. This view possesses four constructs: (a) personal experiences, (b) organizational norms, (c) industry norms, and (d) cultural norms. Each of these constructs is considered to influence ethical decision making through its moderating effects on perceived ethical problems, perceived alternatives, deontological and teleological evaluations, ethical judgments, and intentions. Dubinsky and Loken (1989) offer still another model of ethical decision making to be used in marketing as an alternative to those just presented. This model is rooted in social psychology and approached from the theory of reasoned action. This theory assumes that individuals are rational, that they utilize available information when deciding how to behave, and that their behavior is under volitional control.

The components of this theory include intention, determinants of intentions, attitude toward the behavior, determinants of attitude toward the behavior, and determinants of subjective norm. *Intention* is the individual's subjective probability that he or she will engage in the behavior. The intention to perform or not perform the behavior is the immediate determinant of behavior. *Determinants of intentions* include the individual's attitude toward the behavior of interest and the subjective norm. *Attitude toward the behavior* refers to an individual's judgment concerning whether engaging in a certain behavior is good or bad. When an individual more favorably evaluates performing a behavior, he or she is more likely to intend to perform the behavior. The subjective norm, or one's family, coworkers, or superiors, enters into this explanation. The individual's perception of whether others who are important to the individual think he or she should or should not engage in a certain behavior affects the behavior. In other words, the more an individual perceives that important others think the individual should engage in the behavior, the more likely the person intends to do so. It is concluded then that performing some ethical or unethical behavior may be a function of attitudes or subjective norms. *Determinants of attitude toward behavior* are based on the individual's salient behavior beliefs and outcome evaluations. To further explain, behavior beliefs are considered one's salient beliefs that performing a certain act will lead to specific consequences or outcomes that will be positive or negative. For example, with fictitious pricing, one's salient belief may be that this act will increase sales volume or will incur ill will among customers. The outcome evaluations include the person's evaluation about whether each outcome produced from the behavior of interest is good or bad. In this example, the

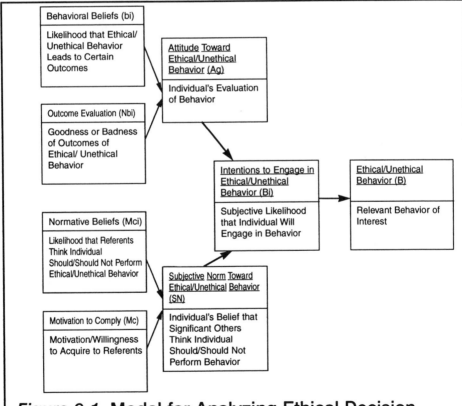

Figure 9-1. **Model for Analyzing Ethical Decision Making in Marketing.**
From "Analyzing Ethical Decision Making in Marketing" by A. J. Dubinsky and B. Loken, 1989, *Journal of Business Research, 19,* p. 86. Copyright 1989 by Elsevier Science, Inc. Reprinted by permission of the publisher.

markets would view increasing sales volume in a positive light, but view negatively the concept of ill will among customers. When it is perceived that a particular behavior generates mostly positive outcomes, the individual will have a favorable attitude toward that behavior. *Determinants of subjective norm* are determined by an individual's normative beliefs (belief that certain groups or individuals think a certain behavior should be performed) weighted by the motivation to comply with specific important others.

Applying this model to ethical decision making in marketing, Dubinsky and Loken (1989) state the following:

> Moving from right to left [on Figure 9-1] the theory espouses that the immediate determinant of engaging in ethical/unethical behavior (or action) is one's intention to perform the behavior. Intention is influenced by the individual's attitude toward the behavior and/or subjective norm (i.e. perceived social influence/pressure placed on the individual to perform or not to perform the behavior). Attitude is determined by one's salient behavioral beliefs about the outcome associated with performing the behavior and evaluations of those outcomes. Subreferents think he or she should engage in the behavior and motivations to comply with these referents. (p. 85)

For example, a potential referent from top management, such as an athletic director, may want an unbiased presentation of the results of a research project involving graduation rates of athletes. If the people doing the research and writing the project report believe this is what the athletic director actually desires, then they are more likely to engage in behavior that will achieve this end. Motivation to carry out this task in an ethical manner is reflective of the referent's desire to have the study done in an honest and forthright manner. Thus the subordinate will carry out the task to the extent that the significant other wishes.

One advantage to the model proposed by Dubinsky and Loken (1989), as interpreted by some, is that it does not assume the individual perceives the behavior as having ethical content. This is in contrast to those models suggested through deontological and teleological philosophy, which require that the person see the situation as containing ethical content. As explained by Dubinsky and Loken

> the cognitive components underlying behavior in the theory of reasoned action are considered independently of whether the behavior is perceived as ethical or unethical ... In fact, for many ethical behaviors in which marketers are interested, individuals may be unaware of a behavior's ethical content; that is, its "rightness" or "wrongness" may not be salient. (p. 89)

This is exemplified by a salesperson in a sporting goods store who has a positive attitude toward giving gifts to customers because of the favorable consequences of giving away gifts, not because the behavior is perceived as ethical.

Harvard Business Review readers indicate that the ethical problems they would most like to see eliminated are (a) gifts, gratuities, and bribes; (b) price discrimination or unfair pricing, or both; (c) dishonest advertising; (d) unfair competitive practice; (e) cheating customers and unfair credit practices and overselling; (f) price collusion by competitors; (g) dishonesty in making and keeping contracts; and (h) unfairness to employees and prejudice in hiring. The readers of the *Harvard Business Review* note mostly marketing issues in their list of ethical concerns. This may due to the broad scope of responsibility of the marketing managers and researchers (Baumhard, 1961; Brenner and Molander, 1977). In studies by Hunt, Chonko, and Wilcox (1984) and Chonko and Hunt (1985), marketing managers and marketing researchers were asked to list the ethical issues that posed the most difficult ethical or moral dilemma for them. Marketing managers included in their list of concerns (a) bribery, (b) fairness, (c) honesty, (d) price, (e) product, (f) personnel, (g) confidentiality, (h) advertising, (i) manipulation of data, and (j) purchasing. Marketing researchers had major concerns regarding (a) research integrity; (b) fair treatment of outside clients; (c) research confidentiality; (d) marketing mix and social issues; (e) personnel issues; (f) fair treatment of respondents; (g) fair treatment of others in company; (h) interviewer dishonesty; (i) gifts, bribes, and entertainment; (j) fair treatment of suppliers; (k) legal issues; and (l) misuse of funds. The primary ethical concerns here dealt with balancing the demands of the corporation against the needs of the client.

The sport manager deals constantly with the issues surrounding marketing. If the points made regarding responsibility are employed, the sport manager is responsible not only for knowing not only the components of the product with which he or she is associated but also the true needs of consumers or clientele, and knowledge of how the product can truly meet the needs of the consumer. The manner in which the behaviors and activities associated with obtaining this knowledge and bringing the product-consumer relationship together necessitates ethical decision making. Responsibility extends not only to individuals with whom one is working but also to the product and organizational goals. In an effort to sell the product to the consumer, it is easy to lose sight of one's own personal and professional goals as a sport manager and the goals of the consumer.

KEY CONCEPTS

factors related to financial survival and success   marketing abuses

Obligations to Consumers

When questioning whether or not businesses have responsibilities to their customers or consumers, it would seem that based on the general principle of fairness, businesses do. Consumers' expectations of businesses include receiving quality goods that are safe and reliable products. This is the case whether the goods are tangible or considered services. When investigating the ethical basis of our expectations, one must realize that one is free to choose either to buy a product or not buy it. Generally one is not coerced into the decision to "buy." This would mean that the buyer determines the quality, safety, and reliability of the product. Using the phrase "let the buyer beware" takes on considerable meaning here. Because one possesses the freedom to choose and purchase a product, one is basically agreeing with the concept that one does not need to be protected from the company that produced the product. People are reasonable consumers with the freedom and wisdom to choose for themselves. Bowie and Duska (1990) point out that the concept of "caveat emptor," or "let the buyer beware," is morally flawed in that it places the total responsibility on the consumer and none on the producer of the goods. It would seem that the prudent thing to do would be to make safety and reliability the joint responsibility of the consumer and producer. Because it would be impossible in today's society for the consumer to research the safety and reliability of all products that they are interested in buying, joint responsibility does not make sense. Therefore, the businesses are required to take on more of the responsibility for safety and reliability. Consumer advocate groups serve as additional watchdogs in this process, but the ultimate responsibility is with the company producing the product. The concept of "strict liability" is employed to producers of goods, meaning that they are responsible for unintended and undetected defects in their products.

Considering the potential of how a new marketing mix might entice the consumer to take part in the product or exchange, the marketer needs to consider if he or she will take advantage of consumer weaknesses, such as ignorance or lack of interest by the buyer. How the marketer's strategy and actions will influence the effectiveness of the marketing plan needs to be considered along with how the strategy will influence individual consumers. Social responsibility and ethical questions arise from such situations (Robin & Reidenbach, 1985).

KEY CONCEPTS

responsibilities to consumers	buying freedom and choice
safety and reliability concerns	

Advertising

This particular activity involves not only informing and persuading potential clients or customers of the services or products, or both, that they may desire but also persuading them to purchase the goods. Through various forms of advertising (e.g., in print media such as newspapers and magazines) and bringing the product to the people in this manner, lower prices for products or services are realized. The ethical problems associated with advertising are in the deception associated with this process. That is, products or services are advertised, but the truth in the advertising of the product is either nonexistent or expanded. In other words, what is available is not what was advertised, or not available for the price noted.

Deception in advertising is difficult to define since not all falsehoods are deceptive in advertising. Some of the deception, however, may be considered to be "harmless bluffing" by those responsible for advertising. Michael Jordan does not jump as high as he does just because he is wearing Nike shoes, but the product advertisers would like consumers to believe this is the case. Therefore, if they buy those particular shoes, they will not only jump like Michael Jordan, but also play the entire physical and mental game of basketball with the same skill and finesse that he exhibits. But the thing is, such advertising works. The public responds, and the products are purchased, and consumers are not considered to be hurt by the exaggeration of the product or the harmless bluffing.

Deception in the example noted above is considered by some advertisers to be "part of the game of advertising," or taken in the "commercial sense." Although purchasing the shoes may make consumers feel as if they can play the game like Michael Jordan, in actuality what has been purchased is a bit of confidence and style. This may be considered harmless advertising. Is it?

Deceptive advertising involves the use of false statements or inaccurate information as related to cost, amount, and quality of the product. The cost of items is obviously significant, but when something called the manufacturer's suggested price is used to show the buyer the difference in price and thus the bargain, there is the potential for deception. The manufacturer's suggested price is a device designed by the seller to make the item more attractive to the potential buyer. The amount is another area in deceptive advertising. Packaging techniques make it appear that buyers are getting more for less simply because of the manner in which the item is packaged. It is wise to check the weight and contents of packages. Quality of a product is another factor that is often represented in a deceptive manner. If superior quality is offered at a low price, it is recommended that close scrutiny of the product occur prior to purchasing the item.

The individuals who can be hurt by deceptive advertising and harmless bluffing are those who are considered vulnerable; that is, children, the uninformed, the less educated, the poor, and the sick. Some of these individuals put their faith in the advertised product and may be ultimately hurt by the deception and suffer the wrath of false advertising. Too often individuals purchase products that are not what they expected. Such a practice is not persuasion, but rather manipulation, which violates the principle of maintaining respect for individuals.

A criterion that could be applied here is that of public openness, which indicates that a public practice is not deceptive when the business acknowledges the rules under which it is operating. If as consumers know that there is bargaining potential in a setting and that the price on the item is not the actual price, then there is public openness. Deception enters the picture when there is action indicating one set of rules and behavior indicative of another set. When the rules of the advertising practices are known, then the public is more likely to accept the consequences of various business practices (Bowie & Duska, 1990).

KEY CONCEPTS

truth in advertising   harmless bluffing
deception in advertising   public openness

Moral Dilemmas in Sport Settings

The following are examples of moral and ethical issues as related sport marketing:

1. The promotions director for a minor league baseball team is planning an event day for a game to be held on July 4. During the month of June, the director advertises that the first 500 youths under age 12 who attend the game will receive free baseball caps. There will also be a 7th-inning stretch raffle to give away a television, a camcorder, and a stereo set. Finally, a spectacular postgame fireworks display will be held. On the morning of game day, the promotions director discovers that only 250 caps were delivered; Pat's Electronics store, which donated the raffle prizes, was robbed the night before; and the threat of rain makes the fireworks program tenuous. How should these seemingly unavoidable problems be addressed in light of marketing techniques and social responsibility?

2. Karin Goodwin was named rookie of the year on the Professional Women's Golf Tour after an illustrious college career. Because of her phenomenal first-year success, she accepted an offer by a sports equipment company to endorse their new line of clubs, clothes, and other golf accessories. The owner of the company happens to notice on national television one weekend that Karin is using another brand of golf clubs and she is not wearing the company's logo on her attire. Has Karin breached her endorsement obligations? How should the owner approach Karin and her manager? Suggest a possible explanation for her display during a nationally televised tournament.

3. A sports equipment manufacturer who specializes in producing balls and rubber-based sports equipment has received inside information that a major supplier, a large rubber company in South America, is planning to corner the market on raw materials, thus creating an artificial shortage of rubber and driving up the price for rubber. In anticipation of spiraling costs in a year's time, the manufacturer decides to receive his supply of rubber from a company that produces poor-quality raw material. Consequently, he begins to manufacture goods with this inferior rubber, yet retailers he deals with and safety regulators are not informed, and the

packaging of products remains the same. What are the moral issues of this case from a marketing perspective?

Ethical Analysis

The following discussion will analyze the ethical dimensions and implications of the third example above to demonstrate how moral principles relate to a given case. Readers should try to analyze the other examples and draw their own conclusions and resolutions to any particular problems.

Marketing generally refers to how products are moved from a producer to a consumer. Ethical considerations are raised in this area of management because sometimes the marketing practices of producers are questionable. Producers may not honestly inform the consumer about the product, or the product itself may be faulty, and such information may be withheld from the consumers by the producer.

The sports equipment manufacturer in this case is obviously more concerned about maintaining his profit margin than maintaining the quality of his products. His sole interest is not to be encumbered by a possible increase in the price of the rubber he needs to manufacture his products. Further, he is willing to sacrifice quality in order to ensure he does not experience losses in the future. On the face of it, some of these judgments may be sound from a business perspective; they are not, however, from marketing and ethical standpoints.

There is nothing inherently wrong or morally questionable if a manufacturer decides to produce a lower quality product. In this case, this might be a wise move; perhaps it is the only way the manufacturer can stay in business. On the other hand, there are other features of this case related to marketing that point to several areas that are morally objectionable.

In selling his products to retailers, the manufacturer neglects to inform his buyers that they are receiving inferior goods compared to what they have previously received. Because poor raw materials have been used, the quality, endurance, and standards of the products have likely deteriorated perhaps to the point at which certain retailers would not buy the goods. The manufacturer, therefore, is being deceptive and acting in an unethical manner by not informing retailers that the goods they are now receiving are below the standards they have come to expect. By withholding this information, the manufacturer is doing himself a disservice because in all likelihood, the genuine quality of the products will be discovered in a short period of time and lead to returns and cancelled orders.

The withholding of vital quality changes from safety regulators in relation to the production process is not only unethical but may also lead to serious legal problems. Most sports require the strict use and maintenance of equipment to ensure high standards of safety are in place. In the case of a manufacturer, it would be exceedingly irresponsible and unconscionable to produce equipment where safety is not a foremost concern. No physical-activity participant should exercise or engage in sport with a fear that serious equipment failure will occur as a result of a manufacturer's neglect for safety. When injury to a participant does occur where equipment failure is involved, manufacturers are often named in negligence suits. In this case, the producer knowingly refrains from notifying safety officials and organizations about the lower quality of his products, and thereby tries to avoid the implementation of new standards tests.

Finally, the use of the same packaging for the products is another fraudulent and unethical marketing technique related to the previous point. If the same boxes and instructions are still being used when the products themselves are inferior to those produced in the past, then incorrect and potentially harmful information is being conveyed to consumers. Moreover, there may be safety information, warnings, and safe-use advice, which may pose a threat to users if they incorrectly handle the "new" poorer quality products. Here, the manufacturer may directly be the cause of some type of damage linked to consumers, because they would be the primary users who would read labels and instructions in order to benefit from the products.

In this one case then, there are three separate areas in which unethical marketing practices can occur. They can involve producers and retailers, producers and safety regulators and organizations, and producers and consumers via unsafe packaging. Ethical principles linked to social justice would be important to apply here because there is an obvious element of one person or company influencing the lives of many others in some potentially harmful manner. Ideas referring to impartiality, social good, state interference, liberty, and many other notions could be implicated in assessing this case. The theories of justice discussed in chapter 3 should, therefore, be reviewed before any specific application is carried out.

Summary

There has been increased attention directed toward the concept of marketing and specifically toward the obligations to the consumer by companies and businesses. More public scrutiny is evident because of the abuses of marketing practices. The call for ethics in this realm is loud and clear as are the legal ramifications associated with marketing. In this chapter Dubinsky and Loken's model for analyzing ethical decision making in marketing has been used. Specifically, the model examines intention, determinants of intention, attitude toward behavior, determinants of the attitude toward behavior, and the determinants of the subjective norm, which are explored in order to gain an understanding of ethical decision making in marketing.

Questions for Consideration

1. What are the most critical areas of abuse in marketing that are evident to you?
2. What approaches can be utilized to overcome the negative impressions regarding marketing in our society, specifically related to sport?
3. What are your responsibilities as a sport manager regarding the concept of marketing?
4. What steps would you take to ensure truth in advertising?

References

Baumhart, R. C. (1961, July-August). How ethical are businessmen? *Harvard Business Review, 39*, 6-19, 156-176.

Bowie, N. E., & Duska, R. F. (1990). *Business ethics* (2nd ed.). Englewood Cliffs, NJ: Prentice Hall.

Brenner, S. N., & Molander, E. A. (1977, January-February). Is the ethics of business changing? *Harvard Business Review, 55*, 57-71.

Brooks, C. M. (1994). *Sports marketing: Competitive business strategies for sports.* Englewood Cliffs, NJ: Prentice Hall.

Chonko, L. B., & Hunt, S. D. (1985). Ethics and marketing management: An empirical examination. *Journal of Business Research, 13*, 339-359.

Dubinsky, A. J., & Loken, B. (1989). Analyzing ethical decision making in marketing. *Journal of Business Research, 19*, 83-107.

Ferrell, O. C., & Gresham, L.G. (1985, Summer). A contingency framework for understanding ethical decision making in marketing. *Journal of Marketing, 49*, 87-96.

Fritzsche, D. J. (1991). A model of decision-making incorporating ethical values. *Journal of Business Ethics, 10*, 841-852.

Hunt, S. D., Chonko, L. B., & Wilcox, J. B. (1984, August). Ethical problems of marketing researchers. *Journal of Marketing Research, 21*, 309-324.

Hunt, S. D., & Vitell, S. (1986, Spring). A general theory of marketing ethics,. *Journal of Macromarketing, 6*, 5-16.

Robin, D. P., & Reidenbach, R.E. (1987, January). Social responsibility, ethics and marketing strategy: Closing the gap between concept and application. *Journal of Marketing, 51*, 44-58.

CHAPTER 10

PERSONNEL MANAGEMENT

Chapter Objectives

- to consider ethical practices related to personnel
- to examine hiring procedures and ffirmative action issues

Ethical considerations regarding personnel include basic obligations to employees. The rights that should be guaranteed to employees include the right to liberty, privacy, and fair wages. These rights in addition to the concepts of equal opportunity and affirmative action are addressed in this chapter.

Obligations to Employees

When one considers the employer-employee relationship, it is necessary to examine the rights of each. Although it has been established that employees have certain rights, which include due process in hiring and firing, fair wages, and respect of their privacy, then it is the employer's moral obligation to ensure these rights. Bowie and Duska (1990) point out that questions regarding the conflict between employer and employee rights may arise, requiring a decision to be made between the conflicting positions. In the sport setting, it is the manager's responsibility to decide between the conflicting positions. This task is undertaken by first acknowledging that employee-employer relationships should be contractual. They involve an authority-subordinate relationship, thus opening up greater potential for abuses of power within this relationship. Actually this relationship should be consistent with laws of moral custom, and free of coercion and fraud. The individual who is desperately in need of a sport management position may be exposed more to various forms of subtle coercion than will individuals who have skills that are highly marketable. It is the freedom of the employee that is jeopardized, necessitating the careful examination of one's contract conditions (Bowie & Duska, 1990).

The employee's rights to liberty, privacy, and a fair wage should be explicit within the contract. Regarding the right to liberty, Mill (1859/1956) wrote a century ago:

> The sole end for which mankind are warranted individually or collectively in interfering with the liberty of action of any of their number is self-protection. That the only purpose for which power can be rightfully exercised over any member of a civilized community, against his will, is to prevent harm to others. His own good, either physical or mental, is not a sufficient warrant. (p. 13)

Based on Mill's explanation, once the hierarchy of power (i.e., relationship) and responsibility (i.e., task or job to be accomplished) between the employer and employee has been established, then the employer does not have the right to interfere with the employee's freedom unless there is either harm or evidence of potential harm to the employer, company, or work setting. The most widely used example is drug use. In the broadest view, if the drug use does not bring harm to the work setting (i.e, the employer, product, consumer), then what the individual chooses to do in private life should not be of concern to the employer. Using the concept of harm associated with the sport organization is still another approach to this issue. If there is potential harm to the setting present, then violations of the individual's liberty may be necessary to prevent harm to the company, corporation, or business. Because businesses have been known to control or regulate employees' behaviors regarding dress, family and social life, for example, then any action that the employer feels may negatively affect the profit of the organization, harms the organization and could potentially be restricted (Bowie & Duska, 1990).

There is a close relationship between the employees' right to liberty and their right to privacy. In the drug-use example cited in the discussion of liberty, the right to privacy arises. The issue of privacy has received much attention in regard to the drug testing of athletes. Is such testing an invasion of an athlete's privacy? Why are not coaches and athletic administrators tested as well? The same questions arise with the Olympic athletes. Why not test all who are connected in any way with the Olympics? Why single out athletes? Regarding this point, Bowie and Duska (1990) state that

> some defenders of the market point out that the really important aspect of the market is that it allows us to do business without being hampered by irrelevant considerations such as the beliefs, personal habits, politics, race, sex, or other behavioral and ideological idiosyncrasies of the person we are doing business with. (p. 89)

When this same concept is applied to the employer-employee relationship, it could be concluded that as long as the product that one is interested in purchasing is able to be delivered and its quality is not hampered because of drug usage, the drug issue is not relevant and any probing into an employee's private life in this case is not justified. On the other hand, the relationship between the employer and employee extends beyond the simple market explanation. Rather, it is considered a long-term relationship wherein the employee becomes an agent or representative of the employer. In this case, it is difficult not to pay attention to certain behaviors if they do in fact impinge on job responsibilities or put the company, organization, and possibly the consumer at risk. Bowie and Duska (1990) address this issue by indicating that if businesses are to operate ethically and within the law, then

> ...business activity should conform to the laws and basic moral norms of society. Once this background condition is understood, a business cannot restrict the freedom of an employee when that restriction requires the employee to perform some act that violates either the law or a basic moral norm of society. An employee cannot be ordered to falsify experimental data relating to product safety or to discriminate against a fellow employee on the basis of race. The fact that the falsification of the data or the discrimination would improve profits is irrelevant. (p. 91)

The right to a fair wage brings up issues such as the employer's treating the employee as a human being with dignity and respect, not taking advantage of the employee and not using employees as means to specific ends. As ethical behavior is considered within the right to a fair wage, dependency and autonomy are concepts that should be explored. Enlisting Kant's (1785/1959) second imperative of never using another human being merely as a means to an end is a good approach here. It is important for the employee to retain autonomy and keep in mind that the concept of reciprocity of use prevails. If, however, the equality changes and one party becomes more dependent, the relationship that was freely entered into changes drastically. In other words, if the employee desperately needs the job, then his or her bargaining position becomes weak, and manipulation and coercion may occur on the part of the employer. In this instance, the management would be able to increase profit by paying what the market would bear at the expense of the employee. It is no wonder that unionization and minimum wage laws were enacted (Bowie & Duska, 1990).

Hiring issues and affirmative action are additional concepts that emerge in personnel management. The classical point of view regarding the concept of hiring indicated that the best qualified individual was hired. This is considered to be the best market value. A concept known as employment at will is a practice utilized in publicly owned companies or businesses (Bowie & Duska, 1990; Clement, 1991). This concept was interpreted by businesses as an issue of liberty.

In other words, the employer could hire whomever he wished allegedly in order to get the job done. At-will hiring is rarely public knowledge. Still, many are hired under this concept, and specifically most part-time employment falls into this category (Clement, 1991). Bowie and Duska (1990) state that

> As business becomes public in the sense that its stock is sold on the open market, or there are stockholders other than just the owner, the business needs to be operated in conformity with the primary principle—to make a profit. That means hiring the most qualified, in the sense of those who will serve the company best. (p. 59)

Employment at will is often not compatible with the goals of maximizing profits and productivity. At-will employment often results in various forms of nepotism; individuals may be hired not for their qualifications, but in the name of family loyalty. Not hiring the best qualified in essence, hurts the business. A publicly owned business that uses the at-will principle would be operating legally, but not ethically. Historically, the at-will principle has served to exclude individuals because of their race, sex, nationality, sexual orientation, or religion even when they are qualified to do the job. Such exclusion is indefensible both economically and ethically (Bowie & Duska, 1990).

KEY CONCEPTS

employee right to liberty, privacy, and fair wages   employee-employer relationships
governmental legislation

Hiring and Affirmative Action

Hiring the most qualified individual also brings up the question of equality of opportunity. In the strictest sense, if humankind had historically acted ethically and morally, this discussion on equality of opportunity and affirmative action would not be necessary. Affirmative action requires that available jobs be made public and accessible on an equal basis for all qualified persons. There are two types of affirmative action, weak and strong which require examination (Bowie and Duska, 1990). Weak and strong types of affirmative action are both warranted within society. The weak type requires that jobs be advertised and announced to everyone, including diverse groups. Not only must the job opportunities be announced, but there also must be an equal opportunity to compete for the job. The principle of equal opportunity states that

> persons with the same ability and talents who expend roughly the same effort should have roughly the same prospects of success. Race, religion, sex, and family background should not be relevant

to one's success or failure in the competitive struggle. (p. 60)

Under strong affirmative action, a member of the disadvantaged minority may be selected for a position over another candidate with relatively equal qualifications. In this sense, the minority status is viewed as a "plus factor." This in no way means that an unqualified individual will receive the job. Bowie and Duska (1990) comment further on this problem:

> There is a deontological justification for strong affirmative action in terms of compensatory justice. There was harm done in the past because of racial and/or sexist discrimination. Individuals from disadvantaged minority groups were hurt and consequently they should be recompensed. Besides this deontological argument there is the utilitarian argument that the integration of all groups into the society is an important goal, and thus preferential hiring is an effective means to their integration. We leave unsettled the equally utilitarian argument that preferential hiring is counterproductive because it causes more resentment, racial hatred, and strife than it alleviates. (p. 63)

This issue takes on even greater meaning when the responsibility of businesses is explored. A disputable point is whether businesses have a direct responsibility to promote general welfare or solve the issues and problems of sexism and racism in our society. Government, on the other hand, does have the responsibility to promote general welfare and establish justice and, therefore, could oblige other systems in our society, such as education and business, to devote their power and resources to alleviating social injustices.

KEY CONCEPTS

employee qualifications   equal opportunity

Moral Dilemmas in Sport Settings

The following are examples of moral and ethical issues related to personnel management:

1. Bill Dixon has had a successful physical education teaching and coaching career at Weatherby High School for the past 5 years. As far as students and staff knew, Bill was a bachelor. However, Bill attended the end-of-the-year formal with a male friend. Throughout the evening, it became evident that Bill and Doug were in fact a homosexual couple. Once the relationship became evident, the principal confronted Bill and asked him to leave the formal. He also insisted that they meet immediately to discuss Bill's future at Weatherby. Should Bill's private life be an issue in the

workplace? Does the fact that Bill is a physical education teacher have any special relevance?

2. Two full-time permanent physical education university faculty positions were advertised in several major professional publications. In these advertisements, a clause was inserted to indicate that the positions were contingent upon budgetary approval. During the course of the search and hiring process, the physical education department was informed that one position could be offered only on a temporary 9-month basis. Should candidates seeking employment at the college be notified of this change and the terms of appointment? What main ethical issues are relevant here?

3. The director of the Meadowvale Recreation Department has a position available for an assistant director. The list of candidates has been shortened to three people. The individuals happen to be a white male, a black male, and a white female. Each possesses comparable and equal qualifications and experience. However, the director is concerned about the demographic makeup of the staff and has been informed of this situation by her superior. The staff is mainly represented by black male and female employees. Should race be an influencing factor in the hiring decision? How might the decision relate to affirmative action-related issues?

Ethical Analysis

The following discussion will analyze the ethical dimensions and implications of the second example above to demonstrate how moral principles relate to a given case. Readers should try to analyze the other examples and draw their own conclusions and resolutions to any particular problems.

Hiring is an essential, often first-step, component of personnel management. In many places of employment, especially governmental and other public sector agencies, there are strict hiring procedures that must be followed when searching to fill vacant positions. In some institutions, there are specialized officers who oversee the hiring process within departments to ensure that laws and rules are followed and fair hiring practices are implemented. In the case under consideration, several questions may be asked about the hiring procedure from a moral perspective. For example, does the contingency clause in the ad provide a fair warning to candidates that the position they are applying for will indeed be available? Should applicants be informed when there is a status change in the position they applied for? At what point in the hiring process should this change be conveyed, if at all, to the applicants? What moral obligation(s) does the employer have to prospective candidates?

In answering these questions, we will forgo dealing with any legal issues even though there may be moral concerns attached to unlawful conduct. Although the inclusion of the contingency clause appears to be a legal safeguard for the employer, its application is not broad enough to cover certain moral demands. For instance, members of the physical education department could reason that if one of the full-time positions reverted to a temporary 9-month appointment, each candidate in the pool of applicants still has the potential to secure the remaining full-time appointment. Once the selection is made to hire someone for the full-time position, then a second individual would be chosen from the same pool and offered the temporary job with an explanation as covered by the contingency clause. This sort of reasoning seems plausible at first glance.

One question that could be asked is whether all the applicants should be told in advance of making any firm decisions that the status of one of the positions has been altered. Following the line of thinking above, those in the physical education department feel no need to convey this information to the candidates before making their selections. In effect, the department is withholding information from all of the candidates, information that they (the applicants) might judge important. Why might this information be significant? Some applicants might prefer to withdraw their names from the pool once they learn that there is the potential to be offered a temporary, limited appointment. Perhaps these candidates had no intention of applying for a 9-month job, even on the possibility that this might occur.

Other complications are likely connected to such a case as well. Usually when a department advertises two positions, the job descriptions of each are different, or certainly the needs of the department are likely different. This often means that the department is planning to hire two individuals with dissimilar profiles and qualifications who can work in specific areas of a program. In the case before us, there is no indication that the department is required to disclose which of the two positions might be preferred as the full-time appointment. In other words, candidates would not know that the department has prioritized the hiring of a sport manager on a full-time basis, rather than hire a full-time exercise physiologist. Once again, withholding the status-change information, which might reveal the preferred ranking of positions, from candidates denies these individuals knowledge to make an informed decision. Treating applicants in this way is morally wrong.

A deontological perspective that demands other people be treated with utmost respect and dignity, only as ends and not as means, is a useful ethical guideline to follow here. No person should be deliberately misinformed or be denied access to information when crucial life and career decisions are at stake. Although the physical education department has probably covered its tracks from a legal standpoint, it should immediately make available the status change of one of the positions to all the candidates on moral grounds. Otherwise, the applicants are indeed being duped and exploited, contrary to deontological principles and common decency.

The preceding remarks are especially relevant for anyone who has entered or will enter the job marketplace where the expression "timing is everything" is commonplace. Job applicants need to be informed about working-condition changes immediately as related to a specific position so they can concentrate their search efforts in a more efficient manner. They need to know whether to eliminate certain positions from their lists of potential jobs and remove as many unnecessary contingencies as they can. If prospective employers neglect to provide applicants with certain information so these decisions can be made by candidates, valuable time may be wasted, anticipated commitments may not materialize, the reputation of the department may be jeopardized, and both the employer and applicants may become part of a situation in which distrust and suspicion are prevalent.

In the final analysis regarding this case, the employer has a moral obligation to inform job applicants of any status change related to specific positions in an appropriate and timely manner. Open, honest, and forthright dealings with applicants ensure that the hiring process not only conforms to legal standards but also values moral interests as well. Without establishing such a relationship, the employer, organization, or department may undermine its own integrity.

Summary

This chapter explores ethical concepts with regard to personnel management. These include the rights guaranteed to employees, such as liberty, privacy, and fair wages. The concept of liberty involves individual employee rights versus the employer's right to protect the organization or business. Privacy issues raise similar dilemmas in determining individual rights and those of the interest of the business. Fair-wage issues involve the direct responsibility of the employer. Equitable hiring practices and advertising of job positions were discussed in relation to affirmative action guidelines.

Questions for Consideration

1. In what ways would the concept of hiring at will be advantageous?
2. Were the rights of liberty, privacy, and fair wages extended to you in jobs you have held?
3. What instances of weak or strong affirmative action have you experienced?

References

Bowie, N. E., & Duska, R.F. (1990). *Business ethics* (2nd ed.). Englewood Cliffs, NJ: Prentice-Hall.

Clement, A. (1991). Sports law: Product liability and employment relations. In B.L. Parkhouse (Ed.), *The management of sport: Its foundation and application* (pp. 97-106). St Louis: Mosby Year Book.

Kant, I. (1959). *Foundations of the metaphysics of morals* (L.W. Beck, Ed. and Trans.). Indianapolis, IN: Bobbs-Merrill. (Original work published 1785).

Mill, J. S. (1956). *On liberty*. (C.V. Skield, Ed.). Indianapolis, IN: Bobbs-Merrill Library of Liberal Arts. (Original work published 1859: London: Parker).

CHAPTER 11

LEGAL AND GOVERNANCE ASPECTS OF SPORT

Chapter Objectives
- to generally discuss ethical concerns and sport law
- to examine the concept of governance

Overview of Sport Law

Because the areas of study or specialties within sport law are numerous and expansive, it would be impossible to treat each one independently. Therefore, this section will present an overview of the relationship between ethics and the law pertaining to sport. Although it is the hope that ethics will be followed and fair treatment of all will ensue, some laws may in fact be discriminatory in some cases, thus emphasizing the importance of examining this area.

Antitrust, constitutional, contract, criminal, labor, licensing, and tort laws in addition to legislation and legal precedents and many other forms of law are relevant for behavior in sport in one sense. In another sense, the ethical character of the law may be questioned. Issues regarding the relationship between the employer and employee, equitable hiring and evaluation processes, worker compensation, liability, due process, and discrimination of all populations are constantly challenged.

The legal issues associated with sport have created a need for, and in some cases produced, federal and state legislation specific to athletics. Examples of such legislation in the U. S. include (a) Title IX of the Education Amendments of 1972, which governs sex discrimination in educational institutions that receive federal funds; (b) The Amateur Sports Act of 1978, which governs Olympic sports in the United States; (c) agent legislation that governs the conduct of individuals representing athletes in contract negotiations with professional teams; (d) laws requiring medical personnel to be present at games; (e) legislation of fan behavior toward referees and officials; and (f) laws pertaining to fitness facilities (Wong, 1991 p. 75). The preceding areas, in addition to other laws that apply to all, have been especially noted within sport recently. The general legal areas include negligence, due process, equal protection, unreasonable search and seizure, invasion of privacy, sex discrimination, assault and battery, libel, slander, and bribery statutes. The antitrust laws, which include the Sherman Antitrust Act and Clayton Act, have been directly associated with professional sports leagues "which are composed of private economic entities operated as a business to make a profit" (Wong, 1991, p. 90). The NCAA and college or university athletic programs, specifically football and basketball, have also been included in the antitrust decisions. As noted, the issues associated with sport and the law are expansive. The law, however, represents a minimum standard of care and should be followed in both spirit and letter (Hums, 1990). The ethical and moral actions go beyond the minimum standard of care and require actions that take into consideration the situation and individual(s) beyond just what is barely expected. Hums (1990) brings up some interesting points regarding the law in raising the following questions:

1. Does one uphold the law because one has to, or because it is in the best interests of one's constituents to do so?

2. Does one provide a minimum standard of care so that one does not get sued or so that participants have the safest environment possible?

3. Is Title IX enforced because one fears losing federal aid or because one truly believes in equal access to opportunities for women? (p. 7)

These questions further indicate the interconnectedness of ethics, morality, and the law. In addition to those noted, questions concerning equal access to participation in sport for all could be added; this would include women, minorities, children, differently abled people, HIV-positive persons, and the elderly. The area of individual rights, including drug testing, exploitation of athletes, and sexual harassment, is an area of further inquiry. The question of knowingly teaching improper and dangerous playing techniques to gain an advantage in the game or of using unsafe equipment or facilities that could endanger participants also raises not only questions not only of legality but also of intention, values, beliefs, and concern for the welfare of others, all of which are inherent concerns in ethical behavior.

KEY CONCEPTS

main types of law	federal and state legislation related to sport
the law and minimum standards	relationship between ethics, morality, and the law

Governance

A question that is often raised in U.S. society by sport scholars is "who should have the ultimate governance power for sport in our nation, states, localities, and/or educational institutions?" The United States, as a nation, does not have a minister of sport for sport participation at any level. There is no single person to oversee this area, nor is there a nationwide sports program that ensures participation for all individuals. The United States Olympic Committee has a limited range of governance, and although the NCAA is the primary governing body of women's and men's intercollegiate athletics, it, too, is limited in its power and scope.

The NCAA as a governing body does, however, have power at the level it serves. There is considerable national attention paid to the governance of intercollegiate athletics. *The Chronicle of Higher Education* features a section on athletics that consistently informs readers of the NCAA's governance policy and procedures and violations of NCAA laws.

The certification of college and university athletic programs by the NCAA as a result of the Knight Foundation Commission reports (1991, 1993) is a lesson in ethics in and of itself. The certification self-study items require that reports be made by institutions concerning governance, academic integrity, financial integrity, and commitment to equity. This process involves an examination by all athletic personnel and athletes of the current practices, policies, and changes within the last 3 years in athletic programs. In addition, the mission of the university, program goals, and outcomes are studied. This practice is consistent with ethical examination regarding the individual and the programs. The commitment to equity involves investigating the access of individuals of different gender, race, and ethnicity to all facets and programs with the athletic departments and particularly examines the role of athletics within the institution and the athletes' welfare. Just as it is impossible to truly legislate equality because it is a concept that must exist within each of us in order to work, it may be impossible to have anyone's rights and privileges protected if there is no ethical and moral connection between such behavior and the laws. The same would hold true if there is not any value examination regarding the mission and goals of sport programs. Ethics is not optional. It is required to ensure the welfare of all and should address particular concerns within sport.

KEY CONCEPTS

sport-governing bodies   certification issues   limitations in legislation

Moral Dilemmas in Sport Settings

The following are examples of moral and ethical issues related to legal and governance aspects of sport:

1. Sam has a form of paralysis that does not permit him the use of his legs,

and he is mobile only in a wheelchair. Sam has always had an interest in physical activity, but he has been denied many opportunities to pursue such interests. With the recent passage of the Americans with Disabilities Act, all physically challenged individuals must be provided reasonably with access and opportunities to participate in publically funded and supported programs. Because this act is now in effect, Sam should have few problems pursuing his physical-activity interests. Provide arguments to demonstrate that such legislation is ethical. Suppose Sam wanted to play in a wheelchair basketball league that his community center does not now offer. How should such a league be implemented?

2. A high ranking representative of a nationwide sport-governing body is concerned with certification of college and university athletic programs. Certification is involved with meeting standards related to financial integrity, gender equity, minority rights issues, student welfare, and other similar concerns. How would one ensure that such standards were being followed by college and university athletic programs? How can one be certain that the information provided by individual campuses in the above areas is accurate and reliable? What compliance issues are involved here?

3. The person in charge of a large college intramural program discovers that accident reports filed by student organizers have been inaccurate and that some reports were altered weeks after the accidents occurred. The intramural coordinator is aware of this because one student brought up charges of negligence and eyewitnesses confirmed details that were not on the specific report related to this episode. After checking further, the coordinator discovers other accident reports where false and exaggerated statements are evident. What legal liabilities does the college assume? Were the students morally wrong to "doctor" the reports? Suggest explanations for producing the inaccurate reports.

Ethical Analysis

The following discussion will analyze the ethical dimensions and implications of the third example above to demonstrate how moral principles relate to a given case. Readers should try to analyze the other examples and draw their own conclusions and resolutions to any particular problems.

Those involved in physical-activity programs and institutions assume an additional responsibility to ensure the physical and emotional safety of participants. Instructors, teachers, and coaches work in an environment where participants can and do experience accidents by virtue of the distinct tasks and demands required. Despite the inevitable, every attempt must be made to ensure that safe practices are implemented and that when accidents do occur, sound guidelines are in place to treat accident victims in a responsible manner. A crucial part of the follow-up procedures following an accident is preparing an accident report. There should be a standard form for this report, and all physical-activity employees should be familiar with when and how to complete this form. Clearly the most important feature related to the accident report is that it contains accurate and precise information. Accident reports may be used as evidence in legal proceedings, and the individual who prepares the report must realize this fact. To deliberately exaggerate, withhold, or tamper with vital information on an accident report can create severe legal difficulties not only for an institution but also for the person who completes the report. From a legal standpoint then, it is imperative that those who work in the physical-activity profession recognize the seriousness of this document.

In the case under consideration, therefore, the college definitely has a legal obligation to produce and maintain accurate records when accidents occur. The students are likely considered representatives of the college because they are league organizers, but ultimately the responsibility rests with the intramural coordinator, who is an employee, to ensure that accident reports are completed appropriately. All individuals under this person's charge must be informed of the content of the accident report and of the procedures for gathering and entering relevant information. The coordinator should also stress that every accident, no matter what a student worker thinks, must be acknowledged with the completion of an accident report. No one should risk making a judgment whereby a small matter later turns into a serious situation, and no record was kept of the initial incident. Student workers must be impressed with the fact that accident reports are essential and must be addressed in every circumstance deemed an accident. The preceding then discusses the legal implications of accident reports.

The moral position as related to such documents requires an evaluation based on right and wrong standards. The students who doctored the accident reports were morally wrong because they were not only less than truthful, but they also placed others, mostly the victims, at greater risk. The latter might refer to significant information whereby medical decisions have to be made, and if such information was inaccurate, this could lead to some serious harmful consequences. Such risks were also elevated for the college, because accurate accident reports would likely conform to other pieces of evidence and witness accounts to confirm the nature of the accident. Students were also placing in jeopardy unforeseen consequences that they could not anticipate. For example, perhaps months later, an accident victim experiences a recurring form of injury linked directly to the initial accident. If the accident report is unreliable as a source of information, this may lead to serious repercussions. Because no one can project such possible outcomes, students have a moral responsibility to treat accident reports seriously and minimize any real or potential risks to others. The student organizers themselves may have assessed the situation in several ways to have acted as they did. Perhaps some felt they needed to protect themselves if indeed they had neglected to carry out some specific task, like mop up a dirty or wet gymnasium floor. Perhaps some were led to believe that doctoring the accident reports protected the institution and that this was an expected practice among student workers. Finally, some may have felt that certain accident situations were too trivial or unbelievable, and so a more plausible and reasonable scenario had to be created. None of these possible rationalizations are acceptable from a moral perspective in light of the discussion above. Students have a moral obligation to complete such documents accurately, and the intramural coordinator must teach and monitor this area of student responsibility with greater vigilance.

Finally, in this case, moral principles related to social justice, where again the decisions of a few have an impact on the lives of many, may be implicated. Here, the college likely has a policy or set of procedures to follow when accidents occur, and so these become the action guides that affect student participants. There may also be utilitarian grounds and calculations to determine the right course of action by demonstrating the costs and benefits involved in accident situations. When these factors are assessed together with the goals and objectives of the intramural program, then moral decisions may be upheld and supported by the college, the intramural coordinator, student workers, and physical-activity participants.

Summary

This brief chapter discusses the issues associated with the relationship between the law and governance of sport. The issues that emerge from this discussion are consistent with those noted in other chapters that point out ethical and moral concerns. Laws associated with sport are noted in addition to questions that address the concept of ethics and ensuring minimum standards of behavior. Examples of the governance of sport are briefly discussed, and the process of certification of athletic programs as a result of the Knight Commission reports is highlighted.

Questions for Consideration

1. To what degree are the laws that govern sport and society ethical?
2. Should there be more governance of all levels of sport in our nation?
3. Is the minimum standard of care sufficient to ensure ethical behavior?
4. Will certification by the NCAA ensure that college and university athletic programs operate within ethical standards?

References

A New Beginning for A New Century. Intercollegiate Athletics in the United States. (1993, March). Final Report of the Knight Foundation Commission on Intercollegiate Athletics. Charlotte, NC: Knight Foundation.

Hums, M. A. (1990). *Model for moral development: A life issues approach for a sport management curriculum.* Unpublished manuscript.

Keeping Faith with the Student-Athlete. A New Model for Intercollegiate Athletics. (1991, March). Report of the Knight Foundation Commission on Intercollegiate Athletics. Charlotte, NC: Knight Foundation.

Wong, G. (1991). Sports law: The theoretical aspects. In B.L. Parkhouse (Ed.), *The management of sport: Its foundation and application* (pp. 74-96). St. Louis, MO: Mosby-Year Book.

PART IV

WHAT LIES AHEAD

Wade Austin, (1995). Reprinted with permission.

CHAPTER 12

THE FUTURE OF SPORT MANAGEMENT ETHICS

Chapter Objectives

- to identify potential directions of sport management ethics
- to determine who is responsible for ethical behavior in the sport setting
- to suggest means for moral improvement

Predictions and Concerns

The future of sport and the future direction of ethics and social responsibility within sport management are difficult to predict with precision. However, it appears that as the demographics of our society change and more individuals have access to and the opportunity for participation in sport, no matter their skill and ability, sport programs will increase, thus increasing the market for sporting goods and other sport businesses. As professional leagues expand and broadcast media increase, programming and spectating will also increase. Technology will also offer new approaches to sport that will require increased performance levels and more input and participation by spectators. With such increases, it can be anticipated that the value sport holds for all individuals within society will maintain a high quality and a moral character. The value of sport may increase, but what must be monitored and sustained are the rights and privileges of each individual as a consumer of sport.

Sport Management Ethics: Who is Responsible?

The future of ethics within sport management, although difficult to predict, is the direct responsibility of those studying to be sport managers, those who teach these standards, and those who currently hold such positions. Further, and more generally, it is the responsibility of everyone within North American society. It is the responsibility of everyone because individual values, beliefs, biases, and behaviors are learned through socialization and those responsible for this process. Socialization into and through the sport setting is often a difficult process because society places so much value on achievement and success. The learning fields of sport offer a primary ground for the learning of moral development and the primary ground for violations of moral responsibility.

Although the call for moral reform in sport has been loud and clear, in some instances, it has fallen on deaf ears. In other instances, individuals have responded. The future holds the potential of moral training associated with the sport setting. Physical education classes, among others, offer this potential, but the real possibilities are within the competitive settings of sport at all levels. Few academic settings provide an opportunity for students (particularly the athlete) to examine values, beliefs, and behavior with regard to their practices, but athletes have and should have this opportunity. This type of education is sorely needed, but it is needed early in the educational system. The same is true for those preparing to be sport managers. Such examination and understanding of concepts regarding ethics and social responsibility are required of those preparing for a career in sport management in order for sport at all levels to offer quality potential and opportunity for all.

Reforms for Moral Progress

A rethinking of the role of sport in society as well as within the educational institution is needed. It is hoped that there will be reform regarding the issue of ethics at all levels of sport competition. The possibility for the future includes courses, workshops, and interactions that directly address moral development, responsibility, and ethics in sport not only by the players but also by all those involved.

A significant step has been taken by Sharon Stoll, Director of the Institute for Ethics in the College of Education at the University of Idaho, and Jennifer Beller from Eastern Michigan University, who serves as the Institute's Associate and Research Assistant. After four years of intensive study of moral values and critical reasoning with university athletes and coaches, Stoll and Beller have developed programs that address these issues. Their work on moral reasoning intervention programs with athletes has had marked success. The College of Education Center for Research Theory and Service at the University of Idaho houses ETHICS (Ethical Theory and Honor in Competitive Sports). This program is committed to helping competitors, coaches, and administrators make good choices based on impartial, consistent, and reflective reasoning.

Although moral reform in sport has been the call from various sources, the individuals to whom this call has been directed do not possess the necessary background either in moral and ethical development or in social responsibility. Inappropriately or inadequately trained individuals in these areas have been a detriment to the management of sport at all levels. Youth sport, Olympic sport, professional sport, and all interscholastic sport programs are characterized by the top-down management approach. This means that the organizational structure of such programs proposes that those in the positions of management and administration know what is best for the athlete(s) and such programs regarding values, beliefs, behaviors, and the approaches to develop ethical and social responsibility. Beller and Stoll (1993) suggest that reform measures such as those recommended by the 1929 Carnegie report and the 1991 Knight Commission report, among others, will continue to have little impact because the top-down management approach and decision-making model "violates the fundamental principles of moral/character value education" (p. 4).

At the intercollegiate level of sport, Beller and Stoll (1993) point out that in order for meaningful reform to occur in the United States, the following must occur:

1. Primary participants (athletes) and secondary recipients (athletic directors, coaches, university administrators, and faculty) must be involved in dialogue concerning personal, program, and institutional values, beliefs, and goals.
2. The dialogue must be based in what Meyer and Pruzan (1993) state is an "ongoing, self-reflexive, and value- based" educational model.
3. All shareholders (all players involved) must be involved in the development, implementation, and continued evaluation of program and institutional values, beliefs, philosophies, and goals. (p. 4)

To expand on these ideas for the future, value-based dialogue must occur. This includes authentic dialogue between the primary and secondary shareholders as noted above. For example, within intercollegiate athletic programs, the dialogue would center on the values and beliefs of the program and the shareholders in conjunction with the mission and mission statement of the educational institution (Beller & Stoll, 1993).

The future for sport and the ethical, moral, and responsible behavior within these settings present some difficult challenges for the future. Although Meyer and Pruzan (1993) indicate that educational systems should expand their capacity to redesign themselves in order to be effective in serving the purposes of society and its own purposes, all social systems, sports included, should take part in this same exercise. Redesigning involves interaction between the primary and secondary shareholders in a setting where goals, values, and beliefs can be discussed and evaluated in conjunction with the mission of the programs involved. Drawing from the work of Meyer and Pruzan (1993), the self-designing system demonstrates that it has the ability to meet its own overall goal of contributing to its shareholders' values at any time. In addition, a contextually dependent situation is created in which the shareholders' values in relation to the system depend upon the design of the particular system. The self-redesigning system is in constant fluctuation between harmony, dissonance, harmony, and then dissonance again. The dissonance and harmony occur between the shareholder's actions and values and the shared values and goals of the specific sport program and the program's role within the mission of the larger social community (Beller & Stoll, 1993, p. 12).

It is evident how self-redesigning can occur within sport management. The top-down management style offers the best example. This particular model is paternalistic, indicating that those at the top know what is best for those at the lower levels. Top-down management has the potential not to acknowledge the worth of individuals, their values, and their importance within the organization. If the individual does not have the opportunity to take part in value-based, self-reflexive structure, then the overall operation, strategies, and goals of the organization will be diminished.

The revenue produced, win-loss records, graduation rates, and other award systems are insufficient upon which to ground value-based dialogue. Beller and Stoll (1993) point out that unless those associated with the administration of sport and those involved at other levels as well (e.g., athletes, spectators, and other participants) are involved "in an ongoing dialogue concerning values, beliefs, and program philosophies which lead to mutually acceptable visions and strategies, the system cannot develop a collective identity" (p. 14).

Reform in sport in terms of understanding one's personal values and beliefs, taking part in value-based dialogical interactions, and continually challenging one's values and beliefs in conjunction with the mission of sport programs and businesses is necessary for the future good of sport programs and sport management. Most in the sport community, however, do not seek or want reform. Many like sport in all its forms as it currently exists. Many are afraid to seek the challenge of change. How then does one move to reform?

When sport in its current form is examined and challenged from various perspectives, it is necessary for the sport manager to look for the positive and negative aspects of this environment: how individuals (participants and public) are affected; how the sport's realm is consistent with the values, issues, and problems of a multicultural/diverse society; what value the sport brings to society as a whole; and how moral excellence is achieved and maintained through sport. This is the ethical responsibility of sport managers for the future.

Summary

The future of sport is assured as access and opportunities for participation increase. The value of sport needs to be constantly reevaluated in human lives as does its effect on human moral development. The future of ethics and social responsibility in sport management is the responsibility of all. Those educators preparing individuals for careers in sport management, the students studying in this area, and those already holding sport management positions are responsible for assuring that sport and those associated with sport maintain moral character. Examination of the top-down management style is needed to examine how it affects moral development, ethics, and social responsibility. Ethical reform within sport will occur when self-reflexive dialogue between or among those involved takes place. During such dialogue, values, beliefs and goals must be examined in conjunction with the program values and goals and the ways in which each of these compares with larger society.

Questions for Consideration

1. In what ways will the top-down management style hinder the moral development and ethical responsibility of a sport program?
2. What actions can be taken by specific sport managers to assure the ethical quality of their sport programs or services?
3. In what ways has sport either contributed to or hindered your own personal moral development?
4. In what ways can you assure that sport will retain an ethical quality exemplary of social responsibility in the future?

References

Beller, J., & Stoll, S. (1993). *A praxeological assessment of the need for reform in United States intercollegiate sport through moral education.* Unpublished manuscript.

Knight Foundation Commission on Intercollegiate Athletics (1991, March). *Keeping faith with the student-athlete: A new model for intercollegiate athletics.* Charlotte, NC: Knight Foundation.

Meyer, T., & Pruzan, P. (1993). *Redesigning educational systems through value-based dialogue: Practical philosophy and action theory.* New Brunswick, NJ: Transaction Press.

INDEX

Subject and Author